contents

... and there was telev!s!on

Why all the fuss over television? It is blamed for an assortment of evils, including violence, shortened attention spans, the decline of literacy and political indoctrination. In this scintillating and approachable book, Ellis Cashmore weighs up the theories and the evidence. He argues that much of the panic is without foundation and that the single most important danger posed by tv is that it encourages us to spend too much. Cashmore agrees with many writers that television is an elemental force in today's culture, but he offers us a completely different account of how and why this has come about. It is an evaluation that will surprise, provoke and delight. In essence, Cashmore argues that television is the central apparatus of consumer society and its success is measured not in terms of whether we enjoy programs, but how much we spend as a result of watching them. It is a book that should be read by anyone who watches television and wants to know what it is doing to them.

Ellis Cashmore is the author of several books, including *The Logic of Racism* and *Making Sense of Sport*. He has held positions in the universities of Hong Kong, Washington, Tampa and Aston and is now Professor of Sociology at Staffordshire University, England.

... and there was telev!s!on

ell!s cashmore

London and New York

First published 1994
by Routledge
11 New Fetter Lane, London EC4P 4EE

Simultaneously published in the USA and Canada
by Routledge
29 West 35th Street, New York, NY 10001

Typeset in Times by LaserScript, Mitcham, Surrey
Printed and bound in Great Britain by
T.J. Press (Padstow) Ltd, Padstow, Cornwall

British Library Cataloguing in Publication Data
A catalogue record for this book is available from the British Library

Library of Congress Cataloging in Publication Data
Cashmore, Ernest.
. . . and there was television/Ellis Cashmore.
p. cm.
Includes bibliographical references and index.
ISBN 0–415–09130–6: $50.00. – ISBN 0–415–09131–4 (pbk.): $15.95
1. Television broadcasting – Social aspects. I. Title.
PN1992.6.C278 1994
791.45 – dc20

93-33670
CIP

ISBN 0–415–09130–6 (hbk)
ISBN 0–415–09131–4 (pbk)

acknowledgements

My appreciation goes first to Chris Rojek, senior editor in sociology at Routledge, who urged me to write this book and offered editorial encouragement throughout the process of writing it.

My colleagues at the University of Tampa, Florida, and Aston University, England, have given me valuable advice on various facets of the book. In particular, Mickey Wells in the USA, and George Paton in England, have supplied me with many intellectual and practical resources.

Additional appreciation goes to Linda Scrivens of Aston, who keyed and assembled the manuscript, and Ann McGinnis of Tampa, who keyed drafts of many of the chapters.

Part of the research behind the book was conducted with the financial support of the Dana Foundation of Florida.

Acknowledgments

chapter one

bombardments and bee stings

whatever happened to television?

Dear Vladimir Zworykin
What has happened to the cathode ray tube you made come to life by activating photoelectric cells with moving electrons and patented in 1923? Receiving all those gifts from your invention and its successors used to be such a joy. I remember detective thrillers, like *Dragnet*, and comedies such as *All in the Family* that kept us in stitches. I was also impressed by the seriousness of the many documentaries you gave us and the largeness of purpose of those heavy docudrama-type programmes, like *The Day After*. OK, so the news was a bit rough at first, but then it became more polished and informative. Who else could give us an easy-on-the-intellect summary of events spanning the world all condensed into thirty minutes or so?

And those images: unforgettable – like war scenes from Vietnam, the pageant of the royal weddings and, most unbelievably, the incredible moon landing. It truly is a colorful and bounteous largesse and we have rejoiced in it. It has given us fresh perspectives in life; it has allowed us to explore new possibilities; it has provided the impetus for self-reflection. Most of all, it has amused us hugely. And, let us be honest, it has changed us – which is really what I am writing about.

Obviously, we are like the ninety-nine per cent of the population who own one or more television sets and our viewing habits are reasonably typical. I estimate that my wife and I watch about 18 hours a week; our two children between 22 and 30 hours which is, I understand, the norm. This means that, by the time they leave school, they will have spent 22,000 hours stuck in front of a set, compared with only 11,000 in the classroom. They love it. We all love it. I can agree with the Americans surveyed in 1986, who said they got more pleasure from tv than from food, alcohol, religion, money – or sex.

But, I have to admit this worries me. My daughter, who is a university student, has been telling me for some time that watching television is bad for us. I have always laughed it off when she insisted that it rots the brain, makes us violent, manipulates our buying habits, desensitizes us politically and stops us reading. "Well why do you watch it then?" I would always ask sarcastically. "It's that, or the wallpaper," is one of her replies.

I know there is nothing new about all this – almost thirty years ago the US Federal Communications Commission described television as a "vast wasteland." I had not thought about this too much until recently. It must have been the video cassette recorder that made me ponder; we have two of them. For the first time, we actually seem to be organizing our time around viewing. This would have been unthinkable ten, maybe even five years ago, but now I find myself scanning the weekly tv guides, scrawling all over them with a yellow highlighter pen and then programming the Plus+ code on the handset.

I regard myself as a reasonably intelligent person. I think about what I am doing, including what I watch and what effect this is likely to have on me. My concern is that watching television is no longer just a form of entertainment. Sometimes, I have to remind myself why I am watching it all. Yet, I carry on, as if suspended in some part-conscious state, or gently resisting its magnetic power. It takes effort not to watch nowadays. I joke that we have brought a Trojan Horse into our home and that the soldiers are just beginning to appear.

I hope I am wrong, but I would love some assurance. Can it really be that the invention that has brought so much pure pleasure and undeniable richness to my life has, in a period of 50 years, metamorphosed into an instrument of sheer malice? Whatever happened?

Yours devotedly

EC

Television is fascinating. But not for the reasons its admirers or its detractors claim. Some see it as educationally uplifting and stimulating to the imagination; others see it as encouraging a range of unwholesome behavior, including soporific passivity and crazed violence. I am in neither camp. Television fascinates because it embodies the culture it depicts. In a genuine sense, television is culture today: capricious, intemperate and absorbed by a near-religious devotion to consumption.

At the cusp of the millennnium, we can look back and recognize television as the invention that reflected, shaped and recreated twentieth-century culture. True, it may have nothing of substance to show or say, yet it shows and says it with such poignancy that we cannot take our eyes away. Imagine what life would be like without television. What would happen to all the time we spend in front of the small screen? How about the conversations based on last night's sport or drama, or this morning's news? And from where would we get most of our up-to-the minute information on world events? You might ask equivalent questions about being denied access to the internal combustion engine; this and television have changed us immeasurably.

Both have been welcomed; television as an affordable addition to households. It has brought an agreeable blend of joy and enlightenment to the homes of billions around the planet. And, like the internal combustion engine, television has made the planet immediately accessible, at least in a visual way. It is also inexpensive, costing a tiny fraction of an annual income to buy a set and less than a typical monthly car fuel bill for cable, or satellite. The other costs are disguised in the form of additional pennies on the price of items advertised in commercials.

But there may be yet another price. We know tv's impact on our lives is profound in that it has restructured how we spend our waking hours and maybe some of our REM time too, if we dream of television characters. But, is it so profound that we consumers cannot understand what it is doing to us? I write this from my office in Florida, a state where children between the ages of 10 and 11 watch, on average, six hours of television a day, well over the national average. The fact has prompted a debate about how to decrease, or better still, stop this. Television is seen by many audiences and opinion leaders alike as a passive pastime that stunts young minds.

They find empirical support in the research findings of the British National Federation for Educational Research, which, in 1992, surveyed 754 six- and seven-year-olds. Those with televisions in their bedrooms were far less likely to be good readers (1992). Reading will soon become a "lost art," according to Robert Hughes, who, in his *Culture of Complaint*, assaulted television for its impact on literacy. "It is hard to exaggerate the narrowness of reference, the indifference to reading, the lightly dimpled cultural shallowness of many young products of American TV culture, even the privileged ones," (1993: 103).

Many others have warned of the slow death tv-watching promotes among adults: the death of our critical faculties, of our impulses to probe, of our sheer sense of skepticism. Worse still: television is blamed for a medical dictionary-full of physical and mental ailments. The causal chain may be missing a link or two, but researchers have made connections between television and, among other things, civil unrest, drug use, broken families and, most famously, violence. Arguments between scholars over the role of tv in the production of violent behavior continue to blaze away without much sign of a resolution. Populist sentiments usually fall on the side of the "links" rather than "no-links," probably because it is a relatively simple exercise to explain burgeoning violence and an assortment of other social problems by reference to one source. Much harder to look further afield into social, political and other cultural areas for explanations.

Do the critics have a point? Certainly. Do they exaggerate? Probably. Television viewing, as we all know, is qualitatively different from many other forms of leisure. It is right there in our home; it occupies us in a way film, for example, does not. It requires no special effort, apart from flicking a switch and, even then, that switch may be a button on a remote control. Nowadays, there are no time limits on when that button can be pressed. Television is a source of endless novelty, change, excitement and titillation. It is actually one of the best stimulants ever invented. But, like other great stimulants of our time, it has unintended consequences, the central one of which is a habitual compulsion to watch, even when there is nothing watchable on screen.

For all the awful warnings about how bad tv is for us, there have been very few attempts to allay fears. Jib Fowles seems to have appropriated the only franchise with a minor publication in 1982, revised a decade later into a book, *Why Viewers Watch* (1992). It remains the most extreme and thorough appreciation of the benefits of watching television. "The true purpose of television is to remove mental debris from the minds of viewers," opined Fowles, characterizing tv as "the sanitation of man of the psyche" (1992: 49). Television dispenses fantasies, plain and simple. This is good for viewers because: "A view on reality is not what viewers generally want from television; they want the antidote for reality" (1992: 59). Fowles sees in television a massive therapeutic force tailor-made for contemporary stress-filled society. "Like all fantasy material," he wrote, "television does not so much put things in brains as it does take things out" (1992: 49).

Could it be that television does not do anything to us, save for cleaning out our psyches? It almost defies common sense to suggest we are unaffected by a fixture that occupies so much of our time and thought. In the coming chapters, I will argue that television has had an impact that extends beyond the "psyche," an overused and ill-defined concept with no empirical referents. But for the moment, let me state that the most pressing danger that television holds for us is that it encourages us to live beyond our means. Now, to a second source of support.

"Television is not time-out from thinking, as so many fear," argued Robert Hodge and David Tripp in their book *Children and Television*, "it provides grist for the mills of thought, innumerable opportunities for cognitive growth" (1986: 92). Television is now more significant than books, magazines and even newspapers in conveying the consumer culture. But it is more than a conveyance: it affects our experience of the world by providing cultural maps, reference guides that help us frame our interpretations and responses. This is most evident in politics, by which I include party politics and political events; but also in such diverse areas as crime and sport as well as many other components of our culture.

Our language echoes the language on television; the way we dress reflects tv images. It is no overstatement to say we become conscious of the world through television. Consider the age of young children when they start viewing tv attentively: about two, according to Mariann and Charles Winick in their 1979 book *The Television Experience*. This is confirmed by Hodge and Tripp who argued that "a child takes a real interest in the television set at about 2 years old" (1986: 77). (A two-year-old in the Winicks' study was discerning enough to leave the room when commercials came on.)

Watching television increases the range of our experience and exposes us to images that help us form impressions of the world. At least according to the research findings of anthropologist Conrad Kottak who ventured into a small Brazilian village and discovered that television can "(1) stimulate curiosity and a thirst for knowledge, (2) increase skills in communicating with outsiders, (3) spur participation in larger-scale cultural and socioeconomic systems, and (4) shift loyalties from local to national events" (1990: 189). Bold claims.

stimulant culture

What are the implications of all this on an international scale? US television companies dominate the production and distribution of programs and advertisements. Anyone, anywhere in the world switching on a television set will be unable to watch for long before North American material appears on the screen. US programs and commercials are sold to a global market comprising hundreds of millions of consumers. The "one world" we live in is in large part a result of the scope of the expansive communications network, including almost 3,000 satellites orbiting the earth. And the power lies in the USA, which will, almost by default, assume responsibility for carrying information, providing entertainment and defining culture in far-flung places. To hand this responsibility to the United States might seem like passing an Uzi on a velvet cushion to a psychopathic killer. Our first inclination might be to cringe; our second to duck.

Like it or not, the production and diffusion of US-originated tv material has produced a veritable media empire. And, if television is now both a constituent and carrier of culture, we might ready ourselves for an Americanization rather than globalization process. Later in the book, I will expand on Jay Rosen's point that: "CNN represents a new dimension of an emerging global culture that is already heavily Americanized" (1991: 622). Here, let me simply note that television is the latest vehicle for the spread of American ideas, values or even outright ideology to the rest of the world. Television defines and seals the USA's cultural imperialism. Less developed countries are poorly equipped to hold on to their cultural independence and are almost compelled to accept "first world" perspectives in their news and entertainment. And, while the actual quantity of US-originated programs exported as a proportion of the world's total has declined over the past 30 years, the American influence throughout the world is undeniable. The model of broadcasting refined by the US since the war has become almost universal. This affirms the pre-eminence not only of North American culture, but of the consumerism it bears and conveys.

"Money has been consecrated as a value in itself," wrote Robert Merton in his article "Social structure and anomie," first published in 1949, before the take-off period of television. We "are bombarded on every side by precepts which affirm the right or, often the duty of retaining the goal" (1968: 191). Merton could not have anticipated how aggressive the bombardment would become with the arrival of television as a staple household item. But, the value of money in itself was supplanted by an emphasis on what it can buy. This will come as no surprise to anyone who has spent 30 minutes in front of a tv screen. Except they will not feel "bombarded": probably irritated by the persistent interruption of commercials which keep returning like honeybees; brush them away and they keep coming back for nectar. Such is the beauty of television: it makes a bombardment feel, at worst, like a bee sting. Commercials break up the flow of every program, warning us, exciting us, advising us, but always imploring us to spend money. Even BBC television, still stoutly resisting commercialization, has buckled under the weight of sponsorships and the product placements that invade its shows.

We viewers are habitually tantalized by elements of a lifestyle that is glamorous, instantly gratifying, usually bigger and inevitably better than the one we have. What's more, it is shown as available to us: we can buy it. If television has taught us anything, it is that everything can be bought and sold in the market-place. As such, television has become the central apparatus of the consumer society. It promotes not just products, but a culture in which products have value. Without them and the gratification they are supposed to bring, life is colorless and empty – if commercial advertising is to be believed. As Martin Davidson has observed in his *The Consumerist Manifesto*: "Consumption is now the basic mode for all activity in society, not reading, not using, not appreciating, not producing, but *consuming*" (1992: 203). Television may keep us happy and fulfilled; it also keeps us buying. What other force of nurture works so perfectly to transmit, reflect and perpetuate the consumer society?

Television's ubiquity makes it ideal for advertisers: prospective shoppers are gathered in the comfort of their own homes, readied and receptive. They may be seeking entertainment, but, whether they like it or not, they are also "consuming aspirationally," as Davidson calls it. We demand newer, improved products; we welcome novelty. Television is not solely responsible for turning us into aspirational consumers, but it is the main factor in the equation.

"Improve what you have . . . upgrade your possessions. . . . Renew your commodities." These types of imperatives are built into television. Not only in its overtly commercial advertising, but in its programs, including game shows and news – itself a confirmation of the value of novelty over information. Reflecting on *Dallas* and the genre of which it was part, Christopher Lasch wrote: "Images of luxury, romance and excitement dominate such programs, as they dominate the advertisements that surround and engulf them" (1991: 520).

Toward the end of his celestial railroad journey to *The True and Only Heaven*, Lasch offered his views on today's mass media. Defining "drugs" as "commodities that alleviate boredom and satisfy the socially stimulated desire for novelty and excitement," Lasch saw television not so much as a drug, but as part of the same culture that has actually fostered drug use. "The model of possession, in a society organized around mass consumption, is addiction," wrote Lasch (1991: 520–1). "The need for novelty and fresh stimulation becomes more and more intense, intervening interludes of boredom increasingly intolerable." How many of us have used the remote control like an automatic weapon, squeezing off a succession of channels in a desperate search for something more thrilling than the commercials? Even the briefest moment of ennui must be eliminated. Lasch argues that every available stimulant is used to satisfy our impulses. A similar point has been made by Cornel West in his interviews with bell hooks: "A market culture will promote and promulgate an addiction to stimulation, it will put forward the view that, in order to be alive, one needs stimulation" (hooks and West 1991: 95).

Gone are traditional values, like self-denial or deferred gratification, as determinants of human conduct. Historical developments have seen to it that we can hardly exist without large doses of externally provided stimulation. Advertising and the whole machinery of demand creation have turned us into impatient consumers whose relief lies only in consuming even more and more. The actual articles of consumption are not so important as the fact that they can be reduced to saleable commodities. In this sense, the comforting glow we feel at the end of "movie of the week," the agreeable pride we take in buying a new car and the explosive hit we get from crack cocaine are all gratifications activated by consumer culture. It is a culture "which continually tries to create new demands and new discontents that can be assuaged only by the consumption of new commodities" (1991: 518).

My confidence in Lasch's analysis will become evident in the chapters that follow. Much of my effort is anchored in the argument that television has transformed culture from within, encouraging a shift from the work ethic to the consumption ethic, providing people with experiences that alert them to an ever-expanding range of products and urging them to covet avariciously. Television dangles visions of the "good life" before its viewers; it influences their taste, appeals to their insecurities.

But, in contributing so fulsomely to the rise of consumer culture, television has also become a part of it. Television sets are bought, sold, upgraded and supplemented, just like any other commodity. They are used to satisfy wants, alleviating boredom, easing tension, arousing senses and so on. Television occupies a colossal part of our leisure time and, increasingly, time spent in education training or at work. It may be the most significant artefact of the century in its ability to give shape to and inform daily experience. This is both the rationale and the organizing principle behind this book.

"Serious" books on television have to cope with two mandates: to execute an informed and coherent analysis and to offer an account that will satisfy the most committed television enthusiasts that there is more to watching tv than, well, watching tv. Schematically, this book moves from the generic to the particular, beginning with the big and sometimes abstract questions about television, like "how did it start?" "what is its purpose?" or "why do we watch it?". There is no shortage of answers to these questions and I present a précis of many of them in the first four chapters. Non-academics may be surprised – and possibly amused – by the solemnity with which many scholars approach a medium that is meant to entertain.

The book then looks at issues, items that occupy the attention of even the most occasional viewer, like advertising and violence: too much of both of them on tv, say many. Their predominance has given cultural doomwatchers plenty to worry about, as we will see in chapters five and six. As well as shaping culture, television also reflects it, and chapters on ethnic minorities and women indicate how depictions have in some ways chronicled changes in the social status of these groups. In other ways, television has presented images and narratives that serve ideological purposes. Chapters nine through eleven cover areas that television has changed, such as politics and sport, or has effectively exploited, like crime. In dealing with these, I keep one eye on the screen, the other on the changing trends of postwar society.

There are other issues; far more than I cover in this book, of course. I just identify the principal ones. The book is free of the kind of warnings or prescriptions dispensed by many books on television. I believe there are many purposes to television: selling is the primary one. This might seem strange and a mite instrumental. But there is, I think, evidence enough in the chapters that follow to suggest, at least, that television provides an image of the world in which life, liberty and the pursuit of happiness have become equated with novelty, money and the quest for excess. The inescapability of television means that, in providing an image of that world, it is also creating conditions under which it is daily being realized.

chapter two

a gift arrives

the problem of A to B

We live in fear of science and technology. And with good reason: they come at a price. Sometimes, that price seems unbearably high. Two events in the twentieth century alone remind us of the consequences of trying to defy or control nature. The Holocaust and Hiroshima are hubris to scientific pride. And these are examples of science and technology working efficiently. When they go wrong, we witness Bhopal and Chernobyl. The Promethean fable of being tortured, bound to a rock for the sin of stealing fire from the gods, has been encompassed by a number of fictional works, perhaps the most celebrated being Mary Shelley's *Frankenstein*, in which man re-invents himself only to see his construct wreak havoc. Jurassic Park portrays human self-destructiveness as a concomitant of creation. On television, *Star Trek* and its progeny have occasionally tempered their celebrations of the human conquest of the "final frontier" with cautionary messages.

Television, like any other technological innovation, has its costs. As we will see in the next chapter, some writers reckon we have paid with our brains. What began as a genuine boon to our ability to communicate quickly and efficiently has, according to some, become a bane on our intellects. No longer just a means of communication, television is a plaything, a toy, a means of amusement. Assessing this transformation and its consequences on us is the object of this book, of course; so we should properly begin with an overview of the development of television as a piece of technology.

A case could be made for seeing television as a return to primitive forms of communication. It communicates its messages through oral and visual means, sight and sound. It presupposes no literary skills or ability, apart from being able to see and understand a language. It shows pictures and tells stories and asks nothing more of an audience but that they watch and listen and, even then, only intermittently. This is basically how people communicated prior to the advent of widespread literacy. For most of human history, information and ideas have been exchanged primarily through oral means, sometimes with pictorial embellishments. The human ability to memorize large quantities of data would be barely conceivable today.

Even when written language was used, few would have had the inclination or encouragement to understand it and the high cost of producing written documents would have made them inaccessible to most. Written material would be laboriously drafted and painstakingly copied by hand. Medieval bibles were hand-written in English by monks and scribes over a period of months or even years. So word-of-mouth remained the principal method of instruction until the arrival of printing.

Rudimentary printing blocks made from wood were used by the Chinese as early as the seventh century AD, though it seems the more robust metal type was successfully developed in Korea in the fourteenth century. At around the same time, playing cards and pictures were being printed using carved wooden blocks in Northern Italy. Credit for inventing a matrix into which could be set several individual pieces of re-usable type falls to Johann Gutenberg, who lived in the first half of the fifteenth century. Movable type introduced incredible flexibility and allowed for the printing of large books comprising many words. These became cheaper when expensive parchment was replaced by a Chinese invention, paper, the long term costs of which are now being paid. Ten million books would have taken literally thousands of years to write by hand; but that was the result of production in the first 50 years following Gutenberg's invention. Physical proximity was no longer a precondition for the communication of information and ideas and this allowed for an international cross-fertilization of ideas that became known as the scientific revolution.

Gigantic as its effects were, printing lacked immediacy. If people could not read, they needed someone who could read to them. So it stayed a largely mediated form of communication until literacy became commonplace. In the mid-eighteenth century, 40 per cent of men and over 60 per cent of women in England were totally illiterate; and, even in the late twentieth century, advanced industrial societies have illiteracy rates. Increases in literacy were obviously a direct result of the spread of the printed word, especially after the introduction of mass-produced newspapers at the start of the eighteenth century. When allied to steampower technology for both production and distribution, the newspaper became a formidable instrument in structuring the quantity and nature of information people had about the world.

But the actual information made available by print was only as important as the changes it instigated in people's ways of thinking. Texts are ordered sequentially, so, to make them intelligible. The reader has to read and think in terms of the linear narrative which is how the messages were originally encoded by the writer.

Reading aloud to a group is still popular and would have been even more so before mass literacy. Increased literacy encouraged more solitary, detached reading with the reader's attention silently and privately focused on the text. With attention fixed, the reader would be adept at spotting inconsistencies and other flaws in arguments.

Reading print also demanded the use of imagination. Whether reading alone or listening to a reader, the receiver is bound to exercise more than mechanical skills when decoding the messages. We can surmise that people's imaginative scope and their capacity to relate to "fantastic" events were enlarged. "A sophisticated ability to think conceptually, deductively and sequentially" is the principal property of the mentality promised by the rise of typography, according to Neil Postman, who adds: "a high valuation of reason and order; an abhorrence of contradiction; a large capacity for detachment and objectivity; a tolerance for delayed response" (1985: 63). We will return to the way forms of media affect cognition in the next chapter, but, for now, notice that the consequences of printing went beyond the content of the messages it carried.

Despite refinements in the print industry and improved transportations systems, the burden of physically distributing printed material imposed obvious limits.

Getting the product from point A, where it was originated, to point B, where it would be read, was cumbersome. That is, until scientists and engineers began to think of the air as opposed to land: instead of physically transporting print, why not encode it, send it through the air and let the receiver decode it at point B?

For 450 years, print was the prominent form of mass communication. But, in 1844 Samuel Morse proclaimed a device to transmit combinations of encoded words and letters through electrical pulses along wires. Telegraph communication using Morse code was expensive and inelegant compared with print; but it was quick. It also served to reorient thoughts about communicating through air, by using the natural atmosphere instead of the costly wires required for telegraphing. Wireless communication had been tested by Heinrich Hertz, who, in the mid-nineteenth century produced an oscillator device for generating electrical pulses which could be "sent" along airwaves at the speed of light. Guglielmo Marconi's achievement was to transmit morse-coded signals along "Hertzian waves," as they were called, across several hundred yards to a "coherer," the forerunner of what were to become radios. Though there were others whose contributions were as substantial as Marconi's, the Italian migrant to Britain is conventionally hailed as the "inventor" of radio.

The device had obvious applications in turn-of-the-century Britain, then the centre of a sprawling empire, but without a linking communications network of the kind implied by Marconi's wireless device. Interrupted waves containing code were supplanted by continuous waves on which voice could be superimposed, thanks to the work of Reginald Fessenden. In 1897, Marconi, aged 23, became a director of a £100,000 corporation which exploited the uses of his device. Its military value was immense. Two years later, the Marconi Wireless Company of America was incorporated under the laws of New Jersey and with a similar remit to its British counterpart.

Wireless transmissions through radio waves were used in the 1914–18 war and this stimulated both technical improvements and the mass production of components. Amateur enthusiasts began building their own apparatus, or "radio sets," giving rise to the inexpert radio hams. The general interest in radio was not lost on the British government and North American commercial companies.

The British system was to defray costs by charging a licensing fee, but the American equivalent was less structured. In 1920, the Westinghouse Electric and Manufacturing Company, which made radio sets, built a headquarters in Pittsburgh from which they could transmit on air news of the Presidential election to a few hundred owners of its sets. Within five years, 500 similar stations had emerged for the purpose of transmitting, or broadcasting (as it became known) music, sports events as well as general news and "commercial messages" from advertisers, whose money supported the enterprises. The American Telephone and Telegraph Company (AT&T), sensing the growing threat to its staple, bought the patents of Lee de Forest, whose extraordinary "Audion" tube, a glass bulb detector of radio waves, was ultimately to be the foundation of the electronics industry.

mother of invention

Radio prepared a surface for television by developing a fast national and international system of mass communications: whole populations embraced the idea of involving themselves with a medium which was anonymous, remote, yet simultaneously personal and near. One source fed many. But the motivation behind television had separate origins. Almost immediately after Alexander Graham Bell had exhibited his telephone in 1876, dreamers began wondering, if sound could be transferred along wire, why not vision? In 1879 *Punch* magazine featured a George du Maurier drawing of a couple at home watching a tennis match on a screen above the fireplace. It was a product wholly of du Maurier's creative mind, though within five years of this, a German, Paul Nipkow, had demonstrated a rotating disc with a spiral of perforations through which a beam of light was shone. The disc was placed between an object and a screen made of selenium cells, which activated an electrical current when light fell on them. As the disc spun, pinpoints of light scanned across the screen, transmitting an image of the object in the form of dots.

This mechanical system was the basis for a string of separate developments, the most notable being those of the British Broadcasting Company (BBC), which operated with John Logie Baird's formulation, and the Bell Laboratories. But, it was at Westinghouse, in the 1920s, where a fully electronic device employing tubes was first commercially developed, due mainly to the efforts of Vladimir Zworykin, a Russian emigré who worked for Westinghouse and, later, the Radio Corporation of America (RCA). Before migrating, Zworykin had worked as an assistant to Boris Rozing, who had discovered that an electronic beam in a cathode ray tube left complex luminescent patterns on the front of the tube. In 1907, Rozing patented a system of sending and receiving images based on his tube. While the image of Rozing throwing a switch and shrieking "Eureka! I've invented tv!" as he watched the screen activate is a delightful one, it is also far too simplistic. Rozing's work built on that of several others and still others were experimenting in related areas. Nor was Rozing's device a completely workable system; it was Zworykin who managed to translate it into something more practical whilst working in the USA. But Rozing's idea was innovative and, ultimately exploitable.

In 1923, Zworykin patented his design and, in 1928, produced what he called an "iconoscope" based on Rozing's concept and comprising a receiving screen of thousands of elements that took on an electrical charge when struck by light reflected from the object to be transmitted. The screen was rapidly scanned by a beam from an electron gun which resulted in an electrical discharge that was amplified and transmitted to the receiver, which then reconstructed the discharges into points of light on the screen.

Between Rozing's conceptual breakthrough and Zworykin's hands-on application, a British patent official opened a new file under the heading "Television." Rozing's two cathode ray receiver patents demonstrated theoretically that electronically scanned television was possible. Zworykin made it possible. Yet, it did not become the basis for a mass medium until the mid-1950s. Sheer technological advance was not enough: an external catalyst was needed. The "supervening necessity," as Brian Winston terms it, was the "spare capacity of the electronics industry in 1945/6" (1986: 52).

Winston, in his book *Misunderstanding Media*, argued that defense spending during the Second World War had expanded the US radio industry by between 1,200 and 1,500 per cent. More than 300,000 workers were employed. Demand for radio during peacetime would not keep them busy and only television, by then a demonstrably effective medium, offered any promise.

Before the war, in 1939, RCA had begun regular broadcast of television to a few thousand receiving sets with five-inch screens that produced dim images and only in New York. Three years before this, the British government had inaugurated an experimental service but, with only 2,000 sets sold by 1939, public take-up was slow. The BBC for years operated a system without either a viewing audience or a manufacturing base. The latter was created out of the necessities of war. An efficient communications system had been developed through radio broadcasts prior to the outbreak of war and the research, development, and production stimulated by war itself yielded a vast electronics industry. Winston uses Tolstoy's tale of the giant turnip to illustrate his point: the efforts of a mouse were needed at the end of a line of strong able-bodied helpers to uproot the huge vegetable. The idling assembly lines making cathode ray tubes, like the mouse, supplied the final small, but vital ounce of energy. "The farmer, his wife and all the others are to be found, as it were, in those tendencies within society creating entertainment forms for the urban mass" (1986: 54).

The complementary forms of technology in the manufacture of radio, an established medium, and television, a promising tool but without a tested market, meant that wartime investments need not be wasted if a demand could be found. Much earlier, in 1927, the US Congress had created the Federal Radio Commission, giving it broad powers to issue licenses and assign frequencies. In 1934, it was superseded by a new Federal Communications Commission (FCC) with broader powers afforded by the Communications Act. Its regulatory power might have violated the American spirit of free enterprise, but a war of all-against-all would have been self-destructive for the airways. The BBC, being a government-protected agency, had no such problem. In the 1930s, the FCC, faced with a slightly different situation from the fight over airwaves, adjudicated on technical specifications for systems of transmitting and receiving televised images. After the war, this technical standardization encouraged the growth of a mass market. Incompatibilities in equipment and processes, such as those that later fragmented the markets for video cassette recorders and personal computers, were avoided by the FCC's timely imposition of uniformity.

RCA, which had recruited Zworykin and come to terms with another patent holder, Philo Farnsworth, was favored by the FCC and its standards were adopted. Its rival CBS appealed to the FCC that it was near to perfecting a color system, but it was rejected. Months after the decision, the chair of the FCC resigned to take an executive position with NBC, at that time an affiliate of RCA.

The FCC had actually held up RCA's development up till 1941 in order to prevent a replication of the monopoly AT&T had secured over telephone. FCC's go-ahead was quickly followed by the USA's involvement in the war, which aborted plans. Between 1948 and 1952, the FCC froze license allocations with four major networks and 52 stations. Ostensibly, the reason was the proliferation of stations, which had caused interference to reception, but there was also a battle between CBS and RCA over color systems. (In fact, a full color schedule was not introduced until 1964 and sales of color sets were initially sluggish. In Britain, BBC2 became a full color channel in 1967.) The freeze allowed the two major networks, CBS and NBC, to consolidate their power bases. When the freeze thawed, they shared 80 per cent of the market.

Remember: the diffusion of television had been checked in the 1930s and 1940s, even when the technology was available. Not until 1952, when supervening necessity of spare electronic industry capacity came into play, did television begin to take off. By this time, the BBC had completed a network of major transmitters to reach 78 per cent of the British population; its monopoly was protected from commercial competitors until 1955 when Independent Broadcasting was able to frame its programs with advertising.

The BBC also enjoyed a radio monopoly, so its government-brokered transformation to a television empire posed no threat to its paramount position. In the USA, by contrast, major corporate players had vested interests in the radio industry and clearly television was a danger. The period leading up to 1952 allowed the radio giants to strengthen their position and maintain their stability. Television eventually became the dominant medium and it was owned by radio interests.

Winston made sense of this somewhat artificial obstruction to the growth of television as a mass medium by invoking what he called "the 'law' of the suppression of radical potential" (1986: 67–83). Basically, it operates when a business "invents" a device that threatens to put it out of business: the radio powers had the potential to exploit a technology that could effectively kill off radio, so they had to slow down the rate of progress in order to preserve themselves. Winston saw the "law" recurring in the histories of telecommunications technologies. In this instance, the FCC worked hand-in-glove with the radio corporations to impede change.

To the present day, the FCC is torn between the often conflicting demands of the broadcasting corporation and the public it supposedly serves. "Many critics do believe that the FCC has failed to serve the public interest because it has been 'captured' by the broadcasting industry," wrote Rudi Volti, noticing the similarity with other bodies: "the Interstate Commerce Commission often champions the cause of the trucking industry, as the now defunct Atomic Energy Commission did for the nuclear power industry" (1992: 175).

The FCC's authority to fix standards and grant licenses was instrumental in the growth of the medium, but it was legally unable to assume a quality control function and it was quite possible for it to criticize the very corporations it licensed. In 1961, for example, the FCC chair described US television as "a vast wasteland." At the time, 90 per cent of US homes had at least one set. Such comments obviously did nothing to interrupt the astonishing growth of television. After trudging wearily from a depression and a world war, populations looked for some affordable light entertainment. In 1949, only two per cent of US homes had television sets, then priced by Sears, Roebuck at $149.95.

A year later, 10 per cent had sets and, a year after that, 13 per cent. By 1955, this had leapt astoundingly to 67 per cent and the growth continued: 1963, 90 per cent; 1968, 95 per cent; 1977, 97 per cent. By 1985, 99 per cent of the population had television, over half owning more than one set. In Britain, the growth pattern has been very similar, except staggered.

making people pay

Lord Reith, the first Director-General of the BBC, whose attitudes shaped British broadcasting at least until the mid-1950s when commercial television arrived, pronounced that: "To have exploited so great a scientific invention for the purpose and pursuit of 'entertainment' alone would have been a prostitution of its powers and an insult to the character and intelligence of its people" (quoted in Skornia, 1965: 47). And, in its 1933 yearbook, the BBC vowed to "set its face absolutely against devoting its programmes entirely to amusement."

The heads of US television, on the other hand, had no compunction about insulting their people. Their mission was to protect their positions of power and maintain high profits and, if this mean providing "entertainment", then entertainment it would be. No attempt was made to define taste, or act as a patron of culture.

Harry Skornia, in his 1965 book *Television and Society*, noticed how the British viewed US television as a warning rather than an example and that the decision to allow commercial broadcasting to compete with the BBC in the 1950s, was "prompted by fears that, if it didn't it would be swamped by US programmes from US firms based in Europe or ships off the British coast" (1965: 181–2).

By the time commercial television arrived in Britain in 1955, about 9 per cent of the nation's homes had television sets (in the USA, 67 per cent of households already had sets). The Television Act of 1954 provided for the introduction of commercials, but not the type of program sponsorship that was popular in the USA, where, for example, a CBS series of the 1950s, *Man Against Crime*, could be sponsored by Camel, with the result that only "good guys" could be seen smoking cigarettes. This approach was a staple of US television, which had become excellent in producing highly watchable entertainment, thanks in part to the many writers, producers and artists who had left the Hollywood film industry to work for television.

This migration followed a 1948 Supreme Court decision in the case of the *United States* v. *Paramount et al.* The eight main Hollywood studios lost the control they had previously held over cinemas, which effectively meant that they had no say in how and what movie theaters decided to book. Fearing they could not unload their 400 to 500 films on cinemas, the studios slashed production schedules and cancelled contracts with personnel, who fled to television. As Tinseltown declined, tv ascended, boosted by its own Hollywood-style "telefilms."

The ingredients of US television were successfully mixed in the 1950s: comedies, like *I Love Lucy*, variety shows, Ed Sullivan's being the most popular, drama and quiz or game shows, the biggest of which was *The $64,000 Question* sponsored by Revlon. The CBS show reached number one in viewer ratings in 1957 and was virtually cloned several times over, with prizes exceeding the figure suggested in the original show's title. But, in 1959, revelations that the shows were fixed precipitated an investigation by the government's House of Representatives and forced the networks to drop the shows. (The movie *Quiz Show* focuses on this.) Years later, the show reappeared in different guises.

But, if the game show scam was the low ebb of US television in the period, its high point was its success in exporting its products. The globalization of television is, as we know, an "Americanization." At the end of the 1950s, US television corporations had Byzantine interests all over the world: they either owned or part-owned stations in every continent. By 1959, NBC had sold *The Perry Como Show* to seventeen countries. CBS had *Perry Mason*, *Gunsmoke* (or *Gun Law* as it was retitled in Britain), and about forty other shows playing abroad. While it was fearful of following the American example, Britain warmed to the likes of *Highway Patrol*, *Sea Hunt* and *The Lone Ranger*. These were proven commodities in the home market and, as Harry Skornia reflected at the time: "Profit rather than quality determines too much of what they see from and about America" (1965: 190). It was cheaper for countries to buy US programs rather than produce their own; and profitable for the networks, who took extra revenue from their shows' second runs abroad.

In the ten years from 1967, US corporations tripled their income from the world sales of television programs to approximately $240 million, according to Chin-Chuan Lee in *Media Imperialism Reconsidered* (1979: 73). The flow outward from the US was mainly to other large industrial nations, including Canada, Britain, Japan, Australia, and, to a lesser extent, Brazil, France and Germany. By the end of the 1970s, these countries plus the USA accounted for 62.5 per cent of the world's viewing audience. This was imperialism passing off as the world's communication industry. And as European culture had once been exported to far-flung corners of the empires, so US programs were slid easily into the schedules of other, this time industrial, countries. Canada, being next door to the USA, expressed most concern at becoming a cultural Xerox copy of the US and imposed constraints on the quality of programs imported, but later developments in cable and satellite technologies made it possible for Canadians to receive signals from the USA anyway. Today, at any given moment anywhere in the world someone can ask "What's on tv?" and the answer will be a US-made program. So encompassing are the effects of the USA's early commercial efforts.

US programs were not made for their aesthetic value; only for how much value they had for advertisers. The formula pioneered by radio had been adopted whole by US television and the advertisers' money rolled in, making the production of programs something of a conveyor belt. Cheaply made westerns like *Cheyenne*, which was botched together from old Hollywood footage, became worldwide phenomena. *Dragnet* was the first international cop thriller. Such series had the Hollywood touch, but it was a Hollywood that had long since lost the zest of *Casablanca* or *Gone with the Wind*.

An event that both symbolized the globalization and created new methods of televising was the launch of the Telstar Communications satellite in 1962. Once in orbit, the satellite could relay all forms of communication, including television, around the world and "live." The small (three feet diameter, 170lbs) metal sphere travelled in an elliptical path, its perigee 593 miles and apogee 3503, taking less than two-and-three-quarter hours to orbit the earth. It stopped working in its 1242nd orbit, but not before it had demonstrated the possibilities of extra-terrestrial intercontinental telecommunication. Radio telephony had been in use since the 1920s, but was poor quality. Crude undersea cables had first been laid in 1849, though the first permanent transatlantic link was completed in 1866, obviously not for the coverage of television, but for telegraphic messages. The commercial potential of combining cable and satellite was not fully realized until the 1970s, though cable as a television medium was in use for years before.

The origins of cable television and its technological development provide another example of the law of radical suppression. Just 2 per cent of US households owned tv sets in 1949 when broadcast television was available, though not to all. Remote and shielded areas of the country had no reception. Two such areas were Landsford, Pennsylvania, and Astoria, Oregon. Robert Tarlton was a radio sales and service worker, who must have felt a sense of relative deprivation living in Landsford, only 65 miles away from Philadelphia but unable to pick up television. The Allegheny Mountains were the offending barrier to tv signals. Tarlton had the bright idea of planting a master antenna, or aerial, on top of one of the mountains, catching the signals from Philadelphia and then distributing them to Landsford's houses via coaxial cable hung on poles. He got together with three other radio dealers to form the Panther Valley Television Company, charging $125 for installation and $3 per month subscription for a system that brought in three Philadelphia stations.

At around the same time, 1948–9, Ed Parsons, who ran a music store in Astoria, hooked up a wire that ran from his home to a local hotel and into his music store, where he attracted customers by showing programs from Seattle stations. The FCC could touch neither: technically, they were not taking direct signals, but rebroadcasting. The concept was a simple, but workable solution to the problems faced by remote areas where reception was difficult or impossible. Arriving as it did at the time of the FCC freeze, it was a threat to the dominance then being consolidated by the major networks. Basically, anybody, with standard equipment, could hook up their own cable system and tap in; and this made it troublesome.

In Britain, the potential of cable transmission was snuffed out at a much earlier stage in its growth. In the 1920s, radio reception was weak in some areas of the country, like the Northeast and the South coast, prompting the installation of methods of rediffusing services through wires. The danger was spotted and the BBC, in concert with the General Post Office, rationalized its opposition by harkening back to its insistence on information and culture in contrast to the pure "entertainment" that might be picked up from overseas stations and rediffused.

But, in the States, maverick cable systems gained steadily, so that, by 1961, there were 700, and in 1962, 1325, with 1.2 million subscribers yielding $40 million. Subscribers had become habituated to paying for their television. The money went to the private cable operators rather than the originators of the programs.

The FCC had, in its airwaves allocation, privileged urban areas in the interests of giving advertisers the biggest markets. Cable carried the messages beyond at no extra cost and with no additional services. Grumbles of "parasitism" led to court cases through the 1960s but cable came through the decade unscathed. United Artists Television sought protection of their materials under copyright laws, but the US Supreme Court ruled in favor of the cable company which, it declared, was acting like an ordinary viewer in receiving signals, which it merely enhanced and distributed. Yet the FCC's minor successes were significant. For example, it ruled against a firm that wished to use a community antenna (CATV) to import distant signals into Wyoming on the grounds that it would virtually put paid to the local stations (those within 60 miles of the cable headquarters). It confined cable to local rebroadcasting and, in 1972, brought operators into its fold by requiring them to get an FCC certificate of compliance for which they paid a fee based on their size. At the time, there were 2,750 systems serving six million homes unevenly distributed in mainly rural pockets across the United States.

Still in the same year, Time Inc.'s Home Box Office (HBO) began its unique service to 365 cable subscribers. The idea behind it was to charge an extra fee above the basic cable subscription in exchange for full-length feature films and "live" sport uninterrupted by commercials. The technology that permitted this was demonstrated in the 1940s when Hollywood tried to stem the popular growth of tv by essaying a scrambled signal which could be unscrambled in the form of a film for those who wished to pay.

While it used the cable system, HBO was essentially a different animal: it offered original programs and distributed them nationally by bouncing them off satellites to local cable operators. For two years, HBO's progress was slow (57,000 subscribers on 42 cable systems) and the FCC did not encourage satellite-delivered services. Instead of augmenting the major networks, HBO had the potential to become a competitor. The project loomed even larger with the emergence of ESPN, MTV, CNN and C-SPAN, all of which originated their own specialist programs and offered them at no extra cost to basic cable subscribers.

If any event signaled the switch in fortunes for domestic satellite tv, it was the Muhammad Ali–Joe Frazier heavyweight title fight which was beamed live from Manila, Philippines, in 1975 by HBO. Over the following decade new satellite-cable linked networks proliferated over the States, some offering esoteric services like the Home Shopping Channel, a televisual mail order catalog, and the Weather Channel (24-hour reports). HBO and "premium" channels drew their revenues from subscriptions, while the others generated theirs from advertisers and local cable operators.

The cables gnawed at the terrestrial network's store of viewing audience in every season from 1976/7 till 1992, when the combined ABC, NBC and CBS share was 63 per cent. By this time cable was available almost everywhere in the USA (about 90 per cent) though its market was – and is – fragmented. It reaches about 60 per cent of all American households. Despite much rhetoric to the contrary, cable is not threatening to the networks which still exploit the majority of North American market and so keep the interest of the advertisers, which, in turn, generates enough money to make perennially popular programs like NBC's *Cheers*, which cost an estimated $3 million per episode – an amount beyond the reach of most cable stations – shortly before its finish in 1993.

For the most part, cable has stayed free from FCC interference. On occasion, it has invoked the first amendment to protect its content from government intervention (*Miller* v. *State of California* and *FCC* v. *the Pacific* being key rulings). FCC's intrusions have been limited to a 1966 requirement that all cable systems must carry all local broadcast stations along their wires. In 1984, the FCC, in the spirit of deregulation that was then sweeping the US, relaxed all of what minimal restrictions there were, including the ability of local governments to fix subscription rates. As cable operators enjoyed exclusive franchises in their local markets, they could please themselves about what they charged. Prices rose rapidly. This became a contentious issue in 1992 when consumer groups pushed for regulatory legislation. In 1986, the networks were allowed to cross-own a maximum of twelve stations, so that any threat to them implied by cable's then rising popularity would be neutralized by staking financial interests in them.

Satellite technology, inspired by Telstar rather than the thousands of miles of cables laid in the 1960s, made cable television, as we now recognize it, possible. In fact, by 1970 at latest, it was theoretically possible for homes to bypass cable wires completely and pick up signals from any commercial satellite within range with a relatively inexpensive receiving dish. Direct Satellite Broadcasting (DBS) was talked about, but never commercially explored. Not that this stopped viewers setting up their own dishes and effectively circumventing subscription fees. The 1984 Cable Telecommunications Act made the unauthorized reception of a coded or scrambled signal such as HBO's an offence, though the piracy of the air kept pace; as Doug Stewart revealed in 1989, "As many as half the 1.5 million decoders now in use in the USA are unauthorized 'black boxes.' Their owners watch all the tv they want and never have to pay" (1989: 160).

About the same time, new satellite dishes came onto the British market. Compared with North American viewers, who, with a cable subscription, could have about 50 channels at their mercy for about $25 a month, British viewers were hard done by, at least in terms of quantity, for much of US cable's output could have actually used the "vast wasteland" comment as an inspiration rather than admonition. The BBC had an unchallenged monopoly until 1955, when Independent Television arrived. Both initiated second channels under their respective umbrellas, and a fifth earthbound channel was started in 1994. Cable was first developed in 1946, but was legally forbidden to originate programs until the 1984 Cable and Broadcasting Act, under which eleven franchises were granted. A year later, only twelve per cent of British homes had been passed by cable and the prospects were grim. Plans for DBS had been laid since the early 1980s and, after several false starts, commercial transmission began in 1989. Rupert Murdoch's Sky group and the Screensport/Lifestyle network owned by W. H. Smith and later sold to Canal Plus, ESPN, and ABC before going to Eurosport, began Europe-wide operations from two satellite "transponders," Astra and Marco Polo. Viewers had to buy a receiving dish for about £200, then pay monthly subscriptions of about double the US average basic cable rate. Premium subscription channels, like the Movie Channel (equivalent of HBO) were scrambled and additional payments were needed for a descrambler, known as a "smart card."

Television has always had to be paid for, of course. The painless extraction of money from consumers was once disguised in the form of an extra few pennies on the price of washing powder, breakfast cereal or any other item that advertised on the medium. In Britain, the BBC refused to admit advertising (despite pressure to do so from Margaret Thatcher, when she was Prime Minister), but charged for a license. Cable made people dip into their pockets for subscriptions, as did satellite tv; and premium channels made them dip deeper for newer films or sports events. Pay-per-view (ppv) was an extension of this: it provided a particular event for a set price. For example, in 1991, TVKO began monthly transmissions of world championship boxing. Cable subscribers, whether individuals, bars, hotels or whatever could access this for between $25 and $40. BSkyB bought exclusive rights to English Premier League Soccer in 1992 and charged viewers for two games per week throughout the season; more on this in chapter nine.

In the USA, a cable subscriber with a full complement of premium channels and an interest in at least one ppv event per month would pay about $70 per month, plus whatever advertising costs are passed on to shopping bills in 1994. A British satellite subscriber, who was also a movie and soccer fan would fork out approximately £45 a month, including a license.

Technologically, satellite dishes and cables are a thing of the past already, though Winston's "law" of the suppression of radical potential seems likely to operate in such a way as to keep them running for the foreseeable future. Digital television technology would effectively allow for over-the-air cable transmission using techniques originally developed for computers and compact discs. As many as twenty channels could be squeezed in to Britain's broadcasting frequencies. For obvious reasons, existing television corporations have not greeted the idea with open arms and, according to Jonathan Miller, writing in the *Sunday Times*, have attempted to block the new technology (June 7, 1992). With only five channels, Britain has the least competitive terrestrial broadcasting in Europe. Digital technology would open up the airwaves.

I began this brief overview of television's technological history with the observation that we live in fear of science and technology. Television is not greatly feared, of course; certainly not by the millions who watch it night after night. Yet that could be the danger: the fact that we do not recognize that television is threatening. An intelligent audience being insulted, to use Lord Reith's term, is one thing. An intelligent audience that does not know it is being insulted is another. The spell-binding effect of television is what concerns the critics considered in the next chapter. The fact that, like helpless yet amused victims, we do not realize the dire condition we are in makes television a sinister presence in the living room, a technological gift we have welcomed with open arms and taken to our hearts, where it keeps us under its influence.

chapter three

under the influence

the pursuit of trivia

"The methadone metronome," is what the rap band the Disposable Heroes of Hiphoprisy called it. "TV is the reason why less than ten per cent of our nation reads books daily/Why most people think Central America means Kansas/ . . . and apartheid is a new headache remedy," they rapped in "Television, The Drug of the Nation" from the CD *Hypocrisy is the Greatest Luxury* (Island Records, 1992).

Its message is clear from the title: the effect of television on its audience is to give them a temporary feeling of elation and well-being, but it promotes abuse and destructive long-term effects that erode basic faculties, including the ability to think independently and critically. The argument bears strong similarity to Marx's opiate thesis which stated that religion diverted the working class' attention away from wordly matters, specifically their exploitation by capitalists, by supplying illusions of salvation in an after-life. Its political utility to the owners of the means of production is obvious. By the same logic, television could also be seen as a political instrument, keeping people too rapt to concern themselves with important material issues that affect their lives – which is, in essence, what the rap number suggests: "TV is the place where the pursuit of happiness has become the pursuit of trivia."

Almost a half-century before the Disposable Heroes released their product, two independent academic papers advanced a similar argument to set in motion a series of books and articles, all dedicated to exposing the detrimental consequences of watching too much television. The original statements came from entirely different theoretical schools: "The culture industry: Enlightenment as mass deception" was a chapter in the book *Dialectic of Enlightenment* by Theodor Adorno and Max Horkheimer, first published in Amsterdam in 1947; "Mass communication, popular taste, and organized social action" by Paul Lazarsfeld and Robert Merton originally appeared in *The Communication of Ideas* edited by Lyman Bryson, first published in New York in 1948.

Though very different in tone and content, they were both guided by a warning spirit: beware the politically soporific and intellectually degenerative effects of a medium, then busily mass-producing itself all over Europe and North America. A similar spirit is evident in the contemporary works of Neil Postman, Todd Gitlin and others whose contributions we will move to later.

With his peers at the Frankfurt Institute of Social Research, Adorno extended early Marxist analysis into the realm of culture, defined broadly as the product of human efforts to bring nature under control. The Frankfurt School followed Marx in his dissection of the capitalist system, but believed the system had been severely disrupted by technological developments. Previously, nature was accorded great respect. But technology permitted an exploitation of natural resources at a level and intensity never before witnessed and this had served to reorient our relationships to nature and technology. We became free from the fetters of one, only to submit to the domination of the other. As J. M. Bernstein reflected in his introduction to a collection of Adorno's writing: "The very same rationality which provides for humankind's emancipation from the bondage of mystic powers and allows for progressive domination over nature, engenders, through its intrinsic character, a return to myth and new, even more absolute forms of domination" (1991: 4).

The orienting rationality encourages us to disregard intrinsic properties and ask instead what goals or purposes they serve. Work becomes only a means of earning money, for instance. It also inclines us to subsume a variety of different objects so as to allow for the technical mastery of them. Great musical works are collapsed into the category "classical" music for purposes of recording and duplicating many times over. Under modern capitalism, all production, including that of art, is for the market: not to meet human needs, or tastes, but for the sake of profit. Intrinsic properties are sacrificed; particular qualities are ignored. This insensitivity to specific features spreads into all areas of life like a blanket of lava. Everything becomes standardized, homogenized and industrialized, so that Adorno was able to write about what he called the culture industry, in which all products are "tailored for consumption by the masses" (1991: 83).

Adorno referred not only to the uniformity of film, radio, and popular print media, like newspapers and magazines, but fine art and music, which are rendered harmonious in a forced and false way just so that they are easily consumable. Unlike conventional definitions of culture as something that arises spontaneously from the creativity of humans, "the culture industry intentionally integrates its consumers from above." In the process, a mass congeals. The consumers to whom the culture industry is directed become objects (not subjects); targets for market forces. Populations become as standardized and homogeneous as the surrounding culture. This is a marvellous convenience, of course, for it eliminates much of the guesswork from gauging markets. People accept, conform, obey, unwittingly, and perhaps even wittingly, assisting the growth of the industry.

Adorno and his colleagues were Jewish refugees from Germany and had witnessed firsthand the plasticity of entire populations when handled manipulatively by skillful hands adept at propaganda techniques. They had watched the Nuremberg rallies, at which hundreds of thousands of autonomous individuals dissolved into a sea, whose ebbs and flows were guided by the dictates of Nazism. They observed control in action: wills were bent, volition was voided, intentional action was reduced to mere reflex. Hands were extended without, it seemed, conscious deliberation; the mere stimulus of "Heil Hitler" was sufficient. Small wonder that they were persuaded of the ease with which people could be shaped by modern technology to fit any prescribed mold. Nazism, in the monstrous form in which it had surfaced in the 1920s, might eventually have been subdued, but the methods it had revealed for controlling human thought and conduct and reducing individuality to insignificance had lasting effects. Indeed, Adorno later studied the precise composition of what he called *The Authoritarian Personality* (1980).

The freedom that was thought to ensue after the defeat of fascist totalitarianism was, on this account, illusory. For the technology that had facilitated the dictatorship of masses had slid unnoticed into the homes of Europeans and Americans. We became flattened into what Herbert Marcuse, another member of the Frankfurt School, called the "one-dimensional man," choices becoming a matter of consumer preferences, politics becoming a question of whom to vote for and social problems becoming a case of whatever was soluble within a technological framework. Alternatives were marginalized or removed. Everyday life, as the Frankfurt School saw it, comprised buying, working with machines or staying at home to work in isolation. Technology of one kind or another dominated all spheres of activity. This was not enlightenment, as the subtitle of the seminal chapter indicated, it was deception.

One response to the culture industry concept was that it invited elitism. Adorno's critique of consumer capitalism and the debasement of taste it entailed was quite explicit in its dismissal of popular modern cultural forms – as epitomized in television, of course. Adorno rued the decline of "high culture," with all its connotations of esoteric modernism available to only the few, and the corresponding rise of a culture on tap for all. The former was pure, while the latter was polluted by political interests.

To simplify, the culture industry was political in two ways. First, it promised happiness, but delivered only amusement. As Marx saw religion as supplying a relief from work, Adorno *et al.* saw mass culture as an escape attempt from the mechanized monotony of industrial work, helping workers refresh themselves for more labor. In no meaningful way, could this be described as happiness. Related to this was a second use, for, in supplying momentary pleasure, it distracted consumers from contemplating too deeply more urgent matters. "Pleasure always means not to think about anything," wrote Adorno, "to forget suffering" (1991: 9).

Being amused simultaneously removed the thought that there was any alternative to the status quo. Even if it was accepted that mass culture had disguised political utility, there seemed no reason why the Frankfurt School should excuse its beloved opera, ballet, masterly painting and so on, the same type of swingeing analysis it had given more accessible cultural forms.

The culture industry argument has resonances in John Carpenter's film *They Live*, in which earth has been colonized by aliens, who induce humans' conformity by plastering advertising hoardings and television screens with imperatives like "Obey," "Conform," and "Follow rules." So total is the manipulation that humans are never aware of it. Special sunglasses are needed to be able to "see through" the operation. Objectors to Adorno's theory have accused him of depicting humans in a similar way, unable to resist their manipulation because they just do not know about it. No one is quite as passive and gullible as Adorno seemed to suppose.

In two later articles, one on astrology, the other intriguingly titled "How to look at television," Adorno argued that we do, in part, "see through" the attempts of the culture industry to render us submissive. We are not so dopey that we cannot retain an element of self-reflection and keep a critical distance from what is going on around us. Glance at any astrology column and it will dispense free advice on whether today is a good time for business, for love, for making drastic changes to one's life. The advice is based on no more than the purported relationship between planetary movements and earthly affairs. It does not provide anything resembling scientific evidence, yet it permits belief and obedience. Even devout readers are not exhorted to surrender their scientific rationality and commitment to empirical evidence.

Astrology never comes close to scientific status; its appeal is due, in large part, to its incompatibility with the natural sciences. And while there are no doubt hardcore followers who plot their daily lives in symmetry with the stars, most may heed the advice while remaining skeptical. "Oh, I know it's all nonsense, but . . ." might be the legitimating response of someone who adjusts in minor ways to the commands of the stars. Astrology demands so little in the way of thinking and action yet offers so much, that many find it hard to refuse it, even though they do not believe in it. Seeing through something is no reason to reject it, especially when one feels helpless to change oneself or society through more conventional channels.

This suggests parallels with television viewing. "I know most of what's on insults your intelligence, but I watch it all the same." One can almost hear the response of a consumer who has seen through the commercials: "I know all soap powders are exactly the same, but I still prefer . . ." We are able to screen the overt messages or signals of the mass media. Yet Adorno believed there was something more occult at work, "the hidden message" that will "escape the controls of consciousness;" and, in his analysis of television, he seemed to drift towards the *They Live* scenario: "The hidden message . . . will not be looked through, will not be headed off by sales resistance, but is likely to sink into the spectator's mind" (1991: 141).

Adorno admitted that this would be hard to corroborate with exact data, but pushed the argument along to a further point: "The majority of television shows today aim at producing or at least reproducing, the very smugness, intellectual passitivity and gullibility that seem to fit in with totalitarian creeds even if the surface message of the shows may be anti-totalitarian" (1991: 142). This succeeds because of our "multi-layered personalities," which make it possible for us to think critically at one level, yet obediently at another. Adorno gave as an example a comedy show in which an underpaid schoolteacher is continually tried by an authoritarian school principal; so much so that the schoolteacher becomes hard-up and has to hustle friends for food. Amusing situations occur both in her unsuccessful attempts to get food from friends and her encounters with the principal. "Hidden meaning" is in the way the story looks at human beings:

> The character of the underpaid, maltreated schoolteacher is an attempt to reach a compromise between prevailing scorn for the

> intellectual and the equally conventionalized respect for "culture". The heroine shows such intellectual superiority and high-spiritedness that identification with her is invited, and compensation is offered for the inferiority of her position and that of her ilk in the social set up. In terms of a set pattern of identification, the script implies: If you are as humorous, good-natured, quick-witted, and charming as she is, do not worry about being paid a starvation wage.
>
> (1991: 143)

The latent message is smuggled into our minds with a "style which does not pretend to touch anything serious and expects to be regarded as featherweight" but which "sets patterns for the audience without their being aware of it." There is no sinister masterplan behind all this; and the individual writers, producers and other collaborators, all of whom are subject to rules, set patterns, requirements and "mechanisms of control" which reduce "the range of any kind of artistic expression." Adorno called the production of television material *automatized* to fit into formulas, complete with stereotypes and clichés.

"But we know all this!" Adorno reckoned is the first defence against his argument. Today, we are not surprised by what many would regard as scaremongering. In fact, many dismiss the argument, as we will see in the next chapter: television may be as loaded with political messages as Adorno suggested, but we need not rush to the conclusion that we are either duped by them, or "see through them" while still behaving like lambs to the slaughter. The image underlying Adorno's thesis is that of a helplessly passive and compliant victim-viewer. Critical abilities blunted and powers of reasoning diminished, the viewers succumb to the irresistible power of the culture industry so that they become mere absorbers of television's messages, rather than creators of them – as later analysts were to visualize them.

upping the dosage

Much the same image, or model of the human being influenced the work of Lazarsfeld and Merton, whose research at New York's Columbia University established the basis of what was to become known as media sociology. Like members of the Frankfurt School, Lazarsfeld was a Jewish refugee and the influences of personal experiences on his theories are also apparent. He shared a very similar set of concerns about the size and influence of the mass media and about the political uses they could be put to. Lazarsfeld's key article with Merton, like much of Adorno's output, was as much warning as treatise.

"Modern propaganda is a scientific machine," Lazarsfeld and Merton prefaced their arguments in 1948, before the popularization of television. Hitler had used a combination of organized violence and mass coercion; in postwar North America, direct coercion had been minimized. "Mass persuasion" served in its place. The ambiguity of the mass media posed a series of threatening possibilities; including: (a) a conformity to the status quo; (b) a "vulgarization" of aesthetic tastes; and (c) a surrender of critical thinking. None of these suggestions would elicit a murmur from the Frankfurt School, though, remember, Lazarsfeld and Merton regarded them as possibilities, not yet realities.

As adherents of the functionalist school of American sociology, Lazarsfeld and Merton's first response to studying any phenomenon was to ask the primary question "what functions (or dysfunctions) does it serve?" They answered: three. First, status conferral: the social standing, or prestige, of persons or policies is raised when they command favorable attention in the mass media. The relevance to political candidates and their campaigns is clear enough: legitimacy may arrive gift-wrapped if the mass media shows them in the right light. (We will calculate the contemporary relevance of this in chapter eleven.)

Second, the enforcement of social norms: by exposing moral stands, the media can spur organized action. Deviations, sometimes of a gross nature, may – in fact, do – take place, but, it is not until they are made public that concerted action against them takes place. The most extreme example would be a media crusade which provides a center around which disparate groups may organize. The child abuse cases in Cleveland, England, and in New Jersey in the late 1980s would be examples of media crusades which focused public attention and, in the process, reaffirmed social norms of acceptable behavior.

Third, and most interesting for our immediate purposes, is the narcotizing dysfunction: mass communication enables diverse populations to keep abreast of world events and may even provide them with opinions; but, it also leads them to devote less time actually to doing anything about those events and so encourages apathy and inertia. We spend more and more time reading, listening about and viewing events, and so we have not time, or for that matter, inclination, to take action on them. "In this respect," wrote Lazarsfeld and Merton presciently:

> Mass communications may be included among the most respectable and efficient of social narcotics. They may be so fully effective as to keep the addict from recognizing his own malady . . . increasing dosages of mass

> communications may be inadvertently transforming the energies of men from active participation into passive knowledge.
>
> (1948: 106)

Ignoring the fact that it might be argued that the third is no more dysfunctional than the first two are functional and that the three should be seen as complementary, we should acknowledge the resonance of the narcotizing argument, an argument that was to span nearly five decades with little modification. We will move to recent variants of it later, but for now notice the principal metaphor: the narcotics Lazarsfeld and Merton had in mind were not like cocaine, which acts on the brain's cortex and can, evidence suggests, increase perceptual awareness and clear thinking, but more like marijuana, which induces drowsiness, stupor or insensibility. Dozens of writers followed. Among the more notable, Jerry Mander, in his *Four Arguments for the Elimination of Television*, argued that television did not just work like a drug; it was a drug: "Television isolates people from the environment, from each other, and from their own senses" (1980: 168).

Attractive and useful as the narcotic metaphor undoubtedly is, there are a number of drawbacks to using it in a straightforward way. They fall into two groups, the first of which relates to the difference between presenting a powerful provocative and suasive assertion and backing it up with empirical evidence. Research findings from different poles of the spectrum are equivocal.

Common sense seems to tell us that watching television structures the information we receive and, in time, the attitudes we hold about politics, including political ideologies and doctrines, as well as voting preferences. Both main approaches considered here suggest that the broad range of television coverage in free market economies will intensify a coalescence of attitudes towards the right of the political continuum and an accommodation of the status quo. The culture industry thesis strongly argues for a consensus or "massification" of political ideas, while Lazarsfeld and Merton sense a drift towards passivity.

Common sense is sometimes contradicted by empirical research and, in their book *Television and Social Control*, Mallory Wober and Barrie Gunter gathered together the findings of various studies to show that, while attitudes can be changed through viewing and entertainment, "evidence for coherent inculcation of particular ideologies is less widely supported or convincing" (1988: 87). Wober and Gunter, while not directly addressing the two theories, implicitly made them appear simplistic: empirical evidence points to a much more complicated set of political effects with age, status, level of education and other variables having to be factored into the equation. Television has no uniform impact on political attitudes; it depends on social position.

Also, Wober and Gunter cast doubt on the argument popularized by George Gerbner and his associates, who argue that US television has had a powerful "acculturative effect," meaning that political attitudes have been molded into a conservative shape (1982).

Wober and Gunter urged caution in analyzing the link between television and politics, believing the allegedly massive effects must be tempered by taking into account the ages, social backgrounds and values of various sections of the audiences. There is no mass effect on societies. But is there an effect at an individual level?

A strong implication of the views of Adorno, Lazarsfeld and the others is that television has a "deadening" impact and inhibits us from acting in a positive way. Psychologists, studying the desensitizing effects of television, show that this occurs only after repeated viewing of the same presentation. John Condry's exhaustive survey of the research revealed ambivalence on television's capacity to arouse or desensitize and only a tenuous grasp of the behavioral mechanisms involved. "It is unclear the extent to which individual's 'use' television, like a drug, to change their affective state," Condry concluded in *The Psychology of Television* (1989: 114). "People certainly claim this to be the case when asked about why they watch television."

In effect, viewers do not sit back limply and have tv injected into them, they exercise what Condry called the "ability to use television for one's own purposes." The narcotic metaphor still holds, but Condry suggested a more active role for the subject with the "uses and gratifications" model, introduced by Lazarsfeld in a book written with Elihu Katz, *Personal Influences* (Katz and Lazarsfeld, 1985). Unlike the earlier portrayals, this book advanced a conception of the viewer with a lot more choice at his or her disposal; as someone actively seeking out uses for the television and not simply a lifeless doughnut waiting to be injected with jam. Critics attacked Katz and Lazarsfeld for going too far: surely, this understated the role of the media in manipulating the very choices and tastes the writers felt were decisive. At best, the uses and gratifications model taught about how people thought, or wanted to believe, they used the television.

The tension between the concept of the consumer as a conscious and deliberating selector taking an active position in regard to the media and the television as ubiquitous and omnipotent has never really relaxed. We will see in subsequent chapters how adjustments in the tension have led to as many problems as they have solved. Softer terms like persuasion and influence do little to erase the fundamental question of how much capacity the human being has and can exercise in resisting or using the television. Not much, was the answer given by Neil Postman in his short, but inspiring essay which claimed that, in viewing so much television, we were effectively *Amusing Ourselves to Death.*

when the thinking stopped

Thematically, Postman's work was part of a new humanism, which arrived hand-in-hand with a preoccupation with death. This seemingly peculiar coupling is only peculiar until one thinks about it. When Postman wrote the book in the 1980s, death was a natural subject for a world entering the final score years of the millennium. And, for writers devoted to the human as a responsible and intellectual being with species-specific needs beyond those of other animals, the prospect of a surrender to death was disorienting. Why surrender? Because, Postman argued, the main institutions of life, like politics, religion, education and commerce, were being transformed into adjuncts of show business, without as much as a whimper of protest. "The result is that we are people on the verge of amusing ourselves to death" (1985: 4).

Postman's book might have been subtitled "Marshall McLuhan meets Aldous Huxley." The influences of these contrasting writers subtly guides much of the argument. A paragraph or so on each should set up the thesis. The aphorism "the medium is the message" helped McLuhan's *Understanding Media*, first published in 1964, command almost biblical reverence. Television's influence was due almost wholly to its direct style of presentation; the actual content of the programmes was irrelevant. It is rather difficult to comprehend why such an elementary observation had such messianic impact. Human culture is, of course, made possible by language; but we create it and transmit it from one generation to the next through various media of communication. We use visual materials, like hieroglyphs and photographs and oral ones, such as radio. Every different medium establishes new boundaries for possibilities; studying a woodcarving provokes different cognitive processes to looking at a video. The forms of media permit or even demand certain capacities for thought by supplying a framework. Media have *a prioris*, that is classes or categories into which they pour content, whether it be news or entertainment. These structure our experience of the world. After all, few of us actually experience firsthand what we receive through the media.

McLuhan took this a step further by arguing not only that the conduit through which experience was mediated was all-important, but that it changed us permanently. The structure of people's minds moved with changes in the structure of the media. There is a complementarity with Adorno's foretelling of a similar televisual tendency in this respect.

Postman travelled so far along McLuhan's path, accepting the basic point that the medium changes the structure of discourse by its varying demands on the intellect (unlike some other writers who prefer to see similarities in our reading of different media; next chapter). McLuhan argued that new technologies extended existing faculties: a car is a fast horse, which in turn "extended" human feet. Postman, along with an assembly of other critics noticed that, in fact, cars did not extend, but replaced feet. Technologies can almost eliminate human faculties. As Mark Miller remarked, in criticizing McLuhan: "Assisted by the calculator, our students forget how to add and subtract" (1988: 295). A very similar point is made by Postman, who, while agreeing with McLuhan's original formulation, remained skeptical about its implications for television viewers: "Television does not extend or amplify literate culture. It attacks it" (1985: 84).

The attack does not come from a menacing foe bearing a scowl, but one with a smiling face. Postman draws his metaphor from – yet again – drugs, this time Huxley's "soma" as featured in *Brave New World*, the inhabitants of which were continually under the influence (Huxley 1932). In Huxley's fictional dystopia, the goal was to keep people focused on their own satisfaction and confine their needs to ones that could be handled by social engineers. Sensibilities were overwhelmed by the effects of soma: personal love or caring was "unnatural" and disgusting. People lived for their own pleasure and mass doses of soma ensured that they thought of little else save their own satisfaction.

Unlike fellow prophet of doom Orwell's creation *1984*, Huxley's world had no need of prison wardens or Ministries of Truth: external controls were not necessary when the population was so distracted by trivia and shallow entertainments that challenges and even mild social criticism became things of the past, as did anything resembling genuine cultural life. Happiness permeated the entire world. The only problem was that no one knew quite what they were happy about. The affliction of the people was not so much that they were laughing instead of thinking, but, as Postman puts it, "they did not know what they were laughing about and why they had stopped thinking" (1985: 163).

As one might anticipate, Postman saw television where Huxley saw soma. The insight was not entirely original, as in 1983 Robert MacNeil, in a short article, asked the question "Is television shortening our attention span?" His answer:

> You are required, in much popular television fare, to pay attention to no concept, no situation, no scene, no character, and no problem for more than a few seconds at a time. In brief, television operates on the short attention span.
>
> (1983: 2)

Television diverts us only to divert us further, MacNeil argued, "to make time pass without pain". Hence the parallels with soma, as he notes. The ability to focus our attention is "the most precious of all human gifts," and television "usurps" it.

Postman built on MacNeil's gloomy diagnosis and decorated his own argument with examples of how, even in its most strenuous efforts to be serious-minded, television finds it awkward to convey coherent language or the thought process. He cites *Meet the Press* and *Open Mind.* (Britain's Joan Bakewell interviews would fall into this category.) But these are anomalies, as tv aims to achieve applause rather than reflection. And this signifies a profound change in culture: it has been transformed into "one vast arena for show business" (Postman 1985: 80).

Comparing the nature and type of public discourse television permits with earlier forms, Postman concluded that our culture has become degraded. Bearing in mind McLuhan's ideas on media of communication and the demands they place on the intellect, Postman suspected that such media are a dominant influence on a culture's "intellectual and social preoccupations."

Reading a book, or watching a play, or attending a political assembly to listen to a speaker requires us, at minimum, to remain immobile for a fairly long time. We learn a familiarity with words, not just the shape or sound of them, but the meanings they carry. We also assume an attitude of detachment and perhaps objectivity. Television's spread into our homes has introduced a new set of demands on our intelligence, but, in contrast to other writers, Postman did not accept they are of the same order as those of print media. It is "dangerous and absurdist" to think otherwise.

Contrast the scene in Peoria, Illinois, in 1854 with today, suggested Postman in describing a political debate between Abraham Lincoln and Stephen Douglas. Douglas opened and spoke for three hours, sent the audience home for dinner, after which they returned to listen to Lincoln's four-hour response. Seven hours of oratory makes different demands on the intellects of audience and speaker to a televised fifteen-minute political address. Television has transformed us into different creatures; we would not dream of sitting in front of the set for seven hours staring at two politicians. This is not entertaining to us and entertainment is the main reason, maybe the only reason, we watch television. Nothing too informative or abstract. The overall result is a desiccated culture that has been left out to dry as people stay at home, with their tv sets. Their intellects are virtually unused.

Postman's diatribe seemed to gather momentum as he galumphed over televisual religion, news and education. One reacts by wishing he would slow down and consider some of the benefits of television. What about the new vistas it has opened up? The news from all quarters of the world 24 hours a day on CNN or Sky News; Pavarotti concerts from La Scala; premier sporting events "live" from anywhere in the world – television is the first medium to globalize culture in an authentic way. Different languages prohibited print from doing this. Television is visual as well as oral. It has become the town cryer of the global village.

But, it is inert, replied Postman. The information we receive rarely causes us to take action, to re-plan our days or weeks. It requires us to do nothing. Note the agreement with Lazarsfeld and Merton. Historically oral and typographic, or print, cultures derived their importance from the possibilities for action. The sting in their tail was that we did something as a result. To this Postman would add that international news is a "world of fragments, where events stand alone, stripped of any connection to the past, or to the future or to other events" (1985: 110). In prising open the world for inspection, tv breaks it, so that we tend to view it in terms of short unconnected episodes, without context.

"The modern mind has grown indifferent to history because history has become useless to it," wrote Postman. It is as if we have become knowledgeable about world events in the previous 24 hours, but ignorant of them in the previous half-decade. We sense that anything more than a grasp of immediate events is irrelevant. So, paradoxically, globalization has not led to a fuller understanding historically or contextually, according to Postman.

Mark Miller made a related point when he rejected the argument that the purpose of television news is to inform the public. "To tell the public what the newsmen think the public is already thinking" is nearer the truth, according to Miller (1988: 101). His book *Boxed In* continued in the same vein as Postman's. "TV acts as a retardent on social progress," argued Miller. "By emphasising only the most visible events, tv, first of all, conceals social and economic reality in pious rituals that have upstaged the very struggle which produced them" (1988: 148).

Television has depleted our faculties and "corporate engineers keep searching for more ways to computerize our functions" (1988: 295). Miller concurred with all the theorists considered in this chapter when he observed that we have lapsed "into a constant, dull anxiety wherein we can hardly sense the difference between a famine and a case of body odor" (1988: 324).

sophisticated sponges

Todd Gitlin's feat has been to alchemize some of the assertions, arguments, declarations and possibly plain dogma into empirical questions, which he answered in two related books. *The Whole World is Watching*, published in 1980, draws its title from the chant of the Students for a Democratic Society (SDS) when in the presence of US national television cameras. The SDS formed part of a rising New Left movement in the 1960s and Gitlin studied the media's coverage of it during 1965. SDS demonstrations centered on protests against the Vietnam war; and the media at first respected them as legitimate, before growing impatient and trivializing or denigrating them as the manipulations of extremists.

SDS was a new and original phenomenon, owing little to existing political organizations. The media had difficulty "framing" it as a phenomenon. Gitlin showed that its assemblies were, at first, covered in the same way as civil rights protests. Later, they were transmuted to crime stories, thus stripping away all legitimacy. New recruits to SDS were attracted on the basis of the media's depiction of the organization and, in time, they directed the organization towards the types of activities emphasized particularly on television news. As the antiwar feeling spread across the nation and into the "respectable" upper echelons of political and economic leaders, the news portrait of SDS changed so that its activities became legitimate.

Gitlin's work concentrated on the production side of the media rather than its effects on audiences and it is clear, at least in his 1980 study, that he holds a much more creative model of human beings than other writers in this chapter. In his introduction he stipulated:

> Society is not a machine or a thing; it is a co-existence of human beings who do what they do (including maintaining or changing a social structure) as sentient, reasoning, moral and active beings who experience the world, who are not simply caused by it.
>
> (1980: 9)

In this regard, he aligned himself with the writers featuring in the next chapter. But there is a massive irony because our experience is "patterned" by ideology, that is, a "set of ideas that facilitate a ruling class" domination of society by shaping popular consent. "How and where are ideas generated in society?" asked Gitlin. Through a meshing of ideology and common sense. What we as consumers take to be real and natural, how we live, play, know, even rebel, is fixed by ideological limits. Schools and the mass media formulate and convey national ideologies; they do not impose them on us; we receive them and interpret them in such a way as to make life intelligible. The process through which we become convinced by the ideas is known as hegemony and we will return to this concept in the following chapter. For now, notice how Gitlin believes that people "stretch, dispute, and sometimes struggle to transform the hegemonic ideology." Gitlin's work shows how one such struggle was transferred to mainstream cultural institutions courtesy of the mass media and tamed through a process of what he calls "ideological domestication."

Gitlin does not propose that the "established order" simply absorbs all challenges. In fact, it may even need such challenges to survive. And here is the irony: "The self-contradictions in hegemonic ideology give it flexibility to shift with circumstance, and even turn opposition to its own advantage" (1980: 291). Sentient, reasoning, active, etc. as we may be, our "oppositional spirit is transformed and moves into the channels" (1980: 291). We grow from rebels into cynics. And this conception of impotence strengthens in Gitlin's later work and brings his work into closer harmony with the central themes of this chapter.

Inside Prime Time followed up the mass media–New Left study and is a tougher account of the power of television as an agent of control and constraint. It shapes viewers' perceptions, structures expectations, suggests opinions, motivates and inclines towards action, or more pertinently inaction. The "curious power," as Gitlin calls it, of television "begins from the fact that it requires so little of us" (1985: 333).

The substance of the book is an examination of the elements contributing to primetime television, between 8 p.m. and 11 p.m. when about one-third of the total population is glued to the set. Gitlin interviewed producers, writers, executives and other key personnel about the factors that weigh in making programming decisions. He found support for the views of Adorno *et al.*, that tv networks strained toward uniformity in both the content of shows and the way they are packaged. This is no conspiracy; it is an attempt by the television networks to guess mood swings and anticipate shifts in tastes, while at the same time guiding those moods and influencing those shapes. Calculated risks are sometimes taken, but predictability and conservatism generally hold sway, if only for the sake of attracting advertisers, who pull most of the strings anyway. Television's primary customers are not viewers, of course, but advertisers "whose business is to rent the eyeballs of the audience." More on the overweening influence of advertising later in chapter five. The story of the show *Lou Grant* is of special interest to Gitlin. A politically and socially alert content, intelligent themes and credible portrayals were of no consequence to CBS executives, who noticed only a slip in its viewer ratings and cut the show.

Gitlin revisited ideology when, in a blazing rejection of the view that we have become totally sponge-like in relation to the cut-out images often depicted on tv, he argued:

> The audience is sophisticated enough to recognize that media images are stereotypes, and don't hesitate to complain . . . the public no longer takes television for granted as if it were natural, or a wondrous gift of beneficent science.
>
> (1985: 249)

Yet, there is no denying that, sophisticated or not, we are influenced by television, not so much in how we think, but what we think about. And that may be more important. Gitlin acknowledges that television's "force" lies in the point that our guard is down when we watch and we are susceptible to "diversion and ideology." In a slightly self-contradictory passage, he wrote: "We notice and soak up and ignore selectively, although not always consciously" (1985: 333). Television's influence is now so all-pervasive, that we cannot possibly reflect on its symbols, meanings and implications. Television radiates ideology which means "nothing more or less than a set of assumptions that becomes second nature; even rebels have to deal with it." Television, Gitlin argued, "can no more speak without ideology than we can speak without prose" (1985: 333).

In a later edited collection, Gitlin detected that there had been an "over correction" of early, crude models of the media which depicted it as acting hypodermically, injecting ideology into the unsuspecting social bloodstream. In responding to it, some schools – and although he does not name them, he is clearly thinking of cultural studies – have not paid enough attention to "the unifying styles and ideological homogeneities of the contemporary media" nor to "the stultifying forms of popular culture" (1986: 5). If the choice of adjective is significant, then Gitlin sees viewers reduced, neutralized or, at best, impaired as active agents. And in this sense, his efforts contain the same kinds of tension that beset early work in a similar perspective.

If there is a problem in Gitlin's work it is that, in his efforts to avoid the generic pounding earlier theorists had given mass communications, he steered towards a "sophisticated" image of the viewer, soaking up "selectively," as he puts it none too convincingly. Like all the theorists covered in this chapter, Postman in particular (to whom, strangely, he never refers), Gitlin has a depressing message: television is bad for us. Whether it mutes our political voice, sanitizes our thoughts, deters us from action, entertains us senseless, or a combination of all of these, there is no mistaking its evil effects. Only in the work of Gitlin do we recognize a warrantable human presence opposing and reacting and, even then, the ascendant power of ideology all but stamps it out.

The sheer one-sidedness of this worried other theorists. Sure, there were ideological pressures to conform generated from "below" as well as "above." But to theorize at such a level of abstraction and without due attention to the role of the viewers themselves in the process, left an unsatisfactorily lifeless image of society. The response was inventive, yet perplexing, as we will see next.

chapter four

the meanings of cultural studies

reading as construction

Cultural studies has the air of a subject created on a dare. What, someone might have asked, if we studied popular media, like film, magazine and television, with techniques borrowed from structural linguistics, using words that few people understand and arriving at conclusions that totally contradict everyone's expectations? Then, with a nod to postmodernism, we tell everyone our conclusions are not true? One might be tempted to suggest that the subject would be regarded as esoteric, if not inconsequential. Not so: cultural studies has become a most influential approach to the study of popular culture, blending Marxist structuralism, semiotics, poststructuralism and other schools together in a heady mixture. In this chapter, I will try to make sense of a subject that is trying to make sense of everyone else. Its sheer bravura in this respect demands scholarly attention, though, as I will show later, much of cultural studies' success owes more to mannerism than meaning.

But first a caveat, or two. Nothing anyone working in cultural studies writes can ever be regarded as true. This is not intended as a criticism, but as a statement of cultural studies' capacity to inspect itself. "Truth must always be understood in terms of how it is made, for whom and at what time it is 'true'," wrote John Fiske, one of the bellwethers of the approach (1987: 256). In other words, no human has direct commerce with an objective reality and what we all come to regard as truth is a matter of agreement and convention, expressed primarily through language. So, the theories or propositions of cultural studies must be seen in the same light as cultural students analyze the world: as products of particular social contexts, in which particular rules apply and in which a particular language is employed.

Cultural studies, is not, as the casual reader might suppose, about the study of culture, but more to do with, as Fiske summarized, "the generation and circulation of meanings in industrial societies" (1987: 254). Actually, this is slightly misleading because "culture," as defined in this version of academicspeak, has little to do with conventional definitions; it is redefined so that it "encompasses all the meanings" of social experience. This sets an astonishingly wide framework of study, of course. So, it is rather surprising to find that devotees of cultural studies work within a narrow and specific perspective and with a lexicon that bears no resemblance to that of the subjects they study.

Significations, connotative agents, metonyms, syntagms, intertextuality and polysemy form a mere fraction of what Roger Silverstone called the "relentlessly implosive" vocabulary (1991: 234). Reading it is so punishing that one feels rather like Bruce Willis, in the movie *The Last Boy Scout*, who remarks after being assaulted by a prolix villain: "Feels like we're being beaten up by the inventor of Scrabble."

Apart from the observation about the relative flexibility of truth and falsity and an enthusiasm for abstruse language, cultural students are united in their interest in the operation of ideology on the ways we make sense of the world. Cultural studies focuses on the parts played by the way we receive and interpret messages from the mass media. Books, newspapers and other print media are fair game, as are film, radio and television. All, in their own way, perform ideological work in sustaining our consciousness, our acceptance of the world as natural and obvious. What we recognize as reality is but one version; there are others we remain unaware of. Ideology's job is to make sure we stay unaware. This is not achieved via conspiracy, with the political-powers-that-be haranguing us Big Brother-style, but by a subtler, or gentler process of meaning-generation. *We*, in other words, keep ideology going; which is why culture is political.

While there is not always an explicit endorsement of Marxism in cultural studies, there is usually some recognition that those in power will exhaust every possible way of keeping social arrangements the way they are. One of the most effective ways is to persuade the have-nots of the legitimacy, or even the obduracy of society's main institutions. The process of persuasion is hegemony and the messages imparted in that process are ideology. Societies, as a way of ensuring their own permanence, create methods for communicating ideology. The machinery through which the messages are disseminated are called ideological state apparatuses, or just ISAs, by Louis Althusser. The mass media are among these; the family, language, religion, the political system being others. These encourage people to think and act in ways that do not challenge the status quo. If you want them simply to comply, then agents of law enforcement can be called. Hegemony is a more exquisite and less costly way of winning the consent of subordinate groups.

The consent must never be assumed and has to be won over and over again, making the functions of the ISAs indispensible. The subtler the means through which the messages get across, the more effective they are. No one likes to be told they are being persuaded; much better that they genuinely believe in something to the extent where they do not need to reflect on it. Television is perfect: ideology slips through its channels surreptitiously. Unlike the earlier, cruder theories of ideology which saw humans as unwitting and, perhaps even unwilling, recipients of media-filtered political messages designed to keep the masses down and the fat cats in power, cultural studies invites an image of the human as wearing a thinking cap, continually reflecting on past and present, reality and illusion. We might be spoon-fed our ideologies, but we are always careful to chew thoroughly before swallowing them.

Cultural students argue that we are endlessly involved in searching for and finding meaning: everything we do, say, see, generally experience has some meaning for us. Listening to the car radio, watching a movie, viewing a painting: we can recover meaning from these, and any other activity for that matter. In the cultural studies vernacular, we "read" radio, movies, paintings and, most importantly for our purposes, television, much like we read a book. This means that we actively engage ourselves with the medium, using our intellect and reasoning in a creative way, even though we may not be aware of it.

Television appears a perfectly natural representation of reality: a window on the world. But, the cultural studies approach insists that the reason television's images and sounds seem so natural is because its messages are coded in a very familiar framework. "The television audience are spontaneously and continuously confronted with this framework and must negotiate a stance towards it in order to decode and thus enjoy the entertainment in which it is embodied," wrote Fiske, this time with John Hartley in their essay *Reading Television* (1987).

None of this sounds too profound – and it is not. All that cultural studies offers up to this point is: (1) The view that there can be no neutral, objective knowledge of the world and that what passes for truth is a matter of collective agreement rather than a reflection of reality (Thomas Kuhn's *The Structure of Scientific Revolution*, made a similar point earlier (1970), more persuasively and with apposite historical evidence); (2) The idea that when we consume media programs we are, in fact, actively engaged in producing meanings, or, more accurately, decoding them, in such a way that they strike us as commonsensical and straightforward. Much the same argument was advanced by Peter Berger and Thomas Luckmann in their book *The Social Construction of Reality* (1966), the title of which conveys the import of their theory, in which language is afforded priority as humans' meaning-making instrument.

It may come as a shock to learn that there is so much creative intellectual activity involved in giggling at one of Carla's acerbic one-liners in *Cheers*. And there is more: the whole process is profoundly ideological in nature. The reason why we find the gag humorous is because the line, the context in which it is cracked, the show of which they are both part and the series in which they are all embedded is shaped, or coded, in such a way as to elicit preferred meanings. The meanings, in turn, are produced in particular institutional environments and specific historical epochs. *Cheers* invites us to see reality stretched to exaggeration, not direct documentations of reality itself. The show works because the agreement on this is sustained and familiarity is not threatened.

Much of television's output is like this: conventional and conservative. Potentially, "readers" can use television programs, or "texts," as cultural students prefer, "for purposes of shattering, reforming and reproducing the established norms," said Fiske and Hartley (1987: 19) In practice, though, the only "norm" *Cheers* viewers think about is the beer-swigging Mr. Peterson who habitually occupies the barstool to the right of the screen.

The viewing subjects find pleasure in the show, acting quite voluntarily, while still conforming to the dominant ideology. But not in any automatic way because, as Sonia Livingstone (1987) wrote: "If viewing can no longer be seen as a passive intake and response, then neither can television content be viewed as a manifest and discrete message." In Livingstone's view, *Cheers* would be quite an "open" program, in that it "invites its audience to become involved, committed, speculative, evaluative, to fill in gaps . . . identify with some characters, to recognize others . . . to discuss events with family and friends" (1990: 72–3). "The more 'open' a program is, the more viewers may be involved in constructing the meaning of the program and the more their interest may be both cognitively and emotionally enhanced" (1990: 72).

Livingstone's research into "how different viewers see a story" showed that, "despite interest in subversive or feminist interpretations of soap opera, much of the difference in interpretations seem to reflect conventional rather than radical positions" (1990: 83). They seem to make what Stuart Hall called a "preferred reading," that is, one that sits comfortably with prevailing ideology (1980). Hall split the general reading process into three, each division defining a strategy. A dominant reading results from a viewer agreeing with and accepting the dominant ideology; whereas a negotiated reading is produced by viewers who generally fit in with the dominant ideology, but read into the messages more local, or particular inflections. Some readings are oppositional, with viewers rejecting the dominant ideology and the meanings it implies. These are very abstract categories, of course; suffice it to say that Hall's point is that television viewers are not simply passive recipients of tv-chanelled messages loaded with preconstructed ideologies. They actively make meanings in decoding text and these meanings may well be at odds with those preferred by the program's originators.

Unless a television program is highly esoteric and available to only the narrowest range of specialist viewers, its text will be open enough to admit a range of meanings to be negotiated by viewers. The key word here is polysemy, which is favored by cultural students to described the multiple meanings available in any text. In his article "The politics of polysemy," Klaus Bruhn Jensen explored the ways in which audiences "move beyond" preferred meanings to oppositional decodings, especially of news. Yet, the conclusion of his research was that: "Even though the social production of meaning can be seen as a process in which the prevailing definition of reality may be challenged and revised, the outcome of that process is overdetermined by the historical and institutional frameworks of communication" (1990: 73–4). Different viewers may make different sorts of sense from television, but "that sense is bounded by the social definition of genres" (1990: 74).

Jensen's idea find support in books such as *The Export of Meaning* by Elihu Katz and Tamar Liebes and Ien Ang's *Watching Dallas*, both of which found wide variations in the meanings made of the globally popular soap. The Katz and Liebes research examined interpretations of *Dallas* by four different types of Israelis and was intended as a critique of the view that hegemonic messages are "transferred to the defenceless minds of viewers the world over" (1990: 4). These kinds of observations alert cultural students to the dangers of compartmentalizing audience interpretations. To avoid the categories of other forms of media analysis, many have targeted the discourse.

signs and subjects

Discourse analysis describes the systematic breaking down of the process of thinking about or talking about a topic. Watching television qualifies as a discourse. Cultural studies is a very wide church, but, if any single approach or style of study has defined it as a clearly- demarcated discipline, it is discourse analysis, particularly the area of semiology, sometimes called semiotics, which refers in the broadest sense to the study of signs.

In recent years, cultural studies has turned away from the type of generalities offered by Hall and towards the intricately detailed, often microscopic empirical studies inspired by semiologists, the most widely quoted of whom is Roland Barthes. Early semiologists may once have sought for social laws that govern all instances of meaning-production, but today they concentrate on specific areas of discourse and try to unravel the often dauntingly complex network in which meanings are caught.

Consistent with the whole cultural studies approach, semiology interests itself not so much in the content of meaning, but in the methods by which it is produced, the ways in which it is coded and uncoded. The center of attention is the sign, which is used in a conventional dictionary sense, that is, a thing used as a representation of something else. Raising one's hands is a sign of submission, a building whose bricks are crumbling shows signs of decay, a footprint in the mud is a sign that someone has been here. The constituent parts of a sign are: (1) the signifier, which is the tangible part, a physical image, a noise, anything that is available to our senses; (2) the signified, which is what registers with us conceptually when we see, hear, touch or smell the signifier. As one might anticipate, there is never an automatic relationship between the two, though it might sometimes seem that way.

Show a photograph of a panther and the persons looking will register a very similar signified. This is a "highly motivated" sign in which the shape and content of the signifier is determined by the appearance of the specific signified, a panther. But, shout "panther" to an audience of English-language users and the convention of language will determine the signified in the minds of the audience. Show a Florida roadsign depicting a silhouette of a panther and, again, convention will determine the form of signifier and what it is intended to signify, in this case that the driver looking at the sign is approaching panther country.

These are instances of "low and motivated" signs when convention has the strongest influence over the relationship of the signifier to the signified. Words are completely guided by convention as they have no necessary relation with the things they signify; they are arbitrary. There is nothing essential in the word panther that relates to the creature that prowls the jungles and savannahs. Customs, rules, orthodoxies and, in general, conventions create the connection between the signifier (panther) and the signified, or the mental image of the animal.

The sign here is representational in that it simply represents something: a picture of or sound of "panther" means, well, a panther. But it may also signify agility, quickness, sleekness, predacity and a range of other meanings that derive from our particular culture. Semiologists call this the second order of signification and within it signs might operate as myth-makers, or connotative agents. The signs themselves become signifiers of other things: myths, or popular beliefs; and connotations, or values, emotions and attitudes.

Roland Barthes' semiological treatments of photographs and stories as examples of significations have been replicated by students of television eager to maintain culture as the medium of analysis. Cultural supports give force to myths and connotations that are incorporated into social relations and structure, it is argued.

Inspired by Barthes, cultural students have focused on particular television programs, or even tiny fragments of programs and tried to extend their analyses into something resonant. Fiske and Hartley provide an illustration of this when they read a dancing segment of the long-running BBC series *Top of the Pops*. Their analysis could easily be applied to MTV's *Party Time*, in which females feature in organized dance routines. "While based on the circle, the girls dance individually, like disco dancers," the authors begin (1987: 138). "They relate to each other by a common rhythm and common restricted dance vocabulary, but concentrate primarily on their own dance experience rather than on a relationship." Whereas the casual viewer may think this tells us nothing, Fiske and Hartley saw more: "This form of dance seems to reflect the tensions caused by the identity and sexual crises of adolescence."

> What this dance *signifies* then, in the first order, is the sexuality and culturally defined beauty of the female body. In the second order, it *connotes* the adolescent concern with identity alongside its concern with sexuality; the movement into and out of the circle's forms become a connotative signifier of the adolescents' ambivalent attitudes to society, and their problems in resolving the clash between the demands of their own personalities and those of others or of the society to which they have to adjust.
>
> (1987: 138)

The first thing one notices about such a reading is that it involves an alarming amount of reading *into*. What, superficially, appears to be a straightforward dance routine is x-rayed as something infinitely more complex and profound, something that is certainly not available to the senses of the dancers, nor recognizable to the television or "live" audience and which lies far beyond the intentions of the choreographer or anyone else involved in the technical production of the program. Skeptics may spy semiological overkill: the passage reveals far more about the writers' mental ingenuity in the search for exotic plants in barren wastes – if they are not there, imagine them. The interpretation represents a bewildering cross-knitting of past and present, individual and society, youth and age, seeming reality and evident façade.

Television programs, like all other cultural items, are constructed statements: they communicate agreed-upon conventional meanings that are accessible to a wide range of people. Those people take-as-they-find, leaving cultural students to decode in alternative modes that would not be readily comprehensible to the viewer. It is subversive reading in that it upsets or even overturns the casual viewer's interpretation and presents a version humming with irony and connotation.

Reading in this way avoids prescription. It does not, indeed cannot, insist that this analysis is any more valid than alternatives. For the entire cultural studies approach preaches the lack of objective standards, which includes standards of verification. Nor does it issue the prospective discourse analyst with a methodological rulebook, at least not in the same way as standard-issue social research texts do.

LA lore

What might the analyst make of *LA Law*? Here is a successful, long-running series watched by a global audience, purporting to disclose the unseen workings of the USA's justice system. The attorneys' practice at the center of the series harbors an elderly paterfamilias, who is the senior partner, and a miscellany of fortyish lawyers, all of whom have money, status and personal problems insoluble enough to make agony aunts resign. The programs typically juxtapose three narrative stories, one of which is heavy, like AIDS mercy killings, date rape or police brutality, another light and humorous and the other concerning affairs of the heart. Like its predecessor, *Hill Street Blues*, which was also produced by Steven Bochco, the series interweaves the multiple stories, often leaving one open-ended so that it might run for several weeks, or even disappear to return many episodes later.

The approach is aesthetically interesting and serves to encourage viewer loyalty, which presumably accounts for the show's longevity. As a myth-maker, the series works to espouse the virtues of the US legal system and the values it expresses. But, it is no simple morality fable: right does not always triumph over wrong, lawyers get taken in by manipulative murderers; corporations squash penniless consumers; rapists walk free. Not too often, though; and, when they do, something usually happens to them (murderer becomes target for the mob; corporation receives bad publicity; rapist gets gunned down by incensed victim). So, even when the legal system shows cracks, the outside society somehow fills them in.

The show's credibility lies in the apparent fallibility not only of the legal system of which the "Mackenzie, Brackman" practice is part, but of the attorneys themselves. Rules are broken, clients are seduced – as are colleagues – principles are compromised daily. But some form of redemption is usually at hand so that the lecherous Arnold Becker gets his come-uppance, Tommy Mulvaney gets hauled before his boss for a reprimand, and the ends that supposedly justified the means are somehow tarnished. Believing in righteousness of the system and observing both the spirit and the letter of the law are paramount.

Yet this is no crude apologia for the North American legal system. *LA Law*'s strength is in its balance: every week it seems to sit on a precipice. Doubts gently nudge the show to the edge. A racist police officer walks scot-free despite killing an innocent black youth, for example. What are we to make of a criminal justice system that permits this? But wait: as he leaves the courtroom celebrating, the cop is shot by the dead youth's mother. We can extrapolate that the mother will serve a life sentence, but the show glides into its closing credits and we, as viewers, are shielded from the unpleasant moral problems that would, in reality, follow.

The illusion that the moral world is not always neatly dichotomized into right and wrong is sustained; but the abiding commentary is that, in spite of ambiguities and, sometimes, contradictions, the right result ensues. And this, in turn, sustains the illusion that everything is fine. Nobody has anything to worry about in the law and order department. Unlike other, less successful tv dramas, *LA Law* avoids being a painfully alphabetic guide to law and order. Certainly, it is contrived in arriving at its moral destinations, but the routes it takes are circuitous and relatively free of the ethical signposts of other dramas. The plots frequently dive into dark detours before returning to light. The signifiers are well-textured too: no whiter-than-white stereotypes here, but people who, like everybody else, want money and power. But not more than they want justice.

Even the slithery materialist Becker corrupts and is corrupted within a moral framework. We know he has limits. Like the series itself, Becker swims in muddy waters, but emerges relatively clean. His signifier works well because of his lack of purity. As an actual individual he is constituted by popular culture: he is, at once a critic and upholder of that culture; he becomes "real" to the audience because of the ideological site in which he operates.

This latter point is important for discourse analysis, for the individual is never seen as an autonomous free-thinking being with capacity for independent action. Cultures make the individual: we think in terms of individuals as units with identities and personalities, or selves, and consciousness only because this conception is an integral part of our culture and we are encouraged to think in such a way about ourselves and others. Every institution is premised on the concept of the individual. This in itself is a focus for cultural students, who ask: "How come we think about each other as individuals?" "How does the language we use and discourses it is part of contribute to this type of thinking?" In cultural studies, the individual is replaced with the subject, a term that is intended to alert us to the way in which common-sense notions are not obvious and natural, but constructed in historical and present contexts. A subject refers to the individual not as autonomous, but as created in a particular social setting.

Cultural students never actually deny individuality: this is part of our biological constitution. They are just interested in how it becomes socially constituted and the answers to this do not lie in biological realms at all. When we view Becker *et al.*, we are never in doubt that we, as individuals, are looking at and thinking about other individuals as reference points. However far removed the lives of well-heeled Southern Californian lawyers may be, viewers are able to relate to them as subjects; they make sense.

LA Law, like many other dramas, is coded as "real life;" its narrative is linear and its plots are peopled by recognizable human beings, albeit slightly caricatured ones. This is why it works. And also why, after decades of televisual "realism," some series that defy this format, such as *Twin Peaks*, require the epithet surreal.

Cultural studies would also want to analyze the LA lawyers as signifiers of ideological values, as well as representative of individuals. Fiske and Hartley marshaled the empirical research of Gerbner (1970) to argue that heroes are typically "white, male, middle class (or classless) and in the prime of life;" they are attractive and "successful in their violence." The villains are usually not; so that: "The textual opposition between hero/ine and villain/ess, and the violence by which this is commonly dramatized, become metaphors for power relationships in society and thus a material practice through which the dominant ideology works" (1990: 9).

So, in making sense of the show we are, knowingly or not, indulging in an ideological practice, that is maintaining and legitimating the "dominant ideology." Our reward is the gratification that comes from recognising the familiar. In other words, we enjoy the show. According to this view, should *LA Law*'s heroes suddenly grow uglier, develop radical leanings, show criminally violent tendencies, then the show would be less enjoyable and, presumably, even less credible. The fact that female and black lawyers feature prominently in the show complicates and possibly contradicts this argument. And more anomalies could be added by *Miami Vice*, the 1980s show in which villains were designer-dressed and coiffured just like the heroes; *Law and Order*, in which perpetrators of crimes sometimes walked away free and clear; and any number of shows like Bill Cosby's in which the cast was black. The stock response of cultural studies would be that ideology itself is never smooth and seamless, so the wrinkles and inconsistencies reflected in television only add to, rather than detract from, its plausibility as a window on reality.

In his article "Reading 'Wall Street'," Norman Denzin remarked on the metaphorical value of the title of the 1987 Oliver Stone movie (1990). We might do the same to *LA Law*, which signifies more than a physical plane and a legal practice. The opening titles show a car number-plate bearing the legend "The Sunshine State," with connotations of brightness and, therefore, goodness. Los Angeles, unlike the USA's east coast, metropolis New York, is a place where light radiates, so that evil cannot hide from the force of law. LA is also the center of the film industry, where imaginary things are fused with life and sold in the marketplace, where reality can be edited at the push of a button and illusion can be transformed effortlessly into a reality.

So, in a sense, LA is not only a place, but an imaginary site, where disembodied signs and representations circulate in a self-contained, self-referencing universe. Events "made in Hollywood" seem as "real" as the earthquakes that occasionally shake up the residents. *LA Law* comes from the studio but hints that it has the same ontological status as a quake. In one memorable aside, Michael Kuzak tells a colleague he had been watching *thirtysomething* on tv the night before, as if to reinforce the fact that, they may both be part of the same illusion, but *LA Law* is more "real." (It was an in-joke, a riposte to a reference to *LA Law* in *thirtysomething* a month or so before.)

Fans of *LA Law* would no doubt recoil at this rendition which intentionally subverts the meanings they might take from the show. It is probable also that followers of cultural studies would be dissatisfied and may want to offer alternative readings, a response that captures both the strength and weakness of the entire intellectual approach. There is value in triangulating knowledge: opposing established "truth" A with an alternative B, which, in turn, can be challenged by new alternative C, which can then be subjected to new critiques, and so on, yet without settling unconditionally for one version. "Solipsism," the critic might shout: nothing is knowable, according to this; everything is relative and conditional. Cultural studies would acknowledge the criticism and probably feel it unworthy of a reply: on its own account, knowledge of the world is dependent on our own particular upbringing in our specific culture, at a certain period in history; so it has to be relative to time and space. There is no essential or privileged truth: we should always recognize the difference in versions.

the world as an aquarium

Yet, in disarming its epistemological critics, cultural studies does little to appease those who cling to old-fashioned ideas like validity and commensurability. If one reading is just as good as another and they are violently opposed, how do we know which one is better, apart from resorting to our personal preferences? Surely some basic methodological prescription or evaluative criteria is necessary to enable the comparison of like with like. Or perhaps we are to judge every reading in the same way as we would judge the reading of a palmist, a dowser or a clairvoyant, all of whom lay claim to a special form of knowledge and an idiosyncratic way of getting it.

I use this point to preface my more specific misgivings about cultural studies in general and the work of Fiske in particular, for it is he who epitomizes the approach and who has been lauded by David Marc for doing great

> service to the cause of advancing humanistic thought in the twentieth century by practicing a form of inductive investigation in which actually watching TV series is as central to the critical act as looking at paintings is to art criticism or as reading poems is to literary criticism.
>
> (1989: 78)

But is it such a service to humanistic thought? And is watching tv comparable to looking at painting or reading poetry?

David Morley and Roger Silverstone insist that "print, radio, television, video and the computer all require different skills and different modes of attention . . . they create different possibilities for use" (1990:

46). One presumes that different techniques and modes are also brought into play when we relate to like paintings or literary media. Arnold Wolfe made a similar point when he wrote of "the unique ways television makes meaning" (1989: 343). In reviewing Fiske's *Television Culture*, Wolfe criticized his approach for conflicting fundamentally different media and so missing television's uniqueness. Morley and Silverstone warned: "The danger we run if these differences are ignored, is that we will reify the 'reading' metaphor" (1990: 146). "Reading" Proust may involve one in the same order of discourse as reading King (Stephen, that is), even though one of them may encourage a certain use of the intellect. But, surely the structure of the discourse is changed, as are the demands on cognitive capacities, when the medium is different, say listening to an audio tape of King reading aloud one of his own novels, or viewing *The Lawnmower Man* on screen. Or even staring at Robert Mapplethorpe photographs. All, in their way, yield an emotional gratification, but the nature and format of each necessitates different skills of comprehension. To clump them all together as "reading" seems insensitive to the particular nuances of television viewing.

Marc's other main point in praising cultural studies is that it has performed a great service in advancing humanistic thought, by which I take him to mean that the debasement, conformity and massification entailed in some of the theories in the previous chapter have been rejected and the human being, replete with consciousness, has been restored to centerstage. It is typical of cultural studies to oppose the gullibility suggested by mass society theorists: we are now active thinkers, savvy enough to subvert television's power by reading our own versions of its messages and taking pleasure from the process. If there is a "service" in this, then presumably we can look for the liberating dividend.

Linda Benn, writing for *Village Voice*, noticed that, in cultural studies, young people reconstructing their own identities in the image of *Miami Vice*'s Don Johnson or Madonna, are constructing subversive readings of television texts. "While it isn't exactly clear how the desire to resemble someone else is liberating," she wrote, "there *is* a moment in the creation or imitation of a style – especially for adolescents – which bespeaks the sheer pleasure of setting oneself up against another's judgement (usually a parent's) and that contains the seed, perhaps, of subversive knowledge" (1990: S16).

But the pleasure gained may well "be mixed with anger, or frustrated desire, or a keen sense of powerlessness" and "one might ask about the nature of pleasure that cannot offer any real participation, control or gratification" (1990: S16). A similar point was made by Jensen: "The polysemy of media texts is only a political potential, and the oppositional decoding of media is not yet a manifestation of political power" (1990: 74).

Benn accused cultural studies of extoling the subversive pleasure of reading television that is gained by an active audience. In practice, she argued, people are passively "taken in," as is evidenced by George Bush's crude, but ultimately effective ploy of featuring the convicted felon Willie Horton in a television campaign commercial that manipulated racist fears.

We might add to Benn's remarks the fact that, not only are people sometimes "taken in," but they also know it – and approve of it. Research into coverage of the 1991 Gulf War found that most television viewers would not object to being fed false information by television if the lies were in the interests of national security. Audiences felt being misled was acceptable in moments of crisis, according to David Morrison (1991). The research painted a picture of a viewing audience that was at once prepared to be duped, yet also aware enough to know they were being duped and prepared to accept it.

Beguiling as it may be to envision tv viewers as conscious creators of meaning rather than docile airheads absorbing whatever comes on the screen, it may also be too romantic. John Hartley, himself a theorist in the cultural studies tradition, has written of audiences being "paedocratized" by television. "The audience is imagined as having childlike qualities and attributes," he noted especially of North America (1987: 127). He also emphasized the point that "television operates *regimes* of pleasure." There is "heterogeneity of modes of address, points of view, program genres, styles of presentation, codes of recognition," all geared to supply a diverse population with pleasure. This carries no assumption that audiences are childish and prone to external stimulation of the television, of course; television as an institution only imagines that they are.

But maybe they actually are. Maybe their curiosity has been dimmed and their passivity nurtured by the lack of challenging discourses. Television promotes impulse, not calculation, specifically an impulse to enjoy. Discontents are assuaged; we don't watch to become agitated. Quite the opposite. The idea is that television comforts us. It is the perfect conduit for what J. K. Galbraith called "the culture of contentment," a pacifying condition, where the abiding requirements of the population are to accept what is available and not ask for what is not (1992).

This summons up a rather different image to the one offered by cultural studies and one which invites the type of questions and arguments that cultural studies chooses to ignore. Arguments, for example, about capitalism's dependence on consumerism, the exercise of power and the use of television as an instrument of persuasion. About the creation of new demands and appetites that can only be satisfied by the consumption of commodities. About how advertising and commerce govern the depiction of reality in the mass media. About how the portrayals of television might be understood not as propaganda for any particular ideology, conservative or liberal, but as propaganda for commodities – things that can be bought and replaced.

In avoiding these issues that lie beyond the boundaries of the discourse, cultural studies has limited its power to explaining how meaning is made. Why it is made is arguably a more searching question and cultural studies is helpless to address it.

Instead, cultural studies presents a subject cheerfully encapsulated in a sign-filled discourse, pushing, probing, searching for meanings and making them in concert with television's texts, which set the ideological limits for the encounter. This is society as a human aquarium, a self-contained universe housing many life forms; transparent walls enable the cultural student to observe closely. The claustrophobic intensity of its research and the specificity of its language may privilege followers of cultural studies with an apparently rich, albeit esoteric, understanding of the process by which we make meanings. Yet this form is narrow and forbids widening the enquiry to look at how things operate on the outside of the tank. Cultural studies' undoubted strength is in mapping intricately the inner life of the discourse. But, if it does not combine this with the outer institutional structure that makes television possible in the first place, its value is like that of the aquarist to the marine biologist: interesting, but hardly theistic in import.

chapter five

lethal link

mechanical effects

Is there too much violence on television? To answer this question, I am calling on two gurus, both expert in their own ways. My first authority wishes to remain nameless, but is a member of the National Council for Families and Television: "I believe we have made significant improvements in cutting down the amount of violence – usually totally gratuitous – on television in recent years. But, the council still receives many complaints about violent scenes. Recently, the trend seems to be violence against women. This is very disturbing and is sure to have a detrimental impact on the viewing audience. I am particularly concerned about children who are allowed to stay up late to watch what we euphemistically call adult programs."

Next, my seven-year-old nephew: "Nah, it's usually the bad guys getting what they deserve, anyway. I don't mind it when Hulk Hogan or somebody good smashes somebody up. It makes you laugh, so it's phat. Sometimes, you see violence, true violence that is, when real people fight. I suppose they really do fight like that. Most of the time it's make-believe fighting, like *Tom and Jerry* and *The Killer Tomatoes*. That's not what you mean – is it?"

Seven thousand acts of violence seem an awful lot, but that is the amount the average British person experiences second-hand, if they watch television, listen to radio or read newspapers. Guy Cumberbatch, in his contribution to the monograph *A Measure of Uncertainty: The effects of the mass media* estimated that the figure is much higher in Australia, Japan, the USA and continental Europe. "The ubiquity of crime and violence in the mass media has stimulated a whole host of debates about how far the media may encourage anxieties, shape attitudes, define values or excite behaviour in the public," wrote

Cumberbatch (1989: 32). "Not surprisingly the most persistent concern has been that mass media causes violence in society." At first it was cinema, then radio and comic books. But none of these has seemed to contravene laws governing decency and good taste with the incessancy and immediacy of television. So, most concern centers on this medium which seems to serve up nightly shootings, knifings and beatings with voyeuristic dispassion. A logical, though not necessarily accurate, proposition has been that this influences viewers, whose behavior will reflect that of the characters on the screen.

The subject may well qualify for some sort of world record, for at least a thousand research publications from the fields of psychology, psychiatry and sociology have purported to reveal the truth about the link between tv violence and actual violence. Over three-quarters claim that a link exists and give various interpretations of its mechanisms (direct, causal, mediated, etc.), while the others conclude that there is no connection at all and that the fuss is over nothing.

The study that started the fuss was conducted in the 1960s, when television's incredibly fast growth had just begun to slow, but between 90–95 per cent of the homes in the USA and Britain had sets (1963–68). Albert Bandura, a US psychologist, had been noticing how preschool children imitated the aggressive behavior of adults. He wondered if they would imitate violent behavior shown on television. Two groups of children were shown different pieces of film, one showing a human behaving violently towards an inflatable three-foot doll with a weighted base, so that it sprung back upright after being knocked down. The Bobo doll, as it was known, took a beating with a mallet in the one film and the children watching this, when placed in the presence of a similar doll, did a serious number on Bobo. But, the other group of children watched a film of the doll being treated kindly, and, later, reproduced this kindness. The children's behavior had been learned through simple observation, according to Bandura (1973). Even months after watching the film, over 40 per cent of the children in the first group still replicated the behavior. Later experiments by Bandura showed that he could strengthen the child's mimicry by having the violent character on film rewarded in some way, the angle being that a positive value is usually placed on the victor in tv fights.

Similar results came from Leonard Berkowitz's experiments with university students, half of whom were deliberately insulted and so angered before viewing either a violent sequence from a boxing movie or a film of English canals. Not surprisingly, Berkowitz found that those who had been angered by the insults before viewing expressed more aggression than those who had not (1962). Of the group that had been made angry, some were told the violence in the film was justified and these were identified as most likely to be violent after viewing. Berkowitz's results seem very tame from today's vantage point, but he was challenging what had been a strong orthodoxy: that watching fantastic violence on screen led to a reduction of aggressive drives, a type of catharsis. Berkowitz found quite the opposite effect.

The two experiments uncovered what were taken to be basic psychological mechanisms. In Bandura's case, learning through imitation had occurred: human beings became socialized through many channels, one of which was by witnessing and copying. We all do this, of course. In the 1960s, it was not certain whether observing images on what was then a relatively new home appliance would have the same effect. Berkowitz agreed that television could exert an influence on our development, even on our maturity, and the way it did this was by bringing down the normal inhibitions that restrain us from acting violently, even when we are angry or frustrated enough to want to strike out. Disinhibition is the term Berkowitz used to describe, for instance, a male arriving home after a hard day at work, switching on tv to find a bloodbath cop show and turning violently on his wife. Without the cop show, he would still feel angry, but would contain his feelings. The catharsis theories that Berkowitz refuted held that watching a bloodbath would make violence less likely.

Both the Bandura and Berkowitz theories are best approached wearing blinkers. Peripheral vision must not reveal the lying-in-wait influences outside the highly controlled laboratory settings in which the experiments took place. Children, for example, do not imitate everything they observe, nor do they try to. Watching a doll getting bashed in a lab and watching it on tv at home, where distractions precede and follow the viewing, may have quite different results. Watching inanimate objects like Bobo or cartoon characters such as Tom and Jerry getting knocked around may yield different responses to watching human beings acting violently. The anomalies multiplied as more and more studies replicated Bandura's and produced different results. All manner of violence, including urban uprisings, suicides and murders, have been attributed to imitation, or the "copycat effect." It seems a precarious concept on which to hang such a weighty miscellany of behavior.

Berkowitz's analysis, while complementing Bandura's at one level, contradicted it at another, for his argument was that we do not imitate in the sense of creating a new addition to our repertoire of behavior. We already have the disposition and capability for violence. All that stops us is inhibition. Television relaxes this, allowing us to behave aggressively. One gets the impression that Berkowitz saw humans somewhat like Hobbes – nasty and brutish. Only layer upon layer of inhibitions prevent all-out violence. Seen like this, television could be a very dangerous release.

Berkowitz later saw the limitations of his concept and offered an alternative based on the activation of thoughts by the media (1984). Television violence touches off an "associative network" of thoughts, ideas and behavioral inclinations in the viewer and, once primed, this network may be responsible for eliciting, maintaining, elaborating and, finally, acting out violent behavioral "scripts." This replaced the disinhibition concept with a set of possible mechanisms, the outcomes of which were not predictable.

Berkowitz was trying to explain why a person may watch one of the *Batman* tv shows from the 1960s with its usual fight scenes punctured with cartoon starbursts of "Zap!" and "Pow!" yet act aggressively in an entirely different way. The viewer might use a weapon, or attack a nonhuman target. Yet the violent behavior may still have been stimulated by the sight of the Caped Crusader's fist fight, which provides the "script." Other factors affecting and activating the "associative network" include the presence of others, especially aggressive peers, the rewards conferred on the aggressor in the depiction, the viewer's perception of the status of the scene (fantasy or real) and the observer's focus, whether on the actual violence or other aspects of the character and plot.

Obviously, this widens the scope of the original interpretation immensely; so much so that the theory explains everything and nothing simultaneously. Disinhibition may still feature as one of a potentially limitless series of factors that contribute to a violent outcome. But, in contrast to the earlier formulation, it is not the central mechanism: just one of many. More important is the way it combines with other variables to trigger changes in the associate network. Whether this is significantly more valuable than plain common sense is open for discussion.

Doubtless, television influences us, but whether it promotes violence in some direct, or automatic, way is still open to question. We learn through observation and imitation and, given the saturation of populations with television, it seems implausible to suggest that watching tv, especially violent programs, does not provoke some mimicry. There is also support for the view that watching television arouses us in some instances and desensitizes us in others, possibly stimulating us to actions that, in other circumstances, we would have been inhibited from performing. These are basic behavioral mechanisms explored by many psychological studies and, while their results are mixed, they at least reveal the operations or techniques involved in translating television scripts into violent action.

Yet, there is another area in which television impacts on us psychologically and influences our propensity to act violently: in affecting what we believe. How we understand the world, recognizing danger, deciding what action is appropriate in given situations, assessing others and their likely course of action: these and other cognitions, evaluations and actions are in no sense dissociated from our immediate environment and, as television is very much part of that environment, it will bear an influence. The concerns of George Gerbner were how and to what extent. His research at the Annenberg School of Communications, Philadelphia, in the 1970s helped alert people to the genuine importance of television to culture.

heavy viewing, heavy world

Gerbner's first research efforts in the late 1960s described more accurately than ever before what he called the "message system" of television (1970). He wanted to know what the world as depicted in television was like, who inhabited it, what did they do, whom did they do it to? In sum, what messages were being given out. Systematic viewing around the clock, using specific ways of coding, produced a portrait of television's world as comprising more men than women, more young than old, and more professionals and law enforcement officers than manual occupation workers; it was also a world in which an average of over five acts of violence happened every hour between 8.00 p.m. and 11.00 p.m. (Violence was defined as "the overt expression of physical force . . . against self or another.") These were "cultural indicators" and the message sent out by television was: "The world is really like this" (1970; Gerbner *et al.* 1978). And, in an odd way, it was right because viewers began to re-create the world as television depicted it.

The process was called "enculturation" and it entailed accepting ideas about norms and behavior and absorbing these into one's own life. As more and more people did this, so culture as a whole came to resemble the way it was shown on tv. In particular, the violence repeatedly shown on television imparted a clear message and one to which people responded quite earnestly.

People become fearful of violence, they demanded protection and accepted, if not welcomed, aggression in the interests of self-preservation. Violence begets violence and so a kind of self-perpetuating spiral went into motion. This was what Gerbner and his colleagues called a "cultivation effect." Several research projects at the time reinforced Gerbner's finding that television did portray an inordinate amount of violence; even the major US networks commissioned studies. But Gerbner wanted to demonstrate how this, far from being independent of reality, was becoming part of it. Not that the world before television was a peaceful idyll; but it was still nowhere as manic as television would have us believe and the violence was certainly not glorified, nor comic, as some programs showed it. But television had flowed into the mainstream of culture and, as a result, so had its products, according to Gerbner *et al.* (1980; 1982).

"Mainstreaming," in which the apparent facts of television are accepted as truth and acted on, had a certain symmetry with the ideas of Adorno and the Frankfurt School theorists, whom we covered in chapter three, in the sense that: "heavy viewers of all groups tend to share a relatively homogeneous outlook," for Gerbner *et al.* (1980: 15).

Television contributes to the cultivation of an "exaggerated sense of danger or mistrust" and this is seen as independent of the effects of other influences, particularly for the heavy viewers who are most exposed to tv violence. Heavy viewers were defined as those who watch four hours or more per night. Gerbner's research showed that this group had a significantly higher sense of personal risk and suspicion than light viewers, who were the same in all other respects. Television viewing, in other words, was the only thing that separated the heavy from the light viewers. So this had to be the reason for the difference in their outlook, an outlook that was shared uniformly by the heavy viewers regardless of their income differences or social class.

This last point was important to Gerbner because he found, like most other researchers, that the higher your income level, the less you tend to watch television. If you earn plenty of money, then technically, you should watch little tv and have least fear of crime (at least street crime). But, Gerbner found that, if you watch more television than other high earners, then your fear of crime will be very much the same as medium to low earners who view more heavily than the rest of their cohorts. Gerbner's conclusion was that the heavy viewers of all classes had their attitudes cultivated by television. The homogeneity of their outlooks was not replicated among light viewers, whose differences in attitudes were linked to class and other variables.

Gerbner's departure from the more straightforward psychological theories is apparent: he made no claim to have discovered a hidden mechanism, like imitation or disinhibition, that directly connects television violence with actual behavior. Statistically, he found a relationship, but not of a cause-and-effect nature. A heavy viewing, middle-class urban dweller will, like his or her working-class counterpart, be fearful of crime, accepting that the streets out there are as mean and vicious as those shown on the screen. The customer in front of them in the supermarket line looks like the psycho in last week's *Law and Order*, the checkout girl probably carries a gun for protection, the bearded guy walking towards the cheese counter is a dead ringer for the drug-addicted undercover cop in last night's movie of the week, *Rush*. "Thus, the congruence of the television world and real life circumstances may 'resonate' and lead to markedly amplified cultivation patterns," said Gerbner and his colleagues (1980: 15).

Gerbner stopped short of either identifying the psychological process involved in the cultivation, or proposing that having an apprehensive view of reality will necessarily translate into violent behavior, though that would seem to be the implication. Our supermarket shopper might carry a revolver for protection and, on being approached for change by the *Rush* look alike, pump a slug into his chest. Features of the make-believe world become part of the real landscape. There is always the possibility that the heavy viewer's conceptions are based not purely on television, but on a fairly accurate appraisal of what the streets are like anyway. If the store is in parts of New York City or Newark or many other big US cities, chances are that psycho killers do roam the supermarkets, checkout assistants do keep pistols, junkies do turn violent. Some local residents are justifiably concerned about violence and the reason they watch so much television might be that they want to minimize the amount of time they spend out of their homes.

Another alternative to Gerbner's interpretation is that the people who watch a lot of television are pretty anxious about violent crime to begin with and watch television shows where the forces of law usually prevail for affirmation. This opens up Gerbner's argument to the related criticism that certain types of people select certain types of programs to watch. Contrary to Gerbner's studies, other projects have found that people view selectively, according to taste and preference. Australian researchers, Robert Hawkins and Suzanne Pingree, criticized Gerbner for his lack of sensitivity in this respect. Viewers are more discriminating than Gerbner supposed and select the programs they desire to watch (1981).

This did not exactly undermine Gerbner's conclusions, but it did point to a bluntness in his research instrument which may have weakened some of his grander claims. Paul Hirsch found further indelicacies, which he claimed seriously threatened the validity of the research. Taking Gerbner's original data, Hirsch recoded his sample by breaking down the basic categories of heavy and light viewers into small groupings, adding the labels extreme and nonviewers (1980; 1981). Analyzing Gerbner's data the new way, Hirsch found that those people who watched no tv at all were more scared of violence than light viewers and people who viewed more than eight hours per day were less perturbed by the prospect of violence than those who watched between four and eight hours. If this re-examination is to be accepted, it severely damages Gerbner's thesis not only about the nature of the link, but its direction and, indeed, about whether there is a link at all.

One thing is certain and that is: television violence has become quotidian. We accept it as part of our everyday viewing; so much so that we barely bat an eyelid at the sight of physical force, injury or death. While no country comes close to the USA in terms of the daily quantity of violence, studies show that Britain, Canada, Australia and much of continental Europe have enough bloodshed to satiate more gruesome appetites. Film is perhaps a more direct indicator of popular adult tastes in violence because certification can exclude younger viewers from particularly horrific violence. Twenty or thirty years ago, there was outright violence in movies, but nothing of the order of, say, the *Terminator* or *Lethal Weapon* series, where the sheer volume of killings is matched by the ingenuity of methods for achieving grotesque deaths. Even if television productions do not contain comparable violence, the fact that such films quickly find their way into tv schedules means that, in the absence of the most stringent editing, there has been more violence. This opens another avenue of enquiry.

"Does media violence increase children's toleration of real-life aggression?" was the question R. S. Drabman and M. H. Thomas asked in a 1974 article. To answer it, they took a sample of eight-year-old children, some of whom had watched violence on television, and made them witness a real playground fight. They found that the children who had not watched the tv violence before the real fight were more likely to act "responsibly" and seek the help of an adult. From this small study, Drabman and Thomas suggested that exposure to large amounts of televised violence might *desensitize* children to actual violence. Their emotional response to violence on the screen led to a more ready acceptance of real violence. If this is the same for adults, we can surmise that film makers have sensed it and, in an attempt to arouse viewers, have piled on newer and more extreme forms of violence (in the same way that charity appeals are obliged to screen ever-more horrific scenes of poverty and starvation in the attempt to combat "donor fatigue").

Later studies worked out hypotheses based on the idea of desensitization, the most successful one being: that the longer one's exposure to graphic tv violence, the less sensitive one would become to real violence. It seemed a fairly obvious way in which screen violence could produce a toleration or even acceptance of real violence. What the hypotheses did not take into account was the discriminating capacity of the viewer. It may be so that some viewers interpret all television violence as simply "the way it is." More likely is that most of us realize that what we are watching is bogus. This could result in a heightened sensitivity to real violence when it is encountered firsthand. We could also sense the true proportions of violence when actual violence is shown on news and documentaries; when the action is not slowed down into almost balletic motions and the blood does not spurt in eye-pleasing arcs. Watching protesters being clubbed about the head or worse in Tianenman Square was a quite different experience to watching a stage-managed brawl. Contrary to the desensitization predicted, exposure to television violence could enhance our delicacy of feeling about real violence, making us more susceptible to its offensiveness. Both possibilities underline television's potential to change the emotional state of viewers, whether to numb or arouse their feelings, though research in the wake of Drabman and Thomas has not proved helpful in specifying long-term behavioral effects.

Compounding this are the results of a piece of research by Jerome and Dorothy Singer, which found that aggressive behavior among children followed heavy viewing of the much lauded and ostensibly educational program *Sesame Street* as well as maligned cartoons like *Woody Woodpecker* and *Superheroes*, which have plenty of violent action (1986). Perhaps it is something about the way children encode the program that inclines them to violence at a later stage. One implication of this is that the content of the television programe may be less influential than its pace. Plenty of fast, colorful action expressed in short staccato-type bursts may lead to arousal and possibly aggression, regardless of whether or not the action contains any violence.

encoding aggression

The very idea of studying the effects of television on viewers is as appealing to cultural studies as a crucifix is to a vampire. Assessing the effects of television on viewers carries with it the very assumptions cultural studies questions: that viewers are pliant and yielding recipients of television messages rather than active decoders of those messages. As we saw in the last chapter, cultural studies sees tv as a medium that allows for the production of meanings. While it would not satisfy cultural students, the "reciprocal effects" approach in psychology has the advantage of considering the television–violence connection as a two-way relationship in which the viewer is consciously participating. Earlier in this chapter, we encountered the research of Berkowitz (1962; 1984), in which he employed the concept of a script, yet without ever developing its potential.

As in its conventional meaning, the script is a text from which actors work. They *encode* it, *maintain* it over a period of time, during which they might elaborate on it or give it their own interpretation and, in appropriate circumstances, *emit* it, or give it out. A study by two psychologists, L. R. Huesmann and L. D. Eron, published in 1986, used these three phrases to break up the direct link between television and violence suggested by other studies. Huesmann and Eron stressed the importance of the encoding phase when the television is but one of a number of features of the surrounding environment. If, for example, children live in homes where domestic violence is commonplace and in a neighborhood where streetfights are routine, they may pay greater attention to the script on offer. If they are aroused by the script, they are more likely to remember, or maintain it for later, perhaps adding their own inflexions: ". . . if I was the crook in that situation, I wouldn't have just hit the cop over the head with an iron bar; I'd have broken his legs too, so he couldn't get up and chase after me."

Violent television influences the emission of scripts in many ways, through arousal and the supply of cues that are similar to the ones we pick up in everyday life. In a way, television violence, especially that in cop shows, reminds us that aggression is a socially acceptable way to solve problems. So, in the opinion of Huesmann and Eron, tv violence does not automatically translate into actual violence, but it can facilitate and encourage it by providing scripts to be encoded, worked up and decoded at later stages when the situation seems appropriate. This may help explain the long-term cumulative effects of a diet of violent cop shows.

Huesmann and Eron, while not downplaying the role of television, wanted to allow other factors into the analysis, one of which is the individual's ability to interpret and embellish scripts. This marks a departure from the earlier studies of Bandura and Berkowitz, which, in an obtuse way, complemented the mass society theories, depicting humans purely as reactors rather than creators. Huesmann and Eron saw a strong link between exposure to tv violence and actual aggression, even years later, but insisted that the mechanism, or, more accurately, mechanisms are more varied than anticipated by their predecessors.

There are also a number of curious conclusions in their empirical work in different countries. Viewing tv violence in childhood should result in later aggression in females in the USA, but not in males, and in neither sex in Israel. Males, but not females, in Finland are affected by violence on the screen. Context, in other words, plays a significant mediating role. This opens up the possibilities further, but, in the process, weakens the supposed link between television and violence. If there are so many other factors, how can we be sure tv is one of them?

One of the intriguing correlations discovered by Huesmann, this time with another colleague, N.M. Malamuth, was between viewing aggressive television at the age of eight and criminally violent behavior at 30. This undermined the idea of a short-term link between television and aggression, but strengthened the possibility that, over the longer term, the explosive charges laid down by television may be detonated by any number of intervening factors. Aggression, in this view, can be encoded in early life and maintained by an interplay of what is seen on television and what is experienced in real life.

But Huesmann and Malamuth were careful not to exaggerate television's role. "Aggressive scripts for behavior are acquired from observation of media violence and aggressive behavior itself stimulates the observation of media violence" (1986: 138). So, we behave violently at least in part because we have picked up cues from the media and behaving violently also stimulates us to watch more violence on tv. "In both childhood and adulthood, certain cues in the media may trigger the activation of aggressive scripts acquired in any manner and thus stimulate aggressive behavior" (1986: 138). This seems rather like wanting one's cake, eating it too, getting indigestion and then grumbling about it. The theory, if indeed it is one, encompasses all possibilities: it suggests a strong relationship between television violence and outright aggression, but it is a cumulative relationship, one that is built up by a potentially limitless multiplicity of other influences. Huesmann's work tells us of the possible effects of television, but nothing of its combination with other factors, the strength of its effects or the psychological mechanisms involved.

Huesmann's approach at least restores an element of deliberation to the viewer in the initial encoding phase. This discretionary ability was lacking in much of the other psychological portrayals of television violence and its impact. But, in introducing it to his "reciprocal effects" account, Huesmann opened up the endless possibilities that dilute its value as an explanation.

We might legitimately ask whether any explanation based on general principles is either going to be so broad as to be speculative or fanciful, or so narrow as to be useless in understanding what appear to be patterns of violence. A further problem that many of the various schools of thought seem either to ignore or gloss over relates to the way in which people apprehend the violence on television. We suppose that people intuitively recognize fake violence on television and are never tempted to confuse this with the real thing. If so, this will surely have a bearing on how we encode and react to it. But perhaps the recognition is not as exact as we might suppose.

why realism is not real

The classic case of confusing fact and media fiction is the "War of the Worlds" radio broadcast of 1938, when Orson Welles, inspired by H. G. Wells' novel, announced that martians had invaded earth. American listeners mistook the hoax for the real thing, dashing hysterically into the streets. An almost self-fulfiling panic gripped the population as witnesses to the crowded streets picked up second-hand clues about the radio announcement. The fictitious story gained in credibility as more and more people appeared to accept it. No matter that the content of the program was preposterous; the mode of its presentation, the authority of the narrator and the solemnity of his message contrived to make the martian landing seem real. Such is the power of the mass media.

Some might argue that television, because it is a visual as well as audial medium, has more power to influence people's perceptions of reality. Yet the world according to television is completely unlike the one we live in. Soaps are successful because they are realistic: characters are particular, situations are concrete. Their success demonstrates our fascination with realism. Spurning abstractness and idealism, television specializes in showing life as it is without glossing over what is ugly or painful. Its strength is its apparent fidelity of representation, its adherence to nature and its insistence on getting as near to reality as possible. Television reaches its homes with homogenized entertainment coded in a very specific way, so as to make it acceptable and gratifying. Realism is the code adopted by and large in most film and radio. All have avoided any attempt at impressionism or other forms of expressive athleticism and opted for the safety of narrative structures in which purportedly real stories develop in linear fashion.

But there is nothing "real" about realism: it does not even correspond to the way we see the world and certainly not the way we think. It is what we expect of television's efforts to reconstruct reality. And we relate probably in the same way as Adorno's astrology readers relate to practical advice based on nothing more than the movements of planets: "we know it's all nonsense but . . ." People rejoice at fictional marriages, weep at make-believe deaths, get angry with artificial villains. All these are mediated by television. They are usually absurdly caricatured and wholly unlike what happens in daily life. Yet somehow they have meaning for us; we are asked to suspend disbelief and immerse ourselves in television as a natural and authentic representation of the way things are, even though we are mindful of the fact that it is not.

No one seriously believes *The Simpsons* are real, of course. Nor *Quantum Leap* and probably not *Roseanne*. But they are "realistic" in the sense that the characters and actions are tangible and liable to similar restrictions to ourselves. Even time-travelers obey laws of gravity once they set down in a particular period. Stories are stitched together in narrative sequence and we are able to recognize, quite readily, human features in them.

One of the values of cultural studies, which we evaluated in the previous chapter, is in alerting us to the ways in which political messages are diffused through television programs. Not in overtly ideological fashion: but surreptitiously, so that they actually assist our comprehension and enjoyment of programs, making viewing a satisfying, involving experience. We are prepared to believe in television. This seems to be a conditional thing; as long as it does not task us too much, in which case it becomes far-fetched, absurd or just unrealistic.

Exceptions can make the rule and, occasionally we get a quirky item with little coherent story, a mixture of real and fantastic images and cryptic dialogue broken up by incongruous song-and-dance routines. Dennis Potter's tv plays, like *Pennies from Heaven* and *The Singing Detective*, have been smuggled into otherwise relentlessly realistic schedules and to some acclaim. No one could seriously accept such art as a reflection of reality. So, it was interesting that both plays drew criticism for their depictions of sex. David Lynch's expressionist spoof *Twin Peaks* was a risky endeavor that paid off in spades.

Most people do not accept what they see on television as "real." We might suppose an exception to this. Say we captured the wild boy of Aveyron, France, the feral child who lived rough without the company of humans until the (estimated) age of eleven. We might induct him into human society, perhaps introducing him to television once he has mastered the rudiments of language. He might accept television as his window on the world. If so, his disillusionment on venturing into society would be catastrophic. I extrapolate from psychological research findings that children with little information and experience tend to be more gullible about the "truth" of television (Greenberg and Reeves, 1976; Donohue and Donohue, 1977).

Bandura's experiments, which we considered earlier, found that children imitated violence equally whether the scenes they watched featured real actors or obviously mock characters, like a man dressed in a cat outfit. Yet, subsequent research in a similar vein found that children were more likely to react aggressively if they were persuaded that the violence they had witnessed was "real" rather than "fictitious." Similar patterns of response were elicited from adults under experimental conditions. Even something as artificial as a boxing match prompted a more violent response when subjects were told that it was "for real" rather than staged combat. The studies of Huesmann and Eron endorsed this: aggressive behavior was correlated with the perceived reality of television violence (1986).

Obviously, as we mature, we accept the factuality of television less than as children. We seriously accept only a fraction of what we did as a child. This presumably means that we are likely to respond aggressively only to programs that we believe to be faithful depictions of reality, or which at least may be faithful. News events should qualify, as should docudramas and, probably, some fact-based dramas that have the ring of truth. Yet these are precisely the types of programs that researchers find do not stimulate violence among viewers, even heavy viewers. Much more likely is a viewing of an action thriller video, such as the Stallone/Snipes vehicle *Demolition Man*, followed by a spell of senseless violence at a nearby bar. Few would perceive the implausible tale of a cryogenic cop as having much to do with reality. All of which begs the question of why some people might try to simulate aspects of it. One very blunt answer might be that they do not.

It could be that many of the kind of people who rent or buy such a video for home viewing are for some reason attracted to violence in the first place and enjoy watching as well as doing it. Some might merely want to do violence in the first place but will not content themselves by just observing others fake it. Watching Messrs. Stallone and Snipes battle it out could actually reduce the likelihood of behaving aggressively. This is exactly the type of approach Bandura, Berkowitz and the others were opposing. What many writers on the alleged connection seem to assume is that this is an either/or answer: either you believe television leads to violence or you believe it leads away from it. Maybe it is neither: television violence has no effect at all, at least not on most adults, who correctly understand that what they are watching is "real" but not real.

Thousands, perhaps hundreds of thousands of viewers per year write personal letters to the fictional characters who inhabit the world of soaps. Killers occasionally try to use tv to rationalize their actions, as in the 1977 case of Ronald Zamora, then 15, who confessed to murdering a woman in Miami Beach, then later pleaded temporary insanity "under the influence of prolonged, intense, involuntary, subliminal television intoxication." (Zamora watched tv six hours daily, idolizing the cop Kojak; see Liebert and Sprafkin, 1988, for details.) The former viewers may not be as aberrant as the latter, but they are not exactly typical either. The overwhelming majority of viewers maintain enough distance between themselves and the screen to appreciate that, when all is said and done, this is only television.

Support for this view was given by Barry Gunter and Mallory Wober, of the British Independent Broadcasting Association, whose survey of *Violence on Television: What the Viewers Think* revealed that a large majority of viewers, while regarding dramatic tv violence as enjoyable, did not see it is a credible portrayal of reality (1988). They also thought documentary coverage of, for example, Northern Ireland, exaggerated the extent of violence. They were under no illusions about the fabricated status of the violence they were watching and even maintained a scepticism about allegedly "real" violence. Only a small minority saw television violence as excessive or potentially harmful.

In any case, what is so special about television that makes it deserving of attention never afforded other media? Admittedly, John Lennon's killer performed his deed clutching a copy of Salinger's *Catcher in the Rye*, but books are rarely thought to arouse the reader to the point where he or she performs violence. Ditto paintings. No one condemns Rubens' *Rape of the Sabine Women* or Gentileschi's *Judith Beheading Holofernes* for inflaming passions that might provoke unacceptable action. And what of listening to stirring music like the *1812 Overture*? To my knowledge no one has suggested that it does not evoke images of violence; yet no one has accused it of inspiring violent behavior. It may have something to do with the fact that sashaying about art galleries and listening to classical music are mainly middle-class pursuits. Television viewing spans the entire class structure, with the working class doing more viewing than other groups. This tells us nothing about the working class' susceptibility to television violence; but it may tell us something about the assumptions many psychological researchers and policy makers carry with them when they make their pronouncements.

All of us, regardless of class, sex or ethnic origin, harbor some potential for violent behavior. Only the most saintly would deny having had moments when they wanted to strike out against someone. While I have no evidence to support this, my suspicion is that few people get through a working week without experiencing at least a mild urge to commit violence. There are perfectly plain reasons why this does not usually convert into action. Most of us are rational enough to realize that our actions might precipitate an unpleasant retaliation and that, apart from venting our anger, the action will probably not solve any problems. We have also been taught to believe that violence is wrong in most contexts. Television, in many ways, contradicts all these points. Heroes seem to have knockout power that pre-empts retaliation; acts of aggression elicit acceptable solutions and, often, violence is highly valued by all. Contradictions are not always catalysts, however; and the debate about the conditions under which they can be will run on and on.

In their book *Television in the lives of our children*, Wilbur Schramm and his co-authors draw the memorably equivocal conclusion: "For *some* children under *some* conditions, some television is harmful. For *other* children under the same conditions, or for the same child under *other* conditions, it may be beneficial. For *most* children under *most* conditions, most television is neither particularly harmful nor particularly beneficial (1961: 1). *Mutatis mutandis* the same goes for adults.

Protest and advocacy groups may be basing their campaign for more regulation of television violence on a misconception. The viewer is simply not taken in by what appears on the screen; he or she rarely conflates fictional and actual violence. Gay activists and women's group protesters who converged on New York movie theaters at the opening of the movie *Basic Instinct* in 1992 were obviously underestimating the erudition of the audience. Did they really think audiences would believe the contrived hokum featuring a bisexual multimillionairess who habitually stabs men to death with an icepick just after they have sexually climaxed with her? "The characters are stereotypes," warned protesters. Of course they were stereotypes; what made them think they were the only ones who had realized this?

Television viewers are just as discriminating. Those who fear for them and worry that they will be influenced by television in what they think and do, give them little credit for having intelligence. The concern is patronizing and insulting. Much better to accept that thirty-odd years of research on the supposed link between television and violence has brought forth a tangled mishmash of contradiction and uncertainty and that this may be due to the fact that the link, if it exists, is far, far more tenuous than at first hypothesized. So tenuous that it hardly merits the considerable attention it continues to receive.

And yet there is something quite elemental about the continuing debate because it addresses the question of television's role as an agent of change – or stability – and hence its overall effect on our experiences. As Gitlin has written: "It stands to reason that years of television, cumulatively, seep into the imagination in ways more sweeping than any simple influence on behavior" (1985: 334). While he gives no details on the methods through which the permeation takes place, Gitlin's point has an unmistakable ring of truth.

Let us accept conditionally that we are not, in any direct way, stimulated to think or provoked to behave and perhaps not even inspired to believe. What is left? Gitlin's answer is: television "reminds us to think of ourselves as consumers first and foremost" (1985: 334). Television condescends, so that we feel empowered without actually having power to do much, apart from buying the products we see on the screens. The primary vehicle for the condescension is, of course, advertising and this comes under investigation in the next chapter, where we will once more confront the question of what tv does to us.

chapter six

answering advertisers' prayers

no escape

This time, she is confused. His rude interruption as she was enjoying the company of the new man in her life was unforgivable. She had all but put him out of her mind, then he returns with the sweetly surprising news that he loves her. It began in 1987. "Hello; I'm sorry to bother you, but I'm having a dinner party and I've run out of coffee," had been her way of introducing herself to her new neighbor, a smug, fortyish male. She smiles at the memory of returning his coffee, an untimely and slightly embarrassing intrusion when he was entertaining a woman friend.

Their relationship had never actually caught alight, but it smoldered pleasantly for almost a year until, one night, he burst into a soirée holding flowers and apologizing for his lateness. "I think you know everyone except . . ." Imperturbably, he played along with the deception, later announcing his intention to see her in the more intimate environs of his apartment. She obliged.

Business took her to Milan and him to New York. There were contretemps, like the time one of his old flames visited him at a late hour; and when he jumped to the wrong conclusion at the sight of her and her brother – or was it her ex-husband? Now she has turned 40: she still radiates elegance, but remains torn by questions. Perhaps something was missing from their relationship, after all. Her new friend from Italy seemed so much more compatible. Everything had progressed smoothly – until the intrusion.

Television viewers will recognize this not as a plot outline for a drama series, or part of a soap saga, but as a television commercial for Nestlé's coffee, Gold Blend, known in the USA as Taster's Choice. The 40-seconds-long encounters were quite deliberately structured like dramas, each slotting the same two characters, played by Sharon

Maughan and Tony Head, into different contexts and with teasing ends that invited the viewer to wait for more.

Episodes arrived at the rate of two per year. Like a typical soap series, each was left open-ended, presumably so that Nestlé could kill off the series at the first sign of consumer resistance. But, in Britain, Gold Blend sales rose by 15 per cent in the first year (two instalments) and 40 per cent after five years, or eleven instalments. A replica commercial was shot for the States, using the same scripts and actors, but dubbed with American accents and, of course, Taster's Choice as the sting. This was launched in 1990. Sales were up by ten per cent within two years.

Nestlé's advertising agency McCann Erickson, in this campaign, discovered an antidote to a problem that has plagued advertisers in recent years: grazing. Television viewers keep their remote control handsets within reach and, at the first sight of an uninteresting commercial, zap to another channel. In mimicking programs designed ostensibly for pure entertainment, the commercials were able to hook audiences in exactly the same way as soaps: by providing figures with whom viewers could identify, or even admire, and situating them in a long, involving narrative that always approached but never reached a resolution. Usually bathed in soft candlelight and accompanied by piano, the continuous scorpion dance was predicated on the coffee's aphrodisiac possibilities. Ludicrous perhaps; but, when the jars kept moving off the supermarket shelves, the ads had done their job.

Television *is* advertising. Defenders of the BBC and other supposedly commercial-free broadcasting systems are advised to view a BBC Saturday afternoon sports show, which might typically include cricket sponsored by John Player, motor racing with every square inch of every car plastered with logos of Marlboro, Brut, Fiat and miscellaneous branded products, and excerpts from the Virginia Slims women's tennis series. Tobacco advertising is banned. Later in the evening, BBC might show highlights from the Carling Premiership, featuring Arsenal, whose players wear JVC on their shirts, and Aston Villa, whose shirts bear the legend Müller. In between, there could be a re-run of an old *Miami Vice* episode in which "parts of Don Johnson's wardrobe are furnished by Hugo Boss" – as it tells us in the closing credits. Or an *LA Law* featuring Arnold Becker swigging from one of the several bottles of Perrier he keeps in his office. And closing with (to steal a gag from the satirical show *Spitting Image*), *Profile*, a documentary in which the Chairman of the BBC will explain why he will never allow advertising on his network.

The fact that BBC television does not accept direct revenue from advertisers does not render it significantly different from commercial television. Production costs are offset by the often covert contributions of advertisers, in exchange, for example, for product placement in which actual branded merchandise is used in strategic scenes, or throughout. Even the aged BBC radio series *The Archers*, in 1992, began mentioning the names of actual beers instead of the fictitious products it had previously used. When the BBC buys a program from the United States, its price reflects the amount of advertising it surreptitiously contains.

Advertising has penetrated the inner sanctum of the BBC. There is clearly no escape from it. On average, each North American viewer watches 35,000 commercials, each lasting 30 seconds, per year. By the time they are 40 years old a person will have seen approaching 1.5 million ads on tv. British viewers get less exposure to direct advertising (maximum six minutes per hour, by law), but, because of the reasons given above, will still have been exposed to a battery of ads, some latent, some blatant. And viewers pay for it one way or another. Manufacturers budget for about 32 per cent of the price of a bar of soap being spent on advertising, 40 per cent of the price of toothpaste.

Even if we regard ourselves as discerning consumers, invulnerable to television advertising, we simply cannot dodge all the bullets. Probably, because we do not want to. Advertising is, after all, as much a solution as a problem; at least according to some writers.

"It could be argued that advertising nowadays fulfills a function traditionally met by art or religion," Gillian Dyer suggests in her book *Advertising as Communication* (1982: 2). She dismisses the pretense that the primary function of advertising is to introduce a wide range of consumer goods to the public and emphasizes its role in manipulating values and attitudes by "providing people with simple stories and explanations in which values and ideals are conveyed and through which people can organize their thoughts and experiences and come to make sense of the world they live in" (1982: 2). She assembles the support of other writers, including Raymond Williams and Fred Inglis, who have made similar points; advertising offers a novel magic that can solve many problems of life. As religion and, to a degree, art provide frameworks for interpreting experiences and eliminating, or rationalizing, the least pleasant of them, so advertising presents an alternative. A package of goods that may serve the same purpose; and painlessly. All you need to do is buy them. It is an intriguing way of looking at advertising: as solutions to life's problems that can be bought off a shelf or through a mail order catalog.

One senses, though, that this approach misses an important point and that is how the problems to which advertising offers solutions are actually created by advertising itself. In other words, problems have to be collapsed into simple dimensions if they are to be soluble by purchasing disposable goods. This is the achievement of advertising, as we will see next.

creating problems, creating solutions

"In response to the exigencies of the productive system of the twentieth century, expressiveness replaced thrift as a social value. It became imperative to invest the laborer with a financial power and a psychic desire to consume." So wrote Stuart Ewen in his book *Captains of Consciousness* (1976: 25). "Businessmen began to see the necessity of organizing their businesses not merely around the production of goods, but around the creation of a buying public" (1976: 23–6). Mass production is pointless unless there is a mass market ready and primed to consume the products. Over the first twenty years of this century, advertising came to play an ever more prominent role in industry's efforts to cultivate a continuously responsive consumer market.

The concept of creating a market, rather than producing in accordance with the "natural" requirements of people, is not new. Dyer observed that: "Advertising is consistent with most types of human society and in fact was not unknown in ancient Greece and Rome" (1982: 15). News sheets known as mercuries, after the Roman messenger of the gods, circulated around in Britain in the seventeenth century; merchants and traders needed information on prices, shipping timetables, etc. The mercuries carried the announcements of importers, exporters and local retailers specializing, for example, in miracle cures and "cosmatiks."

Not until the twentieth century was the genuine potential of advertising grasped; that is, as a way of developing demand in a way that fitted supply like a glove. Henry Ford's archetype production factory turned out cars at rates that embarrassed traditional methods. The new methods were deadly efficient and the products were all exactly the same, right down to the paintwork. Advertising was given the job of homogenizing distribution as effectively as automation had homogenized production. Individual taste had to be subordinated to universal need; and this meant appealing to qualities that transcended any particular group. So, in the early years of the century, industries began playing with the idea of selling not only a product, but values. Ford cars were not just a means of transport, but a source of status; cosmetics offered beauty, not just face powder and lipstick.

But Ewen feels the most successful ploy of the era was to appeal to feelings of social insecurity as a way of habituating people to "consumptive life," as he called it (1976: 37). This entailed creating desires and habits by bludgeoning people with the message that normal people do not live without products such as nail polish or washing machines. Nor do they have body odor. Written in the 1920s, the sociological study *Middletown* by Robert and Helen Lynd makes special mention of "rapidly changing habits of thought as to what things are essential to living and multiplying optional occasions for spending money" (1929: 81–2).

Here we find an important insight: "habits of thought," or mentalities, were changing. Needs and wants were undergoing redefinition as satisfied customers became a thing of the past. The new customers so integral to industrial society should never be satisfied. They should have their appetites continually whetted, their curiosities piqued, their desires provoked. Only a special type of mentality could respond: potential consumers should be made self-aware, conscious and critical of their deficiencies, all of which could be rectified through the power of purchasing. So, as production proliferated in the period following the Second World War and austerity was replaced by a relative affluence, advertising's job was to remind populations continually that the goals on offer were not optional extras to their lifestyles, but essentials they should be ashamed to be without. In this way, large-scale businesses tried to intrude into the most personal aspects of a person's private life in their chase for the disposable income circulating in the 1950s.

The idea of consumer sovereignty has its origins in this period. Affirming the individual's belief in the supreme power to choose from a range of options was vital to advertising's success. Berating a person for having body odor or not having a food mixer was less effective than undermining a person's confidence for not having these (or having the "wrong" make) then offering the opportunity to put this right. It had to be *their* decision for it to work. In reality, that decision might be so tightly restricted as to be meaningless. But the consumer had to be made to feel comfortably in charge of the process, always expressing a preference, distinguishing essentially identical products from one another.

Advertising's role was to create, exaggerate and sustain the impression that consumers and not producers determined resource allocation in the free market economy. In this way, consumers were able to participate in the mass industrial market, accepting its values as well as its products. Advertising's own tenet that it could not force people to buy anything they did not already want was as false then as it is now. Advertising was, and is, able to manipulate consumers and bear directly on their choices.

But, there is arguably a more important influence and one which came into being later, largely because of television: advertising taught populations to want, to expect, or to crave, a never-ending supply of novelty. We are never content with what we have, whether it be commodities or values. Improvement is now a socially desired goal and this means we have to replace and upgrade whenever possible.

Underlying this education-of-sorts was the reduction of everything to simple dimensions. When Dyer and the others refer to the magical powers offered by advertising, they have in mind the manner in which, having first had a complete set of problems created for us, we consumers can then buy our way out of them. Industrial society threw up new discontents and demands that could be met by commodities. Troubled relationships could be eased with a box of chocolates; health was a matter of eating the right food; depressions could be lifted by a number of means, like pharmaceuticals, a lick of paint for the living room or a soak in a bathtub full of toiletries. Consumerism involved breaking down everything to common elements; to things that could be bought and sold. Electricity, chocolate and the like were consumed quickly and replaced immediately. Consumer durables such as cars and refrigerators would yield a slower flow. Consumerism involved three basic phases: (1) persuading people to accept the value of products; (2) inviting them to prioritize the ones they want, or "need" most; and (3) motivating them to spend money on them. Ergo advertising. And advertising came of age during its innocence-losing liaison with television.

Advertising's foray into moving pictures began in the 1920s. Short films of between one and five reels stuck fairly closely to the realist narratives popularized by the features of the day. Minidramas culminating in commercials for shoes or confectionery would be shown between main movies at cinemas. Here the possibilities of advertising were realized as never before; engaging audiences emotionally and intellectually in an exhibition of images and sound strung together loosely with a plot, at the same time disengaging them from any meaningful activity.

Remember the context: mass production and the factory system needed a workforce prepared to endure the monotonous grind and narrow satisfactions offered by automated industrial work. Ewen's book shows how advertising was seen in many circles as an answer to the bedeviling question of what to do about a discontented and agitated working class which may have been contemplating "deeper changes" in society than those suggested by modern capitalism. Stifling the urge to change may have proved dangerous in the long term.

Mass consumption, on the other hand, was seen as a way of allowing the working class to "act out" its impulses in a socially controllable context. "The logic of using consumption and *mass* leisure as ameliorations for boredom and social entrapment was not merely an underlying trend in advertising," wrote Ewen (1976: 86). "Some ads made explicit reference to the inadequacies of modern existence, and frankly offered the culture of modern industrialism as an *ersatz* for, meaningful activity." He had film in mind: its ability to visualize fantasies made it the perfect escapist medium.

Viewed from this perspective, film advertising could take people's minds off the basic material issues that affected them and turn them towards trivialities. The argument is a political version of the old idea that "if you're feeling depressed, go out and buy yourself something nice." Discontents arising from dull work could be skillfully converted into additions to the market and, according to Ewen, supports for the existing order of things. Passivity and the acceptance of the marketplace were shown to be more favorable for the consumer than more radical conceptions of change. "Why go on strike against your bosses, when you can make yourself feel better by simply buying a vacuum cleaner for your wife?" was effectively the type of proposition put to industrial workers.

People were required to want much more than they needed. This is putting it crudely. But then advertisers put everything crudely; at least until after the Second World War, when advertising began to drop its directness and become more serpentine in its approach. Television made it possible to convey moving visual images more readily than a set of standardized facts about products. Information, actual statements about products, was all very well for print media; television offered many other possibilities. In particular, it was able to keep viewers' attention focused on images while they listened to a message. Radio's messages lacked the enhancement of television's. Besides, people typically listened to radio while doing other things, which was seen, at the time, as a negative; though, in retrospect, exposing people to commercial messages while their guards were down may have been effective. Quite apart from the obvious mechanical advantages of being able to simulate reality closer than other media, television's rapid penetration of con- sumers' homes and its seemingly hypnotic power gave it potential homogenizing influences.

Having mass media was one thing; a mass market was another. Producing one from the other became a probability. Television may have been a nightmarish prospect for the likes of Adorno *et al.*, as we saw in chapter three, but it was hailed as "the vacuum salesman's dream" and "advertising's third dimension,' according to Eric Clark in his book *The Want Makers*, which bears the alluring subtitle "How they make you buy" (1989: 324). "In the early days advertisers sponsored and produced entire programs, thus giving them complete control of their content" (1989: 324).

Sponsors, at pains to showcase their products in the most favorable way, rewrote scripts or re-edited programs in accordance with commercial rather than any other kind of requirements. So, for instance, tobacco companies would insist that only positive characters, the "good guys," smoked cigarettes. Automobile companies would fashion shows so heroes drove a particular make of car. Brewery companies, toothpaste manufacturers, coffee producers, and so on, all made sure scripts reflected their priorities.

On one notorious occasion, the American Gas Corporation sponsored the drama *Judgment at Nuremberg*, but only on the condition that the word "gas" was edited from the soundtrack. Commercials for gas appeared throughout. On another, Camel cigarettes sponsored an NBC news program: its editorial intervention extended so far that it was able to dictate that "No Smoking" signs were not to be visible in any news footage. A program sponsored by the Ford Motor Company contained a scene in which the famous Chrysler Building was deleted from the New York City skyline.

The policy of sponsoring programs slumped in popularity, not so much because of the stringent editing, but because of its ineffectiveness by comparison with spot commercials. Television folklore has it that this was discovered almost by accident when the Hazell Bishop cosmetic company, with relatively small annual sales of $50,000, wanted to advertise on tv, but was too strapped for cash to sponsor a show. It produced a short commercial independently of the programs it surrounded or punctuated. Instead of "Hazell Bishop presents" followed by the name of the show, there were 30-second "messages" slapped in willy-nilly. And with agreeable consequences: sales shot up. Other advertisers adopted the same format. At first suspicious, television companies later warmed to the idea; it allowed their producers new freedom from arbitrary editorializing, though not without a cost. Much of the somber drama, such as Paddy Chayevsky's *Marty* (1953) and Rod Serling's many plays that defined what have been called the Golden Years of the 1950s, were replaced by lighter fare.

Viewers who had been drawn through cataracts of dialogue, swamps of exposition and thickets of social problems were not exactly primed to accept the *faux naïf* messages of advertisers; that the solutions to life's myriad problems were to be found in fresh breath, oven-ready chickens and ladder-free hosiery. A showcase like *US Steel Hour* gave producers scope to explore prosaic themes; as long as rival products did not feature in the scripts. Spot advertisers required something different: programs that created a receptive audience; receptive, that is, to the obviously commercial messages that were intruding into the entertainment at a rate of twelve or more minutes per hour (this has since been reduced by agreement to a maximum of eleven minutes per hour during primetime). Glibness crept into programming, a quality that is still reflected in much television.

Unlike the USA, Britain spurned commercialism; at least ostensibly. The BBC (originally British Broadcasting Company, now Corporation) had been established in 1922 with the purpose of providing a "public service." It has retained this as a motif ever since, presenting itself as a purveyor of arts and culture in contrast to the lowest-common-denominator approach of its North American counterparts. Able to support itself through the revenue of license fees, it had no need of advertisers and resisted all attempts to compromise its central purpose. As with the USA, television came into being through radio and BBC regarded television, introduced in 1936, as no less burdened with didactic responsibility than radio. As a minority medium, BBC television had no trouble in preserving its integrity: there were no obvious competitors and the service was limited. After the war, as we have seen, television's popularity accelerated and, by 1952, it was a fully-fledged mass medium, paralleling the growth in the USA.

American television's experience served to remind many of the baleful consequences of commercialism, so, when pressures mounted for other networks, BBC supporters did their best to justify the monopoly. "Sponsored broadcasting" was likened to bubonic plague by Lord Reith, then General Manager of the BBC. Commercial logic overriding all else, independent television – as it is called in Britain – was launched in 1955. But whereas US television had developed in such a way that the tail was allowed to wag the dog, British commercial tv was determined to dictate the flow and content of its programs. Intrusive commercials at inopportune moments were barred. Instead, "natural" breaks were permitted; these were not supposed to interrupt the rhythm of the show unduly. Sponsorship of the kind favored initially by North American advertisers was barred by the 1954 Television Act. In one notable instance, a consumer advice program called *Jim's Inn* was singled out for its transparent commercial plugs. It was removed from air.

Despite differences in approach and stated objectives, British and US commercial television were both instruments of mass marketing. The British Independent Television Authority (ITA) was intended to perform as a controlling body and did make stipulations about the content and duration of advertising, but the unseen hand that had guided US television was at work in Britain too. Without advertisers, the money would dry up and, to attract advertisers, you needed the biggest possible audience; so, you laid on shows that were likely to claim the attention of viewers. Advertisers may have been sympathetic towards the creative goals of television producers, but they had a job to do: to sell their products. And they had only one measure: sales.

hidden persuaders

Advertisers were thought to stop short of nothing in their quest for sales. Unproven accusations of hypnosis, brainwashing and other forms of mind-bending were rife. One of the documented techniques used by television advertisers, in particular, was the depth approach, inspired by "motivational analysis." This purported to give answers to why we behave the way we do. Once advertisers had the information, they could re-shape our habits and choices, picking at our frailties and weaknesses to make us buy. The title of Vance Packard's celebrated book on the subject, *The Hidden Persuaders*, first published in 1957, conveyed the sinister possibilities of this approach, which Packard himself decided had "seriously antihumanistic implications."

Packard revealed the assumptions held by advertisers: "Typically they see us as bundles of day-dreams, misty hidden yearnings, guilt complexes, irrational emotional blockages . . . image lovers given to compulsive acts" (1981: 14). As consumers, we please advertisers "with our growing docility in responding to their manipulation of symbols that stir us to action" (1981: 14). Packard estimated that, in the late 1950s, "two-thirds of America's hundred largest advertisers had geared campaigns to this depth approach" (1981: 11).

When Packard's disclosures were first published, over 70 per cent of US and British households possessed television sets. In 1981, when over 99 per cent had one set or more, Packard reflected on his book, identifying six key techniques that had become common practice in the intervening period. *Slipping messages into our mind* was perhaps the most alarming development, involving subliminal stimulation. Visual messages could be flashed on screens so quickly that viewers would not be consciously aware of, nor offer resistance to them. The contents of the split-second flash would slip through unchallenged below the consciousness threshold. The message might be a suggestion such as "In five minutes, you will thirst for a 7-Up" or "Wranglers are the coolest blue jeans." Technically, the method was more suited to cinema, where frames move faster, but Packard gave examples of its use in television, for instance in a 1973 campaign for a family game called "Husker Du" which flashed "Get it" repeatedly (1981: 233).

The potential abuses, political as well as commercial, of subliminal stimulation were so obvious that television authorities banned its use in advertising, though it is employed in auto-hypnotic videotapes designed for example, to increase viewers' self-confidence, or their ability to concentrate. The audio counterpart to this is whispered or disguised messages, such as those thought to be used by bands embedding or "backmasking" sounds in their records. Members of the rock band Judas Priest were brought to trial in 1990 after it was claimed that the concealed message "Do it, do it, do it" on their album *Stained Class* led two fans to commit suicide. The musicians were acquitted.

By marketing our hidden needs, Packard referred to what is now a commonplace advertising strategy: attaching desirable qualities to products. Telephone companies include human contact with their products; breweries associate beer with companionship and fun. Consumers are offered rewards beyond the actual product. Another commonly used technique is promising relief from our anxieties and distress. Volvo has been especially adept at this, emphasizing the safety features of its cars. Tire-makers have played out a similar theme, imploring the potential consumer to consider his or her child's safety. The technique simultaneously heightens a viewer's anxiety and tenders a way of reducing it.

"Sex sells" has become an axiom not only of advertisers, but of film makers, writers and virtually any other group that has an eye on the mass market. Packard cited examples of phallic deodorant containers and lipsticks that "come thrusting out of their metal containers in unison, with a fanfare" as illustrations of the built-in sexual overtone, something that has become very familiar to television viewers. Britain's ad for Cadbury's Flake chocolate bar was a phallic classic. Commercials today have brought sex down from the symbolic levels and make promises that are easily inferred. Drinking Miller light beer makes one irresistibly attractive to blonde, generously bosomed members of the Swedish women's rowing team, according to one commercial which was forced off the air in 1992 after feminist protests. Women could effect a similar result by spraying themselves with a perfume called Impulse in a British commercial which saw a male recklessly pursuing the scent of a woman, followed by the explanation, "Men just can't help acting on Impulse."

Parents often buy in supermarkets as a result of urging from their children. One can almost hear a child admonishing his or her mother as she reaches for the generic brand of sweet corn: "Mom, don't buy that; get the one with the Jolly Green Giant." Packard called advertisers' attempts to turn this to their own advantage the psycho-seduction of children and pointed out that its chances of success were heightened by the discovery that young children do not typically demarcate between programs and the commercials – naively, children stumble across a fundamental truth. (More recent research cited in chapter one indicates that children may discriminate more than Packard thought.)

It is almost axiomatic that advertisers are continuously engaged in a ferocious battle to differentiate goods that are, to all intents and purposes, identical. Packard saw one of their central jobs as the sale of symbols and images rather than product itself. Cars were, and probably are, the exemplar here: several dozen models may be very similar, but some marques maintain a status that can be transferred to the owner, if their commercials are to be believed. Packard's observations did not extend to the point where he was able to see emerging a type of law of diminishing returns as applied to status and image. For example, an expensive product hoping to build or retain an upmarket cachet may establish its market presence through advertising on television. But, if, say, Jaguar cars bombarded viewers with ads, their status may suffer. There comes a point at which excessive advertising can "cheapen" a product. Porsche, for example, advertises in selected print media; a television campaign would probably do long-term damage to a marque that is well-established. Nissan on the other hand, directs its 300ZX model to roughly the same area of the market as Porsche, but believes it needs a steady onslaught of dreamy commercials.

Parts of Packard's book read like the work of an excitable conspiracy theorist, but much of it is plausible, even today. There have also been developments that Packard could not have anticipated, including the emergence of television advertising into a virtual artform in its own right. Techniques of persuasion have moved away from the rather clandestine maneuvers written of by Packard. Yet they are probably no less effective. In the next subsection, we will look at three techniques of persuasion not covered by Packard, but which have risen to prominence. The first is outright lying. The others are: using well-known figures to approve products and making commercials resemble recognizable feature movies and/or incorporate popular music.

zap-proofing

Commercials have sometimes overstepped the mark. In the effort to make potential consumers see their brand in a favorable light in comparison with rivals, they have told outright lies. Zenith's claim that "every color tv Zenith builds is built right here in the US by Americans" was refuted by the fact that 15 per cent of its components were imported. Ford boasted of its "tough cars" with "tough engines," almost two million of which were found to be defective between 1974–8. And, in a vintage visual deception, Campbells dropped marbles in the soupbowl before pouring over their "Chunky Soup," which, of course, appeared to be much chunkier than it actually was on account of all the visible meat and vegetables resting on the concealed marbles.

Smirnoff Vodka's commercials were taken off British tv because of their implied promises of a dramatic transformation from the mundane to the spectacularly successful or exciting. A typical tagline was: "I was Mr. Holmes of Household Linens until I discovered Smirnoff" across a picture of a rugged and enigmatic world traveller. Under the picture was strapped "the effect is shattering." Of course, Smirnoff did not elicit such a change; nor did the advertisers expect consumers to take the claim seriously. Their idea, presumably, was to invite potential drinkers to identify with the "after" figure. Still, the official claim was seen as false and the ads were replaced with a different, yet related series.

Such untruths have often worked more effectively than the facts. But not always. Crest toothpaste was launched in the USA following eight years of clinical research on its effectiveness in reducing children's tooth decay. The evidence was used in the initial advertising campaign, but failed to impress: it achieved a 14 per cent market share. Only years later, when the same product was publicly endorsed by the American Dental Association (ADA), did it take off. For the past two decades, Crest has held over 30 per cent of the market.

Crest's appeal to empirically gathered facts presented in a no-frills, unfabricated manner worked eventually because it established the kind of credibility that can only come via a third party. The ADA was a perfect foil in this context, but other advertisers have pursued less abstract endorsements. Linking people to products is an old, but persistent routine. In the late 1940s, Denis Compton, a real-life comic-book-style cricketer, allowed his image to be used by Brylcreem hair preparation. His seal of approval was a key factor in building Brylcreem's recognition. No figures are available on how much Compton was paid, but we can be certain it was a tiny fraction of the $30 million plus Michael Jordan earned yearly from endorsing a whole series of products, including Nike sportswear and Wheaties breakfast cereal. Endorsements pay well and, presumably, they are cost-effective. Recognizable personalities are thought to help make the product recognizable, of course; but there are image associations that are arguably more important to advertisers.

One of the most famous endorsements was that of actor Karl Malden for the American Express Company. Malden's acting career was at a peak in the 1970s thanks to his lead role in the television series *The Streets of San Francisco*, in which he played a detective, Mike Stone. The Amex ad skillfully conflated Malden and Stone, so that the actor remained squarely in role as he extolled the virtues of American Express traveler's checks. It was less the opinion of an ordinary actor, more an *ex cathedra* pronouncement. Parenthetically, we might add that, as Amex's charge card sales plummeted in the 1990s, their advertising agents Ogilvy and Mather introduced Jerry Seinfeld, star of the eponymous NBC sitcom, to endorse their product on US television. Seinfeld's comic forte was in observing life's irksome annoyances and, in the commercials, these included rival credit cards, like Visa.

Other performers who have barely strayed out of role to endorse products include George Cole, who reprised his Arthur Daley character from the British comedy series *Minder* for the Leeds Building Society and Candice Bergen who was very much *Murphy Brown* when outlining the numerous advantages of the Sprint long-distance telephone system to North American viewers.

Endorsers have made few concessions to credibility; many opt for the totally preposterous, like Michael Jackson, known never to let anything as adulterated as soda pop pass his lips, praising Pepsi. The actual content of messages is of only secondary importance. Advertisers are interested primarily in establishing a connection between the personality and their product. This can be done without resort to visuals. Voiceovers by Michael Douglas for Infiniti cars or Martin Sheen for Toyota can have the same effect. The aim is to add to the product's value by increasing consumers' perceptions of its worth. Products appreciate if a high profile figure with extraordinarily high earnings capacity is prepared to put his or her reputation on the line for the product.

The reverse may be true also. Diadora sportswear along with a clutch of other companies that had commercial ties with Canadian sprinter Ben Johnson distanced themselves from him after he was disqualified from the 1988 Olympic Games for taking anabolic steroids. Johnson was rapidly demythologized from the fastest man on the planet to the "world's greatest cheat," cloven hoofs and horns virtually replacing his Diadora spikes and gold medal. A similar mass pull-out was expected after Los Angeles Lakers' basketball player Magic Johnson declared himself HIV-positive. Thinking twice about appearing mercenary toward someone who was owning up to a terminal condition, advertisers holding contracts with him just let them wind down. Endorsement contracts typically contain clauses to the effect that if the figure's actions bring the product into some form of disrepute, the arrangement is nullified.

Given the continuity of much of advertising and the entertainment it engulfs, it is only logical that some endorsing figures find fame and fortune in commercials. Bill Cosby himself attributes his success to his 30-second slots endorsing Jell-O Pudding. Mark C. Miller argued that Cosby performed a similar role in his series *The Cosby Show* in which he played Cliff Huxtable. "Cliff is himself an ad, implicitly proclaiming the fairness of the American system," wrote Miller (1986: 213). He is a "willing advertisement for the system that pays him well" (1986: 214).

Presenting "facts" or recruiting plausible characters to act as independent authorities invites or encourages viewers to believe in a product. Credibility is the sought-after commodity. In recent years, credibility has not been enough and advertisers have met with serious resistance, due principally to a subversive piece of technology.

Advertisers cannot know for sure how readied for a Burger King commercial a typical viewer may be if it is sandwiched between two news portions, one on starvation in East Africa, the other on a bulimia epidemic. What they do know is that most viewers nowadays have a remote control at their fingertips, many of them with memory facilities pre-set for favorite channels. At first sight of commercials, press button "C" for MTV and get a couple of minutes of rock music videos – themselves barely disguised commercials for cds. Remote controls have been a curse for advertisers: people shuttle between channels without leaving their seats. So unless the commercials are vaguely interesting they are zapped off to make way for a short burst of something else.

How do advertisers meet state-of-the-art resistance? With state-of-the-art advertising. They have created ads that are lucid and mettlesome, inducing audiences to forget they are watching commercials for a minute or two. One way of doing this is through the connecting plot structure, exploited by Nestlé in the Gold Blend/Taster's Choice narratives described at the opening of the chapter. The beauty of this campaign was the symmetry it achieved with actual programs. Other products have essayed this form. In particular, two beers – Kronenbourg in Britain and Bud Dry in the USA – appended their commercials with ". . . to be continued" captions in the early 1990s. The intention was to zapproof the ads by engaging the viewer in an open-ended story. Other advertisements strove to become indistinguishable from the programs they framed, or punctuated. This is more easily accomplished in the States where programs slide into ads without an alerting device, such as the "end of part . . ." that intervenes in British tv.

Another tactic has been to hurl deliberately ambiguous signifiers at the camera and leave the viewer to unscramble the message. The "Zen advertising" of Nissan's Infiniti car, launched in the USA in 1989, was notable for the absence of the product. Hill, Holliday, Connors, Cosmpoulos Inc., the ad agency, behind it, won kudos and raspberries for their conceit: showing natural scenes of rocks and trees, but no car. It certainly made Infiniti one of the most talked-about cars in the country, which was reflected in a 30 per cent sales growth by 1991. Thereafter, sales did not grow as anticipated and Hill, Holliday lost the account.

Levi's approach has also been centered on image, more than direct message; the Levi signifiers are all that matter in a long-running spool of British commercials in which no words are spoken. Each episode of a loose-linked series was shot with the inflections of a music video; grainily lit, gleamingly handsome characters (many, like Brad Pitt, stars in their own right) and rock music, every number gaining a new lease of life in sales as a direct result of the ads. Marvin Gaye's "I Heard It Through the Grapevine," T. Rex's "20th Century Boy" and the Clash's "Should I Stay, or Should I Go?" accompanied short stories of good-looking young men for some reason being deprived of their treasured jeans and always hooking up with an equally good-looking woman. The commercials hinted broadly at the sexual properties of Levi's without uttering a word: the association of the glamorous subjects with the logo on the tab worked effectively.

Derivative as the Levi's campaign was of rock videos, it did not stop rock videos cannibalizing themselves further, as Genesis' "I Can't Dance" showed. This swallowed the spider to catch the fly, ingesting a jeans ad set in a pool room, which could have been taken from any number of rock videos, all taking cues from Paul Newman's *The Hustler*. In the Genesis video, Phil Collins and company traipsed about the pool room *sans* Levi's, revealing their boxer shorts. The ad emphasized the point that there are no natural boundaries between commercials and the other forms of discourse.

Any given night's viewing provides evidence of television commercials' increasing congruity with movies in particular, and other art forms in general. AT&T used a series of images that might well have sprung fully formed from Francis Ford Coppola's film *Tucker: The Man and His Dream*. Sega computers plundered Coppola's *Apocalypse Now* for their British Commercials. Ridley Scott's *Blade Runner*, based, with many a postmodernist turn, on a vision of Los Angeles in 2019, has inspired many tv commercials. But, for sheer volume, the Indiana Jones trilogy must take pride of place: commercials for, among other, things, beer, burgers and do-it-yourself stores, have their stylish origins in the derring-do movies.

Other Spielberg films have had their images appropriated by advertisers. In the early 1990s, a BP commercial screened in Britain showed an incredulous youth reeling at the sight of a hightech oil plant in much the same way as characters in *ET, The Extra-Terrestrial* and *Close Encounters of the Third Kind*. The sources were obvious; they were meant to be. Advertisers' attempts to make consumers see their products in a favorable light include offering a format viewers will find evocative of a pleasurable experience, in this case watching a cinematic fantasy.

The *Naked Gun* movies were reprised in almost exactly the same fashion by two independent companies. Red Rock Cider in Britain and Dollar Rent-a-Car in the USA both employed actor Leslie Nielsen portraying his comic detective Frank Drebin in closely comparable scenes that could have been pulled from the movies. Holsten Pils lager in Britain and Coca Cola in the USA digitally reprocessed footage from old feature films and integrated them with newly shot commercial material to give the impression that, for example, comic Griff Rhys-Jones is talking to John Wayne, or Elton John is dueting with Louis Armstrong in natural scenes abstracted from movies. Viewers were not expected to believe their eyes, of course: the impact of the commercials was in their audacity and their power to shock audiences with apparent authenticity. Advertisers aimed at recall, rather than persuasiveness: just nudging consumers hard enough to make them play back mentally the memorable scene featuring Elton and Satchmo and then recall the brand name.

Another way of achieving recall is by linking a product, or range, with a particular piece of music. This has become popular with advertisers in recent years as many numbers have gone out of copyright and become commercially available for use. The Derek and the Dominoes hit of the early 1970s "Layla" was featured in a long-running campaign for Vauxhall Astra cars in Britain. Boots the chemist used Rod Stewart's "Sailing." Dunlop tires' arch use of the Velvet Underground's "Venus in Furs" to accompany its deliciously oblique campaign of 1993 stirred plenty of media discussion.

In fact, it is practically impossible to sit through a break in British television without at least one instantly recognizable hit in the background of an ad. In the States, the practice is less common, though many advertisers re-record old hits and substitute new lyrics to reflect their products. Perhaps the most incestuous move was that of Britain's National Westminster Bank which took Jan Hammer's "Crockett's Theme" from the television series *Miami Vice* and laid it under a series of their own commercials.

Television advertising has not so much mimicked other forms as absorbed them: their styles, properties, images, in general their signifiers, have been assimilated into a creation which has, ostensibly at least, fundamentally different goals. The object of a movie, a music video or even a plain song is to entertain, whereas a commercial's object is to sell a product. As the boundaries between them have dissolved so have the goals. Love them, or hate them, television commercials in the 1990s are radiant and cunning works of art spanning the short gaps between dull and often predictable programs. The poor ones test us, while the strong tease us. Brilliantly populist beer ads (like Britain's Carling Black Label) and enigmatic swerves towards deconstruction (The Gap clothes stores, McEwan's lager) alike amuse in a similar way to regular news and entertainment. This is not necessarily music to the ears of advertisers. Bask as they might in admiration, their primary job remains the same. This leads us to one final question.

does it work?

Demographics. From the Greek *demos* for people and *graphics* for writing, demography is the study of populations, their size, movements, ages, earnings, everything you need to know expressed in detailed statistical form. Television's version of demographics has a rather different intonation: it is a shorthand way of referring to a precise area of the population as defined by age, gender, disposable income and other criteria relevant to advertisers. Advertising agents who buy commercial space on behalf of companies have very definite pictures in mind about who they want to reach with their "messages." If research tells you that the potential market for light beer is young, white, middle-income males, there is little point in slipping commercials between the segments of a daytime soap opera that attracts, in the main, middle-aged females, no matter how many of them watch regularly.

Women have been the most sought-after group by advertisers and the reason for this is no mystery. They spend more money than any other group. Note that they do not earn more; just spend it, which is what counts. Women, who control the buying for their families and watch a lot of television interest advertisers and, by extension, the programmers, who need the advertisers' business. This explains why, for example, NBC in 1992 dropped from its schedules three of its most solid shows, *In the Heat of the Night*, *Matlock* and *The Golden Girls*, all of which were quickly signed up by rival networks. The reason for NBC's move was not because of the shows' popularity; all rode high in the ratings. But, the demographics were not right: the shows appealed to older viewers, who were not avidly sought by most tv advertisers. Straight ratings success has become less important than success with those viewers advertisers want to reach.

Back in the 1950s, a British newspaper called the *Daily Herald* closed down despite respectably high circulation figures. Its readership consisted of more men than women, older rather than younger people and predominantly manual workers. Such readers were of no importance to potential advertisers who wanted consumers, most of whom, according to market research, were young and affluent. Today, the target age is about 22. Network television, especially in the States, is devoted to courting youth as never before; which is why much of the fare of primetime television is about the joys and challenges of youth.

Television advertising is almost exclusively geared to reaching the young audiences that advertisers believe are the only ones willing to shift product loyalties. Advertising sales, always the *raison d'être* for commercial television, became more important than ever in 1992 with the major US networks coming off their worst financial year in history, as two networks, CBS and NBC, failed to make a profit. NBC's clear-out made way for comedies such as *Here and Now* and *Out all Night*, whose main characters were in their twenties. Fox established itself as a force on the basis of youth-oriented programs. *Beverly Hills 90210*, a weekly inspection of high school *angst*, spawned at least four direct descendants with ensemble casts that might have walked across the studio from Levi 501 ads. The themes were: the struggle of being twentysomething, newly employed and needing to make an important fashion statement.

In contrast, CBS, which picked up two of NBC's cast-offs, opted out of the war for young consumers and tried to corner the market for viewers who could actually remember what televisions were like without a video hook-up. With the other three networks aiming full-tilt at youth, CBS essentially had open access to the less commercially attractive, but still considerable market beyond the 18–22 niche. This was perfectly suited to an advertiser like Quaker Oats, which, from 1987, concentrated its campaign for cereals on the over-55 population, projecting a vigorous, mature image personified by its endorser Wilford Bramley, the actor.

With so much specificity and precision in targeting, one might suspect advertising is approaching a science. It is certainly no hit-and-miss affair and advertisers typically pre-test potential campaigns in isolated areas before deciding on their national commitment. Alternatively, they might run a national campaign everywhere except a designated area, which provides a control population, and compare sales and market shares to assess the effect of the advertising. Focus groups enable advertisers to evaluate face-to-face interactions with small samples of a population. Post-testing, as it is called, gauges brand awareness, recall and purchase patterns to establish a campaign's impact.

Yet, if advertising is so clinical in its approach and costs so much, why is the media column of the *New York Times* filled every day with stories of major ad agencies being fired and accounts being switched, of failing campaigns being cut and of companies going broke after over-budgeting on advertising? Simply because, as Hugh Davidson observes: "Advertising is not the all-powerful persuader which many of its critics imply" (1987: 275).

Davidson's manual on "how to make your competitors followers," *Offensive Marketing*, warns against overestimating the power of advertising, especially television advertising. An advertiser in Britain spending £1 million per year buys on average 0.01 per cent of the total amount of commercials shown on British tv. The figure will have shrunk since 1987, when Davidson's book was published, because of the expanding number of channels. In the USA, the percentage would be considerably smaller. As advertising is costly to produce (a typical 30-second commercial will run close to \$1 million or £600,000) and expensive to transmit (up to \$0.5m during the Super Bowl), a lot of money buys only a little time. But, the figures are still not bad. Jib Fowles made an interesting comparison in his *Why Viewers Watch*: "Almost every commercial is seen by more people than have been to every theatrical production put on in the United States since Colonial times" (1992: 205).

Confronted with the question of how effective it all is, Fowles answered "not very" and "quite a bit" (1992: 209). This is not quite as unhelpful as it sounds. Fowles echoed the conclusions of chapter five, which surveyed the contradictory evidence on the link between watching television and behaving violently. There is no scientific consensus about whether one causes the other, nor indeed about tv's efficacy in modifying behavior at all. Similarly, research on the ability of advertising to persuade us into buying certain products has still not turned up any unambiguous evidence.

And yet, as Fowles pointed out, "it is clear that enough people retain the product information and make purchases that advertisers are willing to continue investing in television commercials" (1992: 209). The preparedness to spend colossal amounts of money is premised on the fact that there is no better way to reach such a vast potential market. Even a sliver of the possible 30 million people sitting in front of sets in the States alone is sufficient to justify spending small fortunes. Estimating what percentage of those fortunes is wasted is a speculative exercise. "All but 10 per cent," said Barry Cole in 1970. Fowles reckoned as much as 99 per cent: "If, of all the people who see a repeated commercial, 1% are moved to try the product, then the manufacturer, advertising agency and network can be content" (1992: 210).

British researchers Patrick Barwise and Andrew Ehrenberg arrived at a broadly similar conclusion: that the reason companies have to spend so much money and creative energy on advertising and give television viewers so much of it is because it is such a weak force (1988). It has to pound the viewers' senses to get results. And even then it can backfire, as the notorious Metrecal slimming product campaign reminds us. This was a US company which ran a series of television commercials with the copyline "I am a Metrealic." Consumers were turned off by the obvious connotations of Alcoholics Anonymous and sales declined abruptly. The case suggests a fitting counterpoint to the Nestlé experience and squares with the general argument of this book: that we are not as empty-headed and manipulable as many, including presumably advertisers, seem to think.

Much of the theory behind advertising is stuck in the stimulus–response tradition popularized by North American behavioral psychologists in the 1950s. The question guiding enquiry is: what does advertising do to people? If a commercial is a stimulus, the desired conditioned response of the recipient is for him or her to recall the name of the product and buy it. Behaviorists are fond of using the *tabula rasa* metaphor in which human beings are depicted as blank tablets on which virtually anything can be written. This is a conception of people drained of free will or sense of purpose. Our behavior is an effect; so those who control the causes can do with us as they please, as long as they can isolate the exact stimulus or chain of stimuli that elicit the desired response. The response itself then becomes a stimulus, because its consequences may either increase or decrease the likelihood that it will occur again.

The last point is an important advance on early forms of behaviorism and is credited to the sometimes astounding work of B. F. Skinner, who was able to use "schedules of reinforcement" to teach pigeons to play ping-pong, rats to memorize where food is in a maze and other animals to spell words. Skinner's model of operant conditioning, as he called it, purports to explain an endless range of human, as well as other animal behavior by reference to rewards and punishment: if the initial response to the stimulus (say, a tv commercial) is to purchase and this is rewarding (customer satisfaction), then the consumer will repeat the behavior as the response becomes a stimulus in itself. If the response is negatively reinforcing or, worse still, punishing, then the chances of a repetition are diminished. The appeal of this to advertisers is transparent; but the tricky part is in discovering precisely what tv reinforces.

This is not nearly as straightforward as pigeons getting food pellets dropped into their cages after they have performed the desired pecking, because humans do not behave so mechanically. Often, we do not so much buy things as values; brands rather than actual products. Advertising agencies are acute enough to realize this, of course; which is why they do not always emphasize the performance-based properties of products. They try to attach a preferred meaning, or a set of values to products, so that advertisements deliver much more than product information. "Advertisements *intend* to make us feel we are lacking," wrote Judith Williamson in her book *Decoding Advertisements*, which is a virtual guide on what we are supposed to do with advertisements and what we can do. "Advertising must take into account not only the inherent qualities and attributes of the products they are trying to sell, but also the way in which they can make those properties mean something to us" (1992: 12).

Williamson stands light years from the behaviorist model and aligns herself with the cultural studies approach in her effort to show that advertising works not as a stimulus–response, but "by an exchange of signs, and an enmeshing of the subject in that exchange; a process concealed by the participation of the 'active subject'" (1992: 167). We are not just empty vessels, blank tablets or whatever other metaphor one chooses to suggest passivity. On this account, we actively engage in creating meaning, making sense of the commercials and, in this sense, advertising does "work" – though perhaps not in the orthodox way presumed by ad agencies. It works in a "circular," self-perpetuating motion because we clearly do need material goods. Advertising endows those goods with meaning by making them represent other, "non-material things" we also need; which is why, as we noted earlier, Williamson equated advertising's functions with art and religion (1992).

While this approach cannot assess the influence of advertising on our buying habits, it alerts us to the problems in trying to answer with a single measurement the question of whether advertising works. Fowles' response of "not very" and "quite a bit" (1992: 209) is rather too trite.

We surmise advertisers are one-percenters, acknowledging that 99 times out of a hundred they miss the mark; we can also surmise that they would not spend so much money without getting more back in return. But the precise ways in which advertising works are not to be explained wholly by the unsubtle theories of behavioral psychology. Certainly, the structure of the stimulus–response link may be a start, but the nature of it remains unclear.

Cultural studies in general and Williamson's work in particular prompt more questions than answers, but they are relevant questions about how we, as consumers, make advertising work. We interpret and infer from ads, collapse aspirations and fantasies into items that can be bought off a shelf or from a showroom. "Consumption is now the basic mode for all activity in our society," wrote Martin Davidson in *The Consumerist Manifesto* (1992: 203). I repeat from chapter one: "Not reading, not using, not appreciating, not participating, not producing but consuming." Advertising is the vehicle of consumption. We should see its influence as part of a complex. G. J. Goodhardt *et al.* issued an interesting reminder in their analysis of *The Television Audience*: "Consumers' awareness and expectations have been raised by magazines, films and television, and also by people's greater mobility and education, not merely by advertising as such" (1987: 123).

But we should also recognize the complementarity of all media today: all are to some degree affected by advertising. None more so than television.

If, as I suggested earlier, television is advertising, then it follows that television is more than an integral part of our culture, it is a defining agent of culture. Its ubiquity means that advertising is inside us as well as surrounding us. If this proposition scares you, read no more.

chapter seven

ethnic images

mensis mirabilis

Event one On April 30, 1992, a crowd converged on the Los Angeles Police Department (LAPD) headquarters protesting against the acquittal of four law enforcement officers accused of brutally beating Rodney King, an African American male. The protest spiraled into a full-scale uprising which led to 44 deaths and 1,100 arrests. Television networks, anticipating the response to the verdict, had cameras on hand to document "live" the street violence. When the LAPD failed to quell it, federal officers and military troops moved in at the command of the then president, George Bush.

Television programs were interrupted and bulletins kept viewers informed in the most immediate way. Almost simultaneously, images of blacks firing guns, torching buildings, wrecking cars and looting shops rampaged across screens the world over. In one memorable scene, a white driver was being yanked from his car and assaulted. African Americans were presented in the worst possible light: as angry, aggressive, emotional and – in television's coverage – irrational. They were depictions that seemed to complement popular stereotypes.

Event two On the night the riots broke out, NBC aired the 198th and final episode of the single most popular television comedy in history, *The Cosby Show*. Dwarfed as it was by LA, the passing of the show, which featured Bill Cosby as the benign patriarch of a well-ordered, middle-class, black family, was also a milestone in the black American experience as coded by television and one not unrelated to the uprisings. *The Cosby Show* was the first situation comedy with a predominantly black cast not to marginalize or victimize its subjects: they were educated, secure and mainstream. Earlier shows had depicted blacks as almost pathologically impoverished strugglers.

Cosby was a savior in many people's eyes. He introduced both a new affluent image and an ordinariness to the black experience. Characters were not seen as continually ground down by racism; they were just everyday people who happened to be black. But, for others, Cosby was culpable. The alternative interpretation of his show, and one which links it to the LA riots, was that the prosperous Huxtable family of the show became the nation's and possibly the world's best-known black family; they were well-off and seemingly unaffected by racism. On this account, the white majority had used this image to shore up indifference. "If blacks can be like the Huxtables, why does the country agonize over their so-called problems?" was the reasoning. The neglect of the deteriorating social conditions afflicting LA contributed to its implosion.

Event three Two weeks after Cosby's exit, a fictional, fortyish, white career woman played by Candice Bergen chose to have a baby out of wedlock and prompted a furore that was to lock into the LA riots debate. The series, named after its main character *Murphy Brown*, was the third most popular show in the USA at the time, though only 55th among black tv audiences. The conservative response to LA was that racism was a thing of the past and that the collapse of traditional family values was the real dagger pointing at the nation's heart. If blacks had more stable nuclear families and less female-led one-parent homes, then there would be fewer problems to worry over. Over half of all African American children are born to single mothers, over half of black families are headed by women and well over half of them are below the poverty line. So, it was disarming, particularly for vice-president Dan Quayle, to see a character who epitomized the 1990s' intelligent, well-paid professional woman "mocking the importance of fathers," as he put it, by choosing to bear a child alone, thus undermining the family.

On May 19, Quayle launched an offensive so emphatic that it was almost possible to lose sight of the fact that the object of the attack was only make-believe. It gave President George Bush an embarrassing moment, as only two days before he had announced that a human tissue bank would not be allowed to use tissue from aborted fetuses. Neither Bush nor Quayle were renowned for their support of obviously feminist causes and, in its own way, the slight against Murphy Brown's decision was also against pro-choice women, who campaigned to maintain abortion's legality, but equally to preserve women's capacity to determine their own reproductive functions. This has been embodied in the phrase "the right to choose," which is integral to the women's movement. Such is the pre-eminence of television that Quayle picked on a fictional woman to express his disapproval not only of the growing number of single-parent families, but also of the legal propriety of allowing women to decide what is good for themselves.

One of the traditional beefs about network television on both sides of the Atlantic is that it either relegates minority groups, including blacks and women – who are minorities in terms of power, not size – to peripheral characters, or portrays them as two-dimensional caricatures, stereotypes. So, it is rather interesting that two programs that quite purposely projected minorities in central roles and with quite sophisticated, layered personalities, were harangued and all but accused of contributing to the LA riots of 1992. The propositions were preposterous and unsupportable, but they brought into relief the edginess North America has over the depiction of groups that have been disparaged in history and whose progress in recent times has been, for some, reflected in and, for others, refracted by television. In this and the following chapter, we will see how television has changed its treatment of ethnic minorities and women. We will notice not only major changes in images, but in social circumstances surrounding both groups. First ethnic minorities.

the mind of the country

All media claim to represent reality: they do not pretend to reshape or change it; just to show it "like it is." Many pieces of social research, including some of those covered in the previous chapter, indicate differently: that the media in general and television in particular possess considerable power to change reality, at first by changing perceptions on which people later act. An illustrative finding is that of *Racism and the Mass Media*, whose authors Paul Hartmann and Charles Husband concluded that the media "have not merely reflected public consciousness on matters of race and colour, but have played a significant part in shaping this consciousness" (1974: 146).

The study in question, like many others, focused on "public consciousness," but actually assessed the consciousness of the white majority. This is an important point because the effects of television portrayals of minorities are different for those who are part of those minorities than those who are not. Blacks, or other ethnic minorities, and women may find television's images degrading, insulting and horribly inaccurate among other things; and they may feel threatened in some way. But, they will not necessarily accept them as real. Others may.

The Hartmann–Husband study found this, especially in populations which had little firsthand experience of ethnic minorities and relied on the mass media for their information. Even in multi-ethnic areas, it is possible that whites, especially those harboring racist beliefs, can have their prejudices reinforced by television. With requisite changes, the same argument can be applied to women, themselves appalled by some of television's portrayals of them as the gentler sex better suited to housework than professional careers, but unlikely to believe them. Men, on the other hand, may find substance for their preconceived notions of women's subordination.

The trend has been to focus on the effects of television's images on those with power – white males – and less on the more vulnerable minorities. This appears to be sound practice, as the power bearers are likely to be most influential in either promoting or retarding change in society. But, it also drags us back to the question that ran through chapter five: do people confuse what they see on television with the real thing? Even if 99.99 recurring per cent do not, one could still persuasively argue that the minuscule number of people who do could be seriously and perhaps dangerously misled.

Television has been responsible for perpetrating some of the most grotesque and nauseating images of ethnic minorities. African Americans have been singled out for especially sickening treatment. Television's history reveals that it has dealt with women in stereotypical terms too, though not in such an overtly offensive way. In both instances, television's defence could be that it is merely an instrument for recording images and presenting them, sometimes in a dramatic and amusing framework. But, as James Baldwin once pointed out, the country's image of the black person has not got very much to do with the black person. What the image reflects "with a kind of frightening accuracy" is the state of mind of the country.

Despite historical and demographic differences between Britain and the USA, there is a striking continuity in the images of black people presented on television. Obviously, many US shows were exported to Britain, but even the home-grown productions were filled with the same kinds of absurd stereotypes. Britain has never had to contend with the vestigial institutions of slavery, like the *de jure* segregation of the USA; though its ethnic minority population was effectively excluded in a *de facto* way from some areas of cities, some schools and some places of public resort, like restaurants and nightclubs. But, if the racism that fueled segregation up to and beyond the civil rights period of the 1960s was a hand-me-down relic of slave days mentalities, Britain's equivalent was no less potent. It was driven by a fear or loathing of what one early writer, Sheila Patterson, called "dark strangers" (1963), migrants from Britain's former colonies in South Asia and the Caribbean, who, as holders of British passports, entered the country as citizens in search of an honest living in the period after the end of the Second World War. At first, reactions to the newcomers were muted, but, as economic decline began in the late 1950s, conflict surfaced and pitched battles were fought in the streets. The strangers were uninvited guests, unwelcome competitors for jobs, even though their numbers were infinitesimal (about 0.5 per cent of the total population).

The USA's African American population returned from the war cautiously optimistic after serving in the armed forces and in the arms industry. They soon found that the freedom they had allegedly won was actually another form of captivity and the deprivation, compounded by discrimination, continued unabated. While, technically, the *Brown* v. *Board of Education* case of 1954 signaled an end to racial segregation, old habits were hard to kill and, in 1956, a series of boycotts and protests led by Martin Luther King sparked what was to become the civil rights movement.

The period saw the mercurial rise to power of television as a popular entertainment. By 1958, the time of Britain's "race riots" and the end of King's first year as leader of the Southern Christian Leadership Conferences (SCLC), about 70 per cent of US homes had television sets and slightly less than that in Britain. Television extended the programming patterns that had been established in radio and one of the most spectacularly successful radio shows since 1929 had been *Amos 'n' Andy* which featured two white actors crudely mimicking blacks. The show was transferred to television in 1951, though using black actors as the eponymous couple of bunglers, who personified every possible cliché about blacks. They were stupid, idle, amoral and given to malapropisms. They also seemed to operate in a sealed-in world where there were no whites. In sum, the type of racist stereotypes that most white Americans of the day must have found hilarious. Andy and his clumsy friend were constantly, opportunistically chasing the American dream of material success, but they were comically ill-equipped to capture it and audiences loved watching them fail. Its production was stopped in 1953, but re-runs continued. The 350,000 strong National Association for the Advancement of Colored People (NAACP) tried to block the program even before it had been aired and its pressure continued until 1966 when CBS withdrew it completely. But not before it had sold it to television channels around the world, including Britain.

In the 1950s black Americans featured in three major shows, always in subservient domestic roles. Rochester, Jack Benny's wide-eyed valet played by Eddie Anderson for fifteen years, was an enduringly famous character in Britain as well as the States, though the other two characters did not escape North America. The mammy figure in a white household in *The Beulah Show* and the handyman in the *Stu Erwin Show* were servile and serviceable types.

The Beulah Show, perhaps more than any series of the era, played down the conflict that was then simmering. Its centerpiece was an idealized, white, two-parent family, supported at every turn by a selfless black domestic who cared for the white family more than her own flesh and blood. Neatly packaged white families popped up in all sorts of series and blacks rarely intruded. It must have been some sort of occasion if a Diahann Carroll or a Nat King Cole appeared. Cole, in fact, became big enough with white audiences to command his own show, though he was made to whiten his facial skin. Cole resisted conventional stereotypes: one could not laugh at him, mock him or even be scared of him. He also mixed freely with his white guests.

Yet Cole's on-screen associations with whites contrasted sharply with the outright conflict in such places as Little Rock, Arkansas, where, in 1957, the struggle to desegregate educational institutions brought bloodshed. Cole's show lasted only one year when sponsors, uneasy with the implications of having a black star who could not be ridiculed, pulled out. Featuring blacks in prominent roles, or addressing black issues in primetime programming was considered too risky, according to Kathryn Montgomery in her book *Target: Prime Time*. "Networks were easily influenced by southern affiliates who refused to carry shows that presented blacks too positively" (1989: 15). Meanwhile in Britain, Afro-Caribbeans and South Asians were totally absent from television screens, apart from in American films, such as *Sanders of the River* in which Paul Robeson appeared as a breast-beating tribal chief.

As the 1960s passed, American blacks appeared regularly in the news: they were usually under attack by whites when campaigning for civil rights. And some dramas, like *East Side, West Side*, absorbed the tensions in stories that shunned neat resolutions and left viewers with problems to ponder. "The color question," as it was called, was repeatedly raised, so much so that the show was cancelled after only one season. More commercially successful was *Julia*, which featured Diahann Carroll as a self-confident nurse in an ethnically-integrated environment. She avoided the usual trappings of female stereotypes and, in 1968, presented, for the first time on primetime US television, a black woman character with independence, her husband having been killed on military duty. Carroll was matched in this respect by Bill Cosby, who, in *I Spy*, played the black partner of a white man, Robert Culp. Cosby's character, Alexander Scott, was intelligent – a Rhodes scholar – emotionally complex and, as such, completely undermined the conventional racist stereotype. Both characters suffered from credibility gaps. Blacks claimed that Carroll was a sell-out and totally unrepresentative of "real" black people, the vast majority of whom were working class. Cosby was rebuked for exaggerating black achievement: how many blacks are Rhodes scholars who become bosom friends with whites? Where Amos and company were criticized for remaining in their own hermetically sealed black universe, Carroll and Cosby were slammed for pretending they could move smoothly into white society, conveniently discarding their African heritage en route to a kind of assimilation.

Here we begin to glimpse some of the ideological importance of television referred to in chapters three and four. The shortcomings of regarding television as pure entertainment, designed to sell the eyeballs of viewers to advertisers, is that it misses the political function it serves – as a legitimating force. While civil rights conflicts pockmarked the entire nation and black power erupted in outright confrontation between 1965 and 1967, television comedy and drama stayed virtually silent. Only in news items were blacks seen as they actually were, many of them actively and often aggressively pursuing some semblance of equal treatment. Yet, when blacks emerged from their subordinate "Uncle Tom" and "Aunt Jemima" roles, what were they? Well-adjusted nurses with white friends and Rhodes scholars. It was as if television was somehow assuring its viewers that all they were seeing on the news was unpleasant and probably unjustified, but there was another side to the black experience. This is an example of what cultural studies refers to as television's "normalizing" effect.

In Britain, politicians had watched the cataclysmic developments in the USA with an interest enhanced by the fact that the migrant flow from Asia and the Caribbean continued. The possibility of a repetition of the riots must not have been far from legislators' minds; so they pushed through antidiscrimination laws framed similarly to the civil rights legislation in 1965 and 1968. Earlier in 1962 immigration control had been introduced; this was made more restrictive in 1965 and even more so in 1968. The race issue was on the agenda of social problems, though television had never tried to address it with the existing US methods: ghettoizing, or masking it. An alternative was to expose it and, in doing so invite the audience's derision. *Till Death Us Do Part* had as its comic pillar Alf Garnett, an East London working-class conservative with a full arsenal of ballistic prejudices which he fired at an assortment of groups, but especially Afro-Caribbeans and South Asians. Script writer Johnny Speight spared nothing: he allowed Garnett, played by Warren Mitchell, to give full vent to his hatred in his vituperations against "coons" and "pakis," words which were used, along with other robust terms of abuse, quite frequently in the show.

The show worked at every level. Aesthetically, it was a joy, crackling with wit and comic imagery. And Garnett himself was not a cartoon, but a caricature; just about real enough for audiences to recognize in him elements of real people, replete with their obdurate ideas. His views were ridiculous and some of his behavior pantomimic; but at the same time, a little bit too plausible to be dismissed as complete fiction. There was never any doubt, though, that Garnett was there to be laughed at, not with. The success of the program attracted interest from the States and Norman Lear, a producer with a reputation of taking on challenging assignments, remade Garnett as Archie Bunker and set him in Queens, New York.

But something odd happened in the transatlantic metamorphosis from Garnett to Bunker and a primitively racist, anti-Semitic clown became something of a folk hero of the 1970s. Bunker's foibles were much the same as his alter ego's, though he added a fierce hatred of "Polaks." In the context of US primetime tv, *All in the Family* was revolutionary. It opened up for inspection the race issue, inviting viewers, black and white – but especially white – to laugh at the oafish, tunnel-visioned character. Whites might find in Bunker a few glints of themselves, it was thought. They did: but often they did not disapprove. Bunker had inconsistencies in his arguments, but his saving grace was his nationalism. He was, deep down, a concerned American absolutely committed, blindly committed. It was an aspect of Bunker that drew sympathy. He would quote the constitution, preach simple segregationist philosophies and think nothing of standing up to be counted. These were virtues transmuted from Garnett's vices.

Its second irony was that, in ripping apart the previously valued American ideal of the 2 + 2 family, the Bunker clan replaced it with another. Gone were the harmonies of the *Brady Bunch*: in Bunker's home, views clashed discordantly; people stormed out, they fought. Yet, they always returned and made up. It was as if all the racial problems of the nation were swirling around the Bunker house and somehow, miraculously, they were contained, as it were, *All in the Family*.

As the turmoil of the 1960s subsided, US networks took what was then the adventurous step of launching four new shows, all with predominantly black casts, all between 1972 and 1976. *Good Times* was set in the heart of Chicago's black section and had echoes of *All in the Family* in its interpretation of a working-class nuclear family confronting the types of everyday problems that affect all families, but perhaps black families more so: unemployment, poverty, violence and so on. Into this thoughtful structure the writers introduced a paradoxical figure straight from the *Amos 'n' Andy* school of repertory theater. J.J. was a buffoon, a court jester who would do anything to get a laugh, including dressing up, dancing comically or just talking in his amusingly mannered way. In the mid-1970s, he was an anachronism, clowning inoffensively and, in the process, supplying light relief for the heavy issues that occupied the rest of the family.

A British comedy about two white London rag-and-bone dealers, *Steptoe and Son*, was the template for *Sanford and Son*, set in the Watts district of Los Angeles, with all the characters being played by blacks. Unlike the original, the US version had a few overt racial referents, Sanford Sr. played by Redd Foxx showing that blacks could be just as prejudiced as your common or garden white bigot. Like the other main African American comedy of the 1970s, *The Jeffersons*, *Sanford and Son* provided a national showcase for black talents and an interesting vehicle for expressing facets of the black experience. Yet it also had an ersatz contentment: here was a bunch of blacks locked in an urban ghetto, surviving from hand to mouth and having every attempt to improve themselves frustrated; still, there was a penumbra of satisfaction around their lives. Maybe life in the ghetto was not so bad after all. This was the comforting message sent to an American population, over 80 per cent of which then was white.

Not so comforting was the message drummed out by the television adaptation of Alex Haley's *Roots* which traced the lineage of an enslaved African family over several generations. The epic book is less an entertainment, more an ordeal, forcing a painful reflection on the system of human bondage and its aftermath that permitted – and perhaps still permits – oppression of entire populations. The miniseries bowled along briskly, characters seldom having time enough to develop as the plot accelerated through the generations. *Roots* showed America's history as a social nightmare, yet climaxed with a wakening moment when African Americans, their families somehow still intact despite the assaults, were able to secure a foothold in mainstream society. The subtext of the story was that liberated blacks in contemporary America had triumphed magnificently.

The series was shown in Britain in the same year, 1977. By this time, the sons and daughters of postwar migrants, especially from the

Caribbean, were beginning to challenge, albeit symbolically, white racism. The Rastafarian movement, whose members insisted they wished to return to Africa and fashioned their hair into dreadlocks, appeared in Britain's major cities in the mid-1970s and focused attention on the search for origins as an alternative to becoming assimilated and discarding one's ethnic identity. *Roots*' interlinking of separate stories from several generations had clear relevance. It was even more of a pattern breaker in British television than it had been in the USA. Blacks had tended to occupy only incidental roles in drama and comedy shows. *Love thy Neighbour* was a gauche, though, on reflection, bold attempt to ironize into farce the experience of whites and blacks sharing the same street. The language, though insulting, never reached the pitch of Alf Garnett's, and the black neighbor, played by Rudolph Walker, usually gave as good as he got. Another comedy, *Mixed Blessings*, exposed the travails of a married couple from different ethnic backgrounds. A predominantly black soap opera, *Empire Road*, featuring Norman Beaton as an Afro-Caribbean landlord, and *The Fosters* took their leads from the US shows of the early 1970s. Perhaps the most hideous show of the period was London Weekend Television's *Mind Your Language* which shamelessly worked on the assumption that, if you bundle assorted racist stereotypes together in an English adult nightclass, then the polyglot misunderstandings should be a source of amusement. Its commercial success confirmed that, for many, it was.

These were soon followed by *Ebony* and *Eastern Eye*, news magazine programs, but with ethnic inflections. The idea was that news and current affairs shows followed an established formula which had been created before Britain had become a genuinely multicultural society. As such, those programs failed to reflect anything apart from white priorities. The alternatives, however, soon led to accusations of ghettoization: ethnic minority affairs were being withdrawn from mainstream programs and locked away in one of the speciality series. While the shows attracted white viewers, the ideology informing both series was considered suspect. BBC's *Network East* and Channel 4's *Black on Black* in the 1980s modified the approach by integrating issues that had general relevance, while maintaining a distinct ethnic minority feeling.

Attempts to centralize blacks in two shows, *The Lazarus Syndrome* and *Paris*, yielded commercial flops in the USA in 1979. But the large-scale miniseries format of *Roots* and its sequel, *Roots: The Next Generation* seemed good omens for another epochal drama called *Beulah Land*. This one ran into all manner of trouble, when minority organizations got wind of the fact that the script dealt with slavery crudely and offensively. Protest groups coalesced into a united front and fought NBC in what Kathryn Montgomery called "the most dramatic confrontation between black Americans and network television since the Amos 'n' Andy controversy [of 1951–3]" (1989: 124).

In 1981, it appeared Britain was being visited by the same kind of mood that mobilized black Americans in the 1960s. Afro-Caribbean youths featured in the most serious urban disorders since the war, issuing stern notices that they were not prepared to accept willingly the inferior positions society had, it seemed, set aside for them. The melting pot had been replaced by a witch's cauldron which simmered and spat for another four years before boiling over once more in 1985. These were the early years of Prime Minister Margaret Thatcher's reign, paralleled in the States by that of her kindred political spirit, Ronald Reagan. In both countries, the ideology of the New Right was ascendant: free enterprise, individual initiative, minimal state intervention and unbridled market competition were the hallmarks. Blacks, went New Right reasoning, had benefited from the protection of antidiscrimination laws and copious state handouts; now it was up to them to bootstrap their way out of the ghettos. Television had its own version of a black family that had done exactly that: the Huxtables.

under control

The Cosby Show went on air in 1984 and became an immediate commercial success. The framework of the show was reasonably orthodox: successful professional couple with sometimes unruly, but basically well-adjusted children; tight family unit, inside which all major problems could be worked out; high values placed on family life, the rewards of hard work and fidelity. The unorthodox element was that all the characters were black. Gone were the pathologies of earlier depictions: crude dramatizations of poverty gave way to a portrayal of black life that was almost startlingly normal. Blacks watched the show, presumably, because it showed what they were capable of, given the right circumstances; whites because it showed those circumstances did exist. At least, that is the popular theory for its spectacular success: it shot up the official Nielsen television ratings, claiming the top position in 1985 and holding it until 1989, sliding to seventeenth position in 1992 when it closed. The show's success was not as pronounced in Britain and its simplistic and often puerile plots made it more appropriate for earlier than primetime viewing when a younger audience could be expected.

Cosby, having previously been in *I Spy*, deliberately extended his former role as an interesting and cerebral character, not averse to antics, but clever enough to temper them with reasoned comments. There was no coincidence about this: Cosby personally took great care to avoid clichés, stereotypes and questionable apophthegms in the scripts. He even retained a Harvard University psychiatrist, Alvin Poussant, as a consultant. And, as we saw earlier, praise and criticism came in roughly equal measures. Some cheered the so-called "positive role model" he projected, while others sneered at the false and almost defamatory statement on the condition of black people. Whatever the reaction, there is no denying that the show was something of a watershed. No subsequent program resorted to the shopworn images of blacks and, indeed, some seemed to go too far in their quest for new dimensions of the black experience. *Frank's Place* was an example: an egregious show that eschewed contrived comedy, it was an intrinsic success winning an Emmy award in 1988, but it failed to achieve a solid enough audience to guarantee a long life and was killed off in 1988 after only a year.

Buoyed by Cosby's popularity, tv networks pushed out more shows about blacks. NBC's *A Different World* was spun off *The Cosby Show* in 1987, ABC's *Family Matters* entered in 1989, and Fox's *Roc* in 1991. All seemed stirred by the challenge to present blacks as complex, contradictory and multifarious. Yet, they also seemed simplistic as guides to the contemporary black experience, for in all these shows, and others, like *In Living Color* and *Fresh Prince of Bel Air*, blacks were seen as inhabiting a virtually all-black world. This was not the world of the underclass as in earlier shows, but neither was it a world visited, let alone lived in, by whites, Asians or Latinos. The characters were radically changed but the contexts remained *in statu quo*.

Other shows situated blacks in different terrains. Steven Bochco's *Hill Street Blues* and its sister program *LA Law*, for example, included blacks in their ensemble casts, yet without exaggerating the importance of the ethnicity. BBC's short-lived, but notable *South of the Border*, produced by Caroline Oulton in 1988, revolved around the exploits of two female detectives, one of whom happened to be Afro-Caribbean. The scenes were populated by characters of all ethnic backgrounds, giving the whole series an authenticity, marred unfortunately by risible plots. Storylines were also a weakness of ABC's *Gabriel's Fire* which failed to stand up in the US ratings and never made it to Britain, despite its promising concept of a black ex-con who becomes an investigator for a white female district attorney. The pity of it was that, in both series, it was easy to transfer positives into negatives. By discarding both stereotyped characters and artificial landscapes and casting innovatively, the shows pre-empted the very criticism made of television over the years. The problem was that they also provided ready-made explanations for their failure.

Historically, mainstream television's treatment of black people has run parallel to society's treatment: exclusion or, at best, marginalization, ghettoization, stereotyping; these are the key processes that distinguish the treatment. And they are processes that have, in similar ways, affected the visualization of other ethnic minorities. Latinos, Asians, and native Americans for instance, have featured in many series shown in Britain and the United States.

Crudely etched characters in *The Cisco Kid*, *Charlie Chan* and *Hawkeye and the Last of the Mohicans* were often not too far removed from comic-book distortions and frequently played by whites: though one exception was Jay Silverheels, the first native American to appear in a network series when he was cast as Tonto, famed of the "Him shot in back, Kimosabee; what we do?" lines in *The Lone Ranger* of the 1950s. Leah Eskin's article "The Tonto syndrome" showed how the durable depiction informs conceptions of native Americans even in recent years (1989).

Perhaps the most unusual Latino in early television was Desi Arnez, the Cuban husband of Lucille Ball in *I Love Lucy* and, later, *The Lucy Show*. His character was endowed with the fiery temperament of a stereotype Latin, but the role was quite pivotal in plots and, in reality, Arnez was a producer of the show. The most unusual "Asian" in the 1970s was *Kung Fu*'s David Carradine, a Wasp actor preferred to the martial artist Bruce Lee, who had played sidekick to *The Green Hornet* in 1966–67. "*Kung Fu*'s producers told Lee they didn't believe a Chinese actor could be seen as a hero in the eyes of the American television audience" wrote Clint Wilson and Felix Gutierrez (1985: 102). Lee's popularity in a string of commercial movies such as *Enter the Dragon* suggests it was a flawed judgement.

Cable television brought with it new possibilities for ethnic minorities. The Washington, DC-based Black Entertainment Television (BET) showed music videos, gospel, black college football and other programs considered of specific interest to African Americans. New York's Spanish International Network (SIN) and other Spanish language channels like Telemundo and Univision specialize in soaps, variety shows and soccer. Such cables were effectively a response to the paucity of ethnic minority representation in the major networks and, as such, present part of a critique that has been festering for years.

Wilson and Gutierrez, in their analysis of *Minorities and Media*, stayed within the consensual approach to television when they accused it of stereotyping ethnic minorities. "Basic negative traits," they argued "have never been abandoned totally" (1985: 103). But, has there been so much immobility? The image of ethnic minorities has surely been a moving one: like tumbleweed drifting around a dustbowl, the depiction of minority groups, particularly Afros, has gained in size and substance. Standard issue stereotypes from the 1950s and 1960s have all but disappeared and critics who trade off them neglect the better-rounded characters, complete with strengths, weaknesses, consistencies and contradictions. Attorneys in *Equal Justice* and *LA Law*, medics in the British *Casualty*, the restaurateur in *Baghdad Cafe*. These have complemented the comedy of Cosby, Lenny Henry, Kadeem Hardison *et al.* An obvious reaction is that television has merely replaced old stereotypes with new ones, but the riposte to this is that all television processes individuals into types. Otherwise, the medium just does not work.

True, television audiences have for years had their senses beaten with two main images: blacks as hopeless figures of fun with limited intellects; or as victims crawling despairingly towards drug addiction, crime or prison, usually all three. Part of the reason for this was the underemployment of minorities in television production. All program makers are clearly thoughtful, sophisticated and ambitious. Yet most whites have, up till recently, failed to create subtle signifiers in black characters which mirror their own depth and complexity. As minorities have more input in the creative and technical production of shows, audiences can expect less clearly coded figures and many more, who make no big play of the fact that they are black, but occasionally prod audiences into remembering that this affects their thinking and straitens their options.

The concept of positive role models has always been wonderfully evocative, yet misleadingly imprecise. Much black pressure on television has been to provide characters whom black youth can admire and structure their own ambitions around. The same is not said about white youth who, it would seem, have either no need of them, or – if they do – have plenty on offer when they turn on tv. The status of this changed from apparently legitimate criticism to pure carping when Cosby arrived in 1984. Educated, professionally successful, well-off Cliff Huxtable appeared like manna. But, not so: he was for many at least, a fraudulent misrepresentation of blacks. "Cosby," the *Village Voice* once sniffed, "is not even black enough to be an Uncle Tom." It was a comment typical of the joyless social conscience that sees sin in every success. It also opened up the further question of what exactly constitutes a positive role model, if a well-heeled professional is not one.

The recent history of ethnic minorities in general and African Americans in particular has been recapitulated in television. Their experience of being squeezed to the outer margins of society, of being victimized by slavery and its vestiges and of being dehumanized as chattel to be moved or abused has been documented and parodied. But those who furiously attack television for exploiting this need to give their critique an oil change. The stereotypes have all but vanished, the victims are being supplanted by the successful and minorities are holding centerstage in many productions nowadays. The essential component missed by most critics is plain: control. Whatever the character, or the context, ethnic minorities are controlled, or at worst, controllable. One somehow cannot imagine a television equivalent of Spike Lee's movie *Malcolm X*, or a series about a deviant cop who is black, such as in Bill Duke's *Deep Cover*, or maybe a dealer like the central figure in Paul Schrader's *Light Sleeper* in which the drugs trade is rendered as morally bland as a travel agency. In these, characters are, in some senses, conflicting with mainstream values and institutions. Signposts to "good" and "evil" familiar to tv viewers are missing.

In television, outer turmoil is avoided in favour of enclosed milieux: blacks may have problems, but the problems are always depicted in such a way that they are soluble. Soluble, that is, within existing social arrangements. Cosby's family has become a virtual archetype, but other frameworks in cop thrillers and legal dramas are no less sturdy. Playthell Benjamin, writing on the 1992 riots in LA, argues that some African Americans believe in "a conspiracy to prevent a coherent black perspective from emerging on the issues raised by the riots" (1992: 34) While rejecting this view, Benjamin notes how white journalists and analysts dominated television's "objective commentary" and this produced an "abhorrence of the rioters." In contrast, Benjamin suggests that there was a "widespread identification with the outrage of black Californians" among every African American community.

Television has become too sophisticated to ignore, or even downplay racism. It is the manner in which it is visualized and addressed that deserves attention.

Usually, it is something that can be, to use an inexhaustible colloquialism, "worked out." The evidence of our senses suggests the contrary, leading to the conclusion that television, far from accurately reflecting manifest conflict, actually serves as a counterpoint to it. The format has an elegant simplicity: take an issue, a problem or question to which there is no ready answer and translate it "realistically" into something which is far easier on the intellect. Credibility is maintained by creating characters and contexts that ring true; only the solutions are contrived. Conflict is contained; the situation is controlled. And this is salient in any production, comedy, drama or documentary involving ethnic minorities and the ethnic minority experience.

One minor exception was *I'll Fly Away* which dealt with racial conflicts secreted in pre-civil rights white suburbia. Despite much sentimentalizing, irreconcilable differences were never forcibly reconciled and happy endings stayed elusive. The source of its verity derived at least in part from the show's refusal to berate viewers with messages of the "those who do not learn from history are condemned to repeat it" variety.

Television has never tried to woo ethnic minority viewers. The reason for this is no mystery: ethnic minorities have, for decades, been commercially the least desired group. They are mostly poor, many are unemployed, often living in the worst areas of the city and they are statistically more likely to go to prison than university. All of which means that they will not have a large amount of income to dispose of on consumer products. Once one accepts the premise that television's principal function is to maintain the need for commodities that alleviate boredom and satisfy the artificially stimulated desire for excitement, then the short shrift blacks have received is perfectly understandable. It is only surprising that television has contoured and centralized black characters to the extent it has done. After all, the heavy consumers are the targets and their preferences set the tone.

Until the 1970s and the rise of what Bart Landry calls *The New Black Middle Class* (1988), the black population was little more than a peripheral market without enough spending power to justify even a demographic calculation in the advertiser's budget. Television depictions of blacks were largely designed to meet the main market's expectations, to amuse and fascinate white consumers and to assuage any doubts whites might have had about the controllability of blacks. But, by 1981, African Americans had come to represent a $100 million market, according to Vance Packard; and, by 1992, this had doubled, making it "a socio-economic entity, wealthier and more populated than most independent nations in the world," as J. Fred MacDonald put it (1992: 268).

Packard added: "They [African Americans] spend [comparatively] more on consumer goods than Anglos and are more avid television viewers" (1981: 219). This still holds good: a 1993 study by the Bozell advertising agency showed that tv is watched almost 50 per cent longer in black households than in others – an average of 73.6 hours, as against

50.2 hours per week (*New York Times*, April 5 1993). This has made African Americans interesting targets for advertisers. It is no surprise to find networks avoiding traditional stereotypes in their efforts to sell advertising spots.

Since 1985, when advertising giants BBDO commissioned its first survey of viewing habits among blacks, a gap has opened between blacks and nonblacks: in the 1990s, African Americans watch different programs from all other groups. A 1993 study by the same agency found that not one of the top-ten-rated shows among African Americans was in the national top ten. Eight of the ten shows most watched by blacks featured predominantly black casts. This may be a reflection of the general state of the USA. Or, it could be indicative of a generational divide, younger blacks tending to watch the same programs as nonblacks.

The reasons for this are less important to the networks than the results it brings, the main one of which is that African Americans are now a valuable segment of the national market and need to be addressed seriously. Same goes for Latinos and East Asians, which are fast-growing groups and, in the case of the latter, favorably oriented toward entrepreneurial activities. In Britain, the growth of advertising agencies specializing in tailoring campaigns to ethnic minority requirements signals a change of approach. An expedient change. MacDonald, in his *Blacks and White TV*, captured the main reason for television's adjustment, when he wrote: "TV had to serve black Americans because it financially needed them, not because it was morally supposed to be fair" (1992: 245).

In the past, images of ethnic minorities have been controllable, unthreatening and entertaining. The presence and complexity of these images have increased in proportion to their importance as a section of the potential market. Is the same true of women? Answer in the next chapter.

chapter eight

in pursuit of women

family affair

Since researchers first identified the quintessential consumer as female and between the ages of 18 and 35, television has pandered to women, promoting a vision of the good life in which they play a key part and feeding an obsession with youth, affluence, beauty and glamor. Yet, in another way, the position of women has similarities with that of other minority groups – and I use the word once more to refer to power rather than numbers. Historically, women on both sides of the Atlantic and, indeed, in most parts of the world, have been regarded as bearers and rearers of children, oriented to domestic work and having no significant role to play in society's major institutions, such as politics, commerce and education. The family has been seen as the woman's domain: here she is in her element, nurturing, caring, comforting. All important interpersonal functions. But not ones which, conventional wisdom dictates, change the direction of society.

George Gerbner's studies of television violence in the 1960s noticed, almost as an aside, that women, like ethnic minorities, were under-represented and, when they did feature, were usually cast in roles that reinforced sexist stereotypes about their natural suitability for domestic activities. As blacks' forays into the serious world of business or politics were made farcical, so women's attempts to break out of the home were roundly satirized. Two US-produced series of the 1950s, *I Love Lucy* and *I Married Joan*, based their huge commercial success on this approach. *The Burns and Allen Show* showcased Gracie Allen as an infantile, airhead wife publicly ridiculed by husband George Burns. Wober and Gunter quote studies from the 1950s which reported that one-third of leading characters in US primetime were female (1988: 91).

This pattern of under-representation continued through the 1980s. Women account for about 51 per cent of the total population.

The 1960s were a decade of release from postwar austerity. Television was both symbolic of and a conduit for this. As a relatively inexpensive electrical appliance available to all classes and all age groups, it became a virtual domestic icon. And, if the public doubted that the days of affluence had arrived, they needed only to look at the screen, filled with images of food mixers, washing machines, refrigerators, cars and other luxury commodities soon to become essentials. For the most part, women were conventionally typed as gentle, affectionate, an anchor for the home; though females possessed of extraordinary powers became a commercially successful theme in *Bewitched*, *I Dream of Jeannie*, *The Flying Nun* and others. "The trend coincided with a wave of magic characters in commercials, dramatizing the occult powers of detergents and cleansers, and made drama and commercials highly compatible," Erik Barnouw noted in his *Tube of Plenty* (1990). To the present day, women in advertisements are deliberately made virtually indistinguishable from dramatic characters. (In the early 1990s, for example, Candice Bergen appeared in Sprint telephone commercials while her *Murphy Brown* series ran on network tv – as noted in chapter six).

The theme, later extended in the superhero *Wonder Woman*, cleverly paralleled and parodied changes in society: women being restored securely to their "rightful place" in the patriarchal family after the war effort, in which many had worked in industry, but subverting norms with their secret gifts. In *Bewitched* and *I Dream of Jeannie*, they could cheerfully shoulder the burdens of child-rearing and homemaking, while their husbands went out to work, but only because they had magic at their disposal.

It was rare to find a woman outside the family home in the 1950s and early 1960s. The nuclear family encased women in all sorts of series even in spoofs like *The Addams Family* and cartoons such as *The Flintstones*. But one character demonstrates the transition of women from homemakers to workers as the 1960s turned. *The Dick Van Dyke Show* hit stereotypes like tripwires as it raced to the top of ratings in both the USA and Britain: successful male ably supported and often assisted by his perfect wife who took care of domestic duties, including child-rearing (they had a son) and always managed an aesthetically pleasing appearance. The sexual division of labor in which Rob Petrie took care of business while Laura, played by Mary Tyler Moore, ran the home produced connubial bliss. Play was made of the male's total ineptitude in domestic affairs: once asked to revise a whole work project because of small but important flaws, he says to his wife: "It's like washing a whole shirt if just the collar and cuffs are dirty," and Laura has to inform him that she does exactly that.

But Moore's role was looking distinctly anomalous amid the social changes of the late 1960s. The women's movement urged women to reconsider their traditional subservience and strike out for what was then called "women's liberation." The freer availability of the contraceptive pill and legal abortion revolutionized the control women had over their fertility, giving them, for the first time in history, a genuine independence. The ability to determine their own reproductive functions was critical in the shaping of women's status from the early 1970s; and this was reflected in the decreasing significance of maternity in television. Mary Tyler Moore slid away from her original subordination into a new show, this time with her as the central character, a single woman in her thirties pursuing a career at a Minneapolis tv station. One of the characters in the series was spun off into *Rhoda*, another comedy series about a working woman. The seamless shift of Mary Tyler Moore into her own CBS show was congruent with the times and made all the more relevant by the fact that Moore herself went on to head her own production company.

Other series incorporating women parting with convention included *Julia*, which we mentioned previously, and *Maude*, a spin-off from *All in the Family*. Unlike the two Moore series, neither transferred to Britain. *Maude*'s parent show had violated all sorts of taboos in satirizing racism and its progeny, introduced in 1972 with Beatrice Arthur in the title role, broke new ground. The central character was a four-times divorced woman in her forties, living in New York with a divorced daughter who had a son. The plot had her becoming pregnant and choosing to have a legal abortion. (Abortion, though legal in New York was not made legal in all US states until the *Roe* v. *Wade* decision in January 1973.) This seems unexceptional today, but at the time it was a *cause célèbre*. Letters of protest poured in to CBS, a formidable coalition of church and anti-abortion groups was met head on by the feminist National Organization of Women (NOW) and the show's commercial sponsors, under the threat of boycott, grew jittery.

While the idealized family was still the framing device for many series, including *The Waltons*, alternative domestic arrangements, allowing women more open career opportunities, were seen. A British comedy, *Man About the House*, later Americanized into *Three's Company*, had two young single working women living with a single man; and while the humor was often prurient, its premise was unusual enough to be seen as having "relevance." This buzzword was attached to any US series regarded as addressing social issues in the 1970s. As women's issues were high on most agendas, they featured in a glut of dramas, most conspicuously perhaps in *Lou Grant*, often held up as an example. It was, as Gitlin commented, "the first television series to defy formula on occasion by refusing to tie up loose plot ends" (1985: 11). Its central character was, in fact, abstracted from *The Mary Tyler Moore Show*, though the element of comedy was totally missing from the sometimes sonorous spin-off which was dumped in 1982, despite decent ratings. In its slot, CBS scheduled *Cagney and Lacey*, a prescient series about two female police officers in New York City.

The concept of having women in prominent law enforcement roles had been successfully explored in *Charlie's Angels*, a whimsical, light drama, in which three bimbos were given secret assignments by an unseen male, Charlie. Unlike its soror's fantastic tales, *Cagney and Lacey*'s plots were as plain as water. But the characters worked like a couple of Alka-Seltzer tablets and the show fizzed. Executive producer Barney Rosenweig had fought tooth-and-nail to persuade CBS to take the series. At one stage, when it looked doomed, he recruited the support of NOW. The material was topical, but never dealt with in an overtly sensationalistic way. Chris Cagney and Marybeth Lacey were opposites in several respects and this gave the scripts scope for probing alternative positions. For instance, one episode had the officers investigating a series of bomb attacks on abortion clinics and routed its plot in such a way as to expose each partner's different perspective on the abortion issue. Private lives were cross-indexed to public issues throughout the series. BBC's *South of the Border*, as we have seen, followed the pattern of having women cops, though less interestingly than the exemplar.

It is noticeable that, after *Cagney and Lacey*, few drama series dared obliterate women from their principal roles. *Hill Street Blues*, which in a sense picked up the loose ends left undone by *Lou Grant*, the sometimes Brechtian *Moonlighting* and that social weathervane, *thirtysomething*, all placed women in active parts. *Murder She Wrote* defied rating odds in the early 1990s, featuring an elderly Agatha-Christie-type spinster as a character in whodunit plots and with great commercial success on both sides of the Atlantic. Joan Hickson's portrayal of *Miss Marple* was almost symmetrical. In these shows we find women operating interdependently with men, or independently of them. We have also seen women desperately trying to salvage their independence through violent means. *The Burning Bed* (released on video in Britain) sympathetically portrayed a battered wife, eventually driven to killing her husband.

No-nonsense cops, learned mystery writers and the like convey impressions of women as "doers," active individuals far-removed from the reactive houseslave types. Television has monitored changes in women's status as so many characters have spurned the option of a family or revised their role within one in order to pursue a career. Those careers have often been traditionally dominated by men. Women have also crept up the hierarchies so that they are no longer seen as factotums. This has obviously worked wonders for demographics-watchers who have linked the rise of the fictional action woman with the purchasing power of real women since the late 1960s. But, there is another story to tell, this one also marked by movement but at a pace so slow it could be mistaken for inertia. We refer, of course, to the story of women in that most enduring of all television genres, the soap.

soaps without end

We may be at the Southfork ranch in Texas or the Rovers Return pub in Manchester, or even in Cell Block H of a women's prison in Australia. The conventions are the same. Mutual loyalties co-exist with personal tensions. People talk candidly with each other about intimate problems. Close-knit neighborhoods with nuclear families, or their functional equivalents, form a kind of matrix for interweaving, open-ended dramas. Families are central to soaps, the large extended type, like the Ewings, less apparent than the smaller conjugal unit. Women often lead, and usually dominate affairs far beyond their own families. Alexis Colby has the same kind of meddling bombast as Ena Sharples, formerly of Britain's perennially best-watched show, *Coronation Street* (which can soak up as much as 74 per cent of the nation's viewing).

Women are cast very prominently in all soaps, though not always in the glamorous positions of tycoons, or tycoon's wives. More often they suffer brick-like, supporting others and unflinchingly accepting their duties. It has been argued that the phenomenon's international popularity stems from the relentlessly matrifocal perspectives: events in the public sphere are filtered through individual women, their perceptions, thoughts and feelings. There is an almost shameless honesty about the women characters disclosing their innermost feelings to each other – and, so, to millions of viewers. Self-revelation is obviously engaging.

In terms of their characterizations, their interconnecting plots and their inherent repetitiveness, soaps are the most "realistic" of all television forms. AIDS, abortion, dyslexia, rape and unemployment are grist to the mill that crushes the debates of the day into personal crises. But so too are Versace clothes, personal Lear Jets, multimillion dollar takeovers and wines that cost as much per bottle as an average manual worker's yearly wage. Soaps are able to construct artificial worlds, but ones with which all viewers can easily identify. Why? Because the contexts are not important; the human relations are. Regular viewers empathize with Alexis' Machiavellian attempts to sabotage a megadeal in *Dynasty*, as they can with Mandy's attempts to find a new job in *EastEnders*.

In using personal themes as their motor, soaps have been able to transcend contexts completely to become classlessly, globally popular. Day-to-day relationships may be different in Denver, Colorado, than in Brookside Close, Liverpool, but not so hugely different that viewers cannot recognize recurrent themes in each. Technically, it would be possible to situate a soap on the moon and have a fair chance of success. BBC's audacious Spanish haven of palms, azure skies and bronzed bodies, *Eldorado*, almost mocked its intended viewers, who were presumably suffering grim British weather as they watched. But the contours of the personal relationships in the show were not so different from those in the original birthplace of the soap, *Peyton Place*.

Some feminists laud soaps for being the only genre to show women in strong active roles. Others decry them for perpetuating the sexist stereotype of women-as-stalwart, always there in times of trouble. Whatever the political line, there is no doubt that central roles in all soaps have been reserved for women; this is an absolutely vital convention that will never be subverted. Clearly, it has something to do with the amazing success of soaps among female viewers, the majority under the age of 45. Students of demographics love them: soaps are watched habitually by precisely the kind of person likely to hold the reins to the family budget. Better still, people watch them in an "active mode," totally involving themselves in the narratives and encoding the commercials that punctuate them in the same way, according to research by Jim Marshall and Margaret Tulley (1992). This is a bonus for advertisers, but, then again, a glance back into recent history tells us that the first soap operas were quite blatantly showcases for commercial products, usually household cleansers. Hence the name.

Inspecting the bland daily lives of ordinary folk, thrown into occasional crises, would seem to offer little commercial potential. Yet, in the 1930s and 1940s, US radio serials such as *Ma Perkins* and *The Romance of Helen Trent* held women listeners in a strange grip. Barnouw notes how women looked to them "for guidance on personal problems. Many expressed a dire dependence on serials" (1990: 73). This dependence persuaded advertisers that radio commercials at each end of the episodes could be "successful instruments of merchandising."

The British equivalents were less instrumental, more designed to attract a loyal and consistent following, particularly from women, who were more likely to be at home during the day. *Mrs. Dale's Diary*, as its name implies, was a daily chronicle of life as seen through the eyes of a woman. Its fascination was matched by *The Archers* which, by 1951, was the most popular BBC radio program, and which still runs today. The matriarchal narratives of the early radio shows, with their almost Dickensian multiplot structures were adapted to television, though without obvious success, in the 1950s. US television offered daytime fare of self-rending psychic quests, while the BBC stuck with the meat and potatoes of *The Grove Family* in early evenings.

US networks' early efforts were daytime advertising vehicles masquerading as entertainment. But they were low-budget affairs and filled airtime. Life on soaps was just one featureless day after another, the serials were distinguishable from drama by their endless deferment and postponement of incident and action. This was the whole point: to follow themes rhythmically so as to tow viewers along day after day; to ensure, as Christine Geraghty put it in her *Women and Soap Opera*, that "the audience is more concerned with continuance than resolution" (1992: 12).

Britain's independent affiliate Granada Television was derided when it launched its first twice-weekly early evening serial *Coronation Street* in December 1960. The *Daily Mirror* newspaper reckoned it was "doomed from the start with its dreary signature tune and grim series of terraced houses and smoking chimneys." More than thirty years on, having enlarged from two to three nights a week, plus an omnibus edition, the show regularly holds the number one spot and with its original signature tune. The US networks maintained their inexpensive daytime output, *Peyton Place* gathering a loyal following from the mid-1960s. One of the CBS's nondescript soaps, *As the World Turns*, shot to fame in November 1963, when it was interrupted by the news of John F. Kennedy's assassination. To the oft-heard question "where were you when Kennedy was shot?" millions still reply, "Watching *As the World Turns*."

The social changes of the late 1960s and 1970s were, as we have seen, re-processed by television, which gave women new roles. Women were not simply judged by their physical attractiveness or their steadiness in times of crisis. At least, not in much mainstream television: in soaps, the song remained the same. Women might have become temporarily disaffected from their homemaking role, but reassuringly, they always returned. The few who, like *Coronation Street*'s Elsie Tanner, self-consciously spurned the "little woman" role ran the risk of being called scarlet women.

In *Dallas*, CBS produced a weekly series of self-contained episodes which later mutated to a serial with the open-ended structure of cheap soaps, but without the tawdry scenery and costumes. It hurled the tackiness of daytime serials to the winds, opting instead for a lavish, glitzy portrayal of life at the top. The money, as they say, was there on the screen. Consistent with the style of daytime soaps and their British counterparts, *Dallas*, which first aired in 1978, framed public events through the interpersonal relations of two clannish families, whose feuding gave the serial an appealing bite. Just like the other soap families, the Ewings and the Barnses were able to absorb any crisis, whether it be breast cancer, adultery, bankruptcy or death. While the characters were far-removed from the "ordinary" figures of other soaps (they did not even wear the same clothes twice), decent acting compensated. The program, shown at night both in the USA and Britain was a success, nay a phenomenon. By 1980, it was dominating the front pages of national newspapers with headlines like "Who killed JR?" The particular episode that bore that title drew the third largest tv audience ever (over 34 million households in the US alone). By 1982, *Dallas* was being shown in 90 countries and watched by an estimated 350 million people.

The show's women were fussy, attractive, dependent and strictly service. In a way, *Dallas*'s great rival, *Dynasty*, came much closer to subverting the genre's gender convention, when it cast Joan Collins as the scheming, high-powered she-devil, Alexis, who seduced and secateured men in roughly even amounts. Quite the antithesis of the homemakers of many other soaps, Alexis was rich and independent enough to have men depending on her. Forever attaching and detaching herself from relationships, she hovered on the brink of remarriage, veering away as if reneging on a business decision. Viewers reacted to her in much the same way as children hiss at an evil queen in a pantomime.

One might think there is little relation between the high-gloss prime-time duo and the grainy *Coronation Street*, by the 1970s joined by other soapy variants, like *Crossroads*. But, there is a similarity, as June Root pointed out: "British soap operas are good at dealing with real-life emotions and the detail of domestic life: *Dallas* and *Dynasty* offer the same feelings spiced with larger than life fantasy and languid images of sexual passion" (1986: 63). We might add: the ever-present family as a protective carapace from the outside world, the ceaseless invasion of social problems expressed through individuals, and what Ella Taylor called the "decentered form" that emphasizes a series of characters, not one individual, as the focus (1989).

Earlier in this chapter, we documented the gradual dissolution of the matriarch role in many television shows as professional women stepped into the van. Soaps strongly defined a countertrend, returning the family as the primary group – so strong in fact that, by the mid-1980s, soaps were ruling the ratings on both sides of the Atlantic and spawning all kinds of offspring like *The Colbys*, *Falcon Crest* and *Knots Landing* in the US and *Brookside*, *EastEnders* and *Emmerdale Farm* in Britain. Series which had all but played themselves out in their native Australia were lent a new lease of life in the late 1980s when British audiences willingly adopted *Neighbours* and *Prisoner: Cell Block H*, which specialized in splenetic, lesbian frictions and confessional revelations in a claustrophobic women's prison. The undoubted success of soaps as a media phenomenon has attracted the attention of some theorists, eager to fathom their appeal, yet reluctant to address the obvious.

rewriting the scripts

As one might imagine, devotees of cultural studies have had a field day with soaps. *Dallas* in particular has cultivated a virtual subdiscipline. Dallasologists include Ien Ang (1991), Elihu Katz and Tamar Liebes (1986) and Sonia Livingstone (1987). Their studies reveal how the viewers decode markedly different meanings from the same program, thereby enhancing its potential relevance. *Dallas* can mean all things to all people. This prevents us from rushing to the conclusion that soaps' popularity is all down to their conservatism. While television in the 1970s left behind the uncomplicated image of happy families and replaced it with the workplace, the soaps continued to portray the family as a site of intimacy and humanism, with women occupying traditional roles. This may be partly true, but we need also to appreciate that there are many other readings.

Soaps' relationships are a critique of the alienating corporate world; beleaguered female characters are knocking patriarchy; their men are hideous caricatures of a world gone mad on power. Why do more women watch than men? Perhaps because they "see connectedness in their interpersonal relationships and view issues more personally," if Randall Scott's research is to be believed (1990: 440). Fred Inglis' conclusion is that "the roots of psychosis are in all human beings" and soaps express these:

> To play in the imagination with a literally endless circuit of quarrel and reconciliation, threat of power-loss (whether of sex or money) and of relief from threat . . . is to return to the mechanical rhythms of the libido, with no help from the alter ego.
>
> (1991: 152)

Ingenious as many of these readings are, most of them require either the mentality of a cryptographer or the credulity of a four-year-old. Ordinary faculties of observation tell us that *Dallas* was born of the same spirit that produced the original soaps: it is itself an epic-sized advertisement of a commodified good life, a cornucopia of luxuries, romance, changing fortunes and continuous excitement. The modern capitalist economy is built on the principles of mass production and, as importantly, planned obsolescence. Consumer items have continually to be replaced and upgraded; so too do consumer tastes. The imperative to want newer, better, improved versions of everything suffuses the media in its every dimension, no less so in its entertainment than in its commercials.

There was no secret to the success of the overwrought advertisement called soap opera. It simply titillated the viewers' senses with a cavalcade of stimulants. The characters were greedy, malicious, corrupt, adulterous and, occasionally, gentle; they had the same fads and foibles as their viewers. This made some element of identification possible. They were also so stinking rich that they had everything the consumers were supposed to long for. The mesmeric appeal was not significantly different from that which guides a child to a toy store, not to buy, but to press against the front window and wish.

The logic of consumerism seemed to have a hand in the fate of the primetime soaps. Like the products they hawked, they too had built-in obsolescence. As the 1980s turned, the repetitious Dallasty charm began to evaporate and the stories became ever more ridiculous. Plot discontinuities in *Dallas* were erased by having an entire series retroactively become one of Pam Ewing's bad dreams. It was a hopelessly contrived device designed simply to bring Bobby Ewing back from the dead after actor Patrick Duffy's absence prompted a drop in ratings.

Dynasty became virtually indistinguishable from the earlier satires like *Soap*, *Mary Hartman, Mary Hartman* and the feature movie *Soap Dish*. Slipping genre for a while, it introduced aliens and flying saucers in a daring, or more probably, desperate move, but one which stretched viewers' credulity beyond breaking point. The shows tumbled further down the ratings. *Dallas*, *Dynasty* and their imitators measured production costs in millions of dollars per episode, which meant that television networks needed to reel in huge advertising revenues. Drops in popularity were noticed by advertisers whose hesitance made *Dallas* and co. unviable by 1991, when their exits from the top 50 indicated their sell-by date had passed.

Low-budget soaps, devoid of the Dallasty ostentation, continue to thrive in Britain's day and early evening periods and US day slots, attesting to the appeal of soaps. Britain's four main home-produced soaps collectively drew almost 854 million viewers across a one-month period in 1992; or, put another way, 100 million hours of viewing. New series come and go, but the formulaic soaps plow on remorselessly; and advertisers flock to them. They represent a bulwark against change. Their themes are topical, but always treated in a way that appeals conservatively to the basic soap grid: answers to problems are to be found in families, in women especially and mothers in particular. The topics shift, but the main themes do not: maternity, intimacy, emotional conflict. In their way, these are every bit as "big" as themes in the "social problem of the week" type telefilms. This does not mean soaps are women's shows; but it inclines us toward the view of Geraghty "that women are the skilled readers by whom the programs are best understood." Geraghty's conclusion was that soaps are "oriented towards" women "in terms of the range of characters offered, the type of stories dealt with and the way in which women characters operate as the norm through whom appropriate judgements can be made" (1992: 167).

While soaps have kept wives and mothers in their more traditional gentler-type roles, other series, such as the aforementioned *Murphy Brown* and its sister show *Designing Women* in the USA, and *Birds of a Feather* and *Rides* in Britain, have advanced different interpretations in attempts to combine commercial success with social responsibility. *Rides* proved an interesting exercise about a group of women owning and running a taxi firm. Critics of television's treatment of women have been disarmed by the greater number of women now appearing; their attack on gender stereotypes has been blunted by the increasing number of complex portrayals of working women, often in powerful positions. The *Prime Suspect* series, which featured Helen Mirren as a senior detective investigating homicides, illustrates this. They were commercial successes in 1991–94 in Britain and the USA (and later turned into a movie). Given the nature of the medium, one can justifiably expect more of the same.

Such shows also serve to undermine the related criticism that the typical woman on tv is, as Wober and Gunter put it, "believed to become flustered in the most minor crises; she is sensitive, often fearful and anxious, and generally dependent on male help and support in all kinds of professional situations" (1988: 100). To accept this argument requires a suspension of consciousness. Women are surely not presented in this way on television any more. Critiques driven by the proposition that images of women are insulting, degrading and disparaging had force through the 1970s, but, nowadays, they are running on empty. Television just cannot afford to upset women.

Women, especially young women, are the most sought-after group by programmers. As they have most control over disposable income and watch most television, they interest advertisers and, by extension, programmers, who need advertisers' business. In this sense, women are the opposite of ethnic minorities, about whom advertisers have been indifferent, up till recent years at least. The logic is irresistible. But the results have hardly helped dispel the kinds of stereotypes both sets of minorities have grumbled about for decades. Despite major modifications over the years, women and ethnic minorities continue to insist that no amount of rehashing can adequately compensate for the injuries.

Women, as the evidence presented here suggests, have less of an argument than ethnic minorities, particularly African Americans, whose dignity and intelligence was violated as a matter of course up to the 1980s and whose predicaments today are handled in a politically stylized way. Women's television roles have opened out since the early days when they were like walking kitchens; though soaps perpetuate the tradition.

Conspiracy theorists will always interpret such trends as parts of a corporate plot to denude minorities of their cultural and political power by portraying them in essentially powerless roles. Majority and minority alike will continue to labor with the erroneous conception that women and blacks are incapable of performing complex or responsible roles. Like the arguments about the effects of television violence, the disempowerment thesis places faith in the ability of television to convince audiences of its fidelity. We are supposed to see, gasp and soak it up; never think or make critical evaluations. The guiding argument of this book is that viewers have enough critical faculties to realize when they are being entertained, not just being fed a slice of life. Of course, this does nothing to mitigate the damage done to the esteem of women and ethnic minorities who would have been regularly hurt and insulted by televisual versions of them.

Audiences are more effectively persuaded to part with their money than mugged for it. Television's marketing brains have already realized this, as the significant elaborations on old stereotypes have indicated. If women keep a tight rein on the household budget and ethnic minorities hold or improve their market position, their status in television programs, especially drama, will grow. All of this makes television's content seem reducible to the imperatives of the market and the advertisers who coolly seek to manipulate it. Sports have been manipulated more than most. Compressed, converted and sometimes dismembered by tv to suit commercial purposes, sports did not exactly set out a welcome mat for the camera crews. But once through the turnstiles, television became an invaluable tenant, as we will see in the next chapter.

chapter nine

dream match

the McDonaldization of sport

The explosion of noise coming through my six speakers is deafening. Two of the world's most illustrious soccer teams are emerging into a packed stadium in Turin, Italy, ready to play in the planet's most passion-charged soccer league: the Microsoft European League. It is 2005; this is the league's sixth year of operation. Today's main game is between Liverpool Carlsberg and Juventus Danone – most teams incorporate their sponsors' names into their own, now. It is a Phase Two game, similar to the NFL play-offs, and will be televised all over the continent and beyond.

Like most sports fans, I have a bank of ten monitors, the centerpiece of which is an 8′×6′ high-definition screen. Because there is so much televised sport going on at once, I can punch up as many events as I want and switch at a command through a voice-sensitive selector. (It's amusing to think that we had to go to all the trouble of pushing buttons on a remote control years ago.) If, for instance, I have ten soccer games going at once and someone scores a goal on screen ten, I just say "ten" and it comes up on the 8′×6′. Next command is "replay" and the action backtracks ten seconds. My personal control over the service extends to time scheduling. If there is more than one game played simultaneously and I want to watch them in sequence, the digital compression capability of my system allows me to do so without the old-fashioned method of taping and playing-back. The game I want comes through exactly when I want it to.

I pay £45 for ten games of my choice, which is not too bad considering the cheapest seat at any stadium is £55. The games are fed through the optical fiber network run by British Telecom in conjunction with, among six others, the European Football Federation, which replaced UEFA. AT & T performs a similar function in the States. This type of technology made satellite dishes redundant not long after they had been launched in 1989.

There was a hue and cry about having to pay for sports when the concept of pay-per-view (ppv) was thrust on the public in the 1990s. The first ppv sports event was introduced in the States way back in 1980. In the 1990s, virtually all the big boxing promotions went ppv. That seemed bad enough, but there was a storm when American football moved to ppv in 1998, at first just for post-season games, then for the whole schedule, which now includes 20 games per team in a regular season.

When the major US tv networks dropped sports completely in 1997, the NFL decided to set its own ppv system and charge, but Congress passed legislation declaring that certain events, including the Super Bowl, baseball's World Series and certain other blue riband contests should remain available free of charge. The law was rescinded within two years, after the Supreme Court ruled on a touchy restraint of trade action.

The subscription satellite network BSkyB began charging for English soccer in 1993 and, after resistance, fans got used to the idea. There was a clever resolution to the problem of how to fit advertising into what is still a fluid game. Eight-second commercials slapped in at every corner, goal kick, injury stoppage or any other interruption came at the rate of ninety per game. They are not called commercials: just "eights". It was irritating to begin with, but apparently it keeps the subscription charges down. The fans have to take television's word for it.

No one grumbles about charges nowadays. Besides there are several features undreamed of a decade ago. I have a choice of commentaries, for instance; or no commentary at all if I wish. I can also pick from about ten camera angles, including a helicopter shot. I especially like the perspective of the batsman's helmetcam in cricket: it is terrifying to stare at a bowler barreling towards you, ready to propel a hard leather ball at over 100 mph; the ball becomes a blur that pitches up fiercely, sometimes actually hitting the lens. Every innings in a game of cricket has a sponsor, now, as do baseball innings; "This innings is brought to you by Ford – have you driven a Ford this century?" says the voiceover. Purists still insist that television cannot compare with actually attending. Nothing beats the real thing, they argue. For many of us, television beats it every time.

Futurist parody this might be, but it is based on trends that are already well established. Technologically, everything in the scenario is possible; the hard part is persuading television audiences to part with their money. Since the 1940s, tv viewers have expected and received sports for no more than the nominal charge of a few extra pennies on the price of advertised product, or the price of a license. The indications are that this will change, perhaps quite sharply over the next several years. Sports have been as much parts of television's stock-in-trade as soaps, news and crime drama. In the 1990s, many of the grander sports events are either being lured away from the networks by competing satellite/ cable subscription systems, or passed over to the pay-per-view services owned by the media behemoths themselves. NBC offered 24-hour coverage of the 1992 Summer Olympics to those prepared to pay $125 for a fifteen-day package, or $19.95 for a single day. The meager number of viewers and the resulting losses did not inspire confidence. But it was all part of weaning viewers away from the "free" sport they had been getting for the previous half-century.

If ever there was a marriage made in heaven, it was between television and sport. The commercial success of each was almost directly attributable to the other. From the 1940s to the present, sports have grown in proportion to television. Not only have they grown in scale and popularity, but they have been modified into virtual theater. And television's effort at focusing its viewers' attention on sport have paid off handsomely in terms of audiences, Historically, high-profile sporting events attract viewing audiences comparable with television phenomena like the moonlanding, the coronation of Queen Elizabeth, the final instalment of *M*A*S*H* and the "Who killed JR?' episode of *Dallas*. The Super Bowl, for example, annually attracts between 90-120 million US viewers, a figure that enables a television company to demand about $850,000 for a 30-second commercial during the game and emerge with a profit.

The current global popularity of an event such as the Super Bowl is unimaginable without television. American football as we recognize it today is a television-created sport, and its dissemination owes everything to tv. No sports event can be classed as major unless television has exploited it. By definition, a sports event that is not televised is simply not significant except in its own minority terms. This may sound cruel to followers of netball, speedway or any number of other sports that command large followings. But, the amount of time television affords a sport is a measure of how seriously it is taken. Think of any sport that is not regularly featured on tv, then assess its credibility. Television's impact is undeniable; but is it good or bad?

"The effect of television upon sport has been a point of debate for over 30 years?" wrote Garry Whannel in his *Fields in Vision*, "some arguing that television has made sport, some that sport has been ruined, others merely content to bear witness to the unholy alliance" (1992: 203). Television has certainly inspired and probably dictated changes in sports. The obvious ones are superficial: the introduction of time-outs for commercials; tie-breakers in tennis; the reduction of championship boxing from fifteen to twelve rounds; the re-scheduling of Olympic events to suit US East Coast time requirements; the switch from match play to stroke play in professional golf tournaments; virtually any sport that has been featured on television for any length of time has had to accommodate changes to meet tv's demands. Some sports, like one-day cricket and timed snooker, have been distorted into a made-for-television format. Others, like baseball, fall almost naturally into the cadences of television. Some abhor the compression of what was originally intended to be five tense days of leather-on-willow into a simple limited-overs format. Others regard cricket's adaptation as a rational response to a changing world in which deferred gratification has been redefined as standing in line for more than three minutes at a fast food restaurant.

George Ritzer's essay on *The McDonaldization of Society* is full of provocative arguments about how every dimension of our lives is in some way influenced by the efficient and controlled predictability of the world-famous restaurant chain, where customers always get the desired result, usually within seconds of ordering (1992). "It's quick, easy and efficient," Ritzer quotes a supporter (1992: 108). So is watching television. Grand, majestic sports like cricket, no less than the narrow, frenetic basketball, have been McDonaldized, primarily through their contact with television, but also just to stay popular with fans. Not that sports themselves have objected too much to television's intrusions. More usually, they take the money and run. When television takes an interest in a sport, it ceases to be a Corinthian activity and becomes "product;" something which can, as the word implies, be manufactured in large quantities, packaged and sold. While the old guard may resent this, any sport that has attracted television has been aware that it has to produce, or be ignored. Some sports have actively sought the attentions of television, believing it to be their only salvation from obscurity. Field hockey is a case in point. Others, like the exotic sumo wrestling, or the chaotic Australian rules football, have been plucked by Channel 4 in Britain and various US cables and fashioned into watchable programs for the demographically desirable professional, or ABC1 classes.

Television's willingness to rescue some activities from the sporting equivalent of an Ultima Thule – like Kabbadi from Delhi, or tree-sawing from Hopkinton, New Hampshire – suggests a passion for what North America's ABC network likes to call "the thrill of victory, the agony of defeat." Reason? Almost any sport draws television viewers. Sport began innocently, allowing cameras to record its events; but, once its innocence was lost, it began to exact a high price; a price, it seems, television is prepared to pay. It pays in the full knowledge that it can defray costs, either by charging advertisers, who in turn pass on its costs to consumers, or by charging consumers directly in the form of subscription or license fees. Either way, the consumer foots the bill.

from flashing lights to ppv

On April 29 1933, the BBC's magazine the *Radio Times* featured on its front cover a picture of Wembley Stadium with a grid superimposed on its field of play. The idea was that listeners of the English Football Association (FA) Cup Final game radio commentary, would have a visual frame of reference to assist their imaginations. The grid was marked in eight numbered segments and, as the ball passed from one to another, a commentator would call out the number. Meanwhile, the play-by-play commentator would describe the action. Listeners were supposed to sit rapt, their ears by the speaker, their eyes on the diagram. It was an early acknowledgement from broadcasters that as many senses as possible were to be stimulated if audiences were to be involved for long periods, in this case nearly two hours.

Seven years later, in Dartmouth College, Andover, USA, a more elaborate experiment involving an electrically illuminated board enabled local students to follow a football game in Princeton, New Jersey. Flashing lights on the grid plotted the progress of the ball virtually as it moved, for the benefit of a gymnasium full of fans. It was crude and not particularly effective, certainly not compared with the breakthroughs of television. BBC had already televised Wimbledon in 1937 and, in 1939, RCA showed a college baseball game between Columbia and Princeton, but for the benefit of about 400 prosperous owners of $600 sets mainly in New York City. These were the first telecasts of sports events.

Early coverage bore little resemblance to the elaborate spectacles we see today. The *New York Times* reviewed the first television games thus: "The players were best described by observers as appearing like white flies running across the screen. When the ball flashed across the grass it appeared as a cometlike white pinpoint" (quoted in Johnson, 1970: 90). Technology proceeded to outpace consumer change, so that, even in 1948, when it was possible to show an Olympic Games "live" only the privileged few were able to watch the exploits of Fanny Blankers-Coen and Emil Zatopek, most people listening to the events over the radio and waiting a couple of weeks before seeing highlights of the action on the newsreels that played at cinemas.

There was money available for sports. For example, as far back as 1910, the motion picture industry paid major league baseball (MLB) $500 for the right to film and show the World Series. Such was the commercial success of the arrangement that in the next year, the fee was increased sevenfold to $3,500. While MLB accommodated this, team owners claimed that simultaneous information, such as that transmitted by Western Union, the telegraph company which paid $17,000 per annum for five years from 1913, would deter fans from attending games. The view persisted; as late as 1932, the three New York teams banned radio. But in 1939, all MLB teams consented to a radio contract and rights for the World Series sold for about $400,000.

In 1947, Ford and Gillette paid $65,000 for the rights to sponsor baseball's World Series on television even though fewer than 12 per cent of US households could receive it. But, as the number of home-owned sets multiplied, sports governing bodies grew wary of the possible detrimental impact of television on gate attendances. As with radio, it was suspected that people would simply stay at home and watch tv rather than paying the price of a ticket and braving the elements. Despite the appeals of the airwaves, sports remained earthbound for as long as they could: through the 1950s, television cameras were encouraged only at marquee events, where gates would not be hit.

This meant that, for instance, up till 1958, only the Northeast quadrant of the USA had real access to baseball. The major leagues extended no further west than Kansas City and no further south than Washington, DC. In the absence of television, most Americans would never have seen a "live" game from the major league. But, America's National Pastime, as it is known, drew support from the minor leagues, which served as nurseries for the future stars: in 1949 alone, minor league gates totaled 42 million. Ten years on, with the advent of televised coverage of major league games, this figure had shrunk to 13 million. By 1959, only 10 million people paid to see minor league baseball and the number of clubs plummeted from 488 in 1949 and 155 in 1969, to 145 in 1974. In the major league, the effects of television were even more pronounced: from a 1948 peak of 20.9 million, attendances dropped 32 per cent to 14.38 million within five years.

As if to illustrate the point that the drop was unrelated to on-field performances, the Cleveland Indians, between 1948 and 1956 suffered a 67 per cent loss in attendance, despite winning a World Series and a pennant. The Boston Braves' crowds plunged by 81 per cent following their

National League victory in 1948, immediately after which they signed a tv deal for the next three seasons. The situation needed drastic remedial action, so the owner, Lou Perini, moved the franchise to Milwaukee and banned television cameras, apart from the World Series winning games of 1957 and 1958. The gates stayed healthy, prompting Perini to announce: "We have come to believe that tv can saturate the minds of the fans with baseball. We would very much like to guard against this." Perini relaxed his strictures after 1962 and eventually sold out to a group, which wholeheartedly embraced television by relocating the club in Atlanta where a tv-radio guarantee of $1.25 million per year awaited.

Another sport whose gates were hit severely was college football. Between 1949 and 1953, attendance dropped by almost three million. The National Collegiate Athletic Association (NCAA) formed a special television committee and instituted rigid rules for limiting the number of telecasts. Even then, it took ten years before gates rose to their 1949 levels.

Television feasted on boxing, which it left as a carcass in 1964 after eighteen years. In some areas of the USA, boxing was on every night of the week, with promoters eagerly accepting television money to supplement profits. Gradually, the supplements became the main source of profits. Gates slid and promotions were viable only with tv monies. It became a case of devil take hindmost, big promoters with "name" fighters under contract grabbing the spoils, while small promoters went out of business – and with them the young boxing prospects. Two hundred and fifty of the country's 300 small fight clubs shut down in the 1952–9 period alone. At the height of its power in 1955, boxing was watched by 8.5 million homes, about one-third of the then available audience. By 1959, boxing commanded only 10.6 per cent of the viewing audience; which sounds much more impressive now than it did when the market was uncluttered by cable channels. NBC was the first to cut boxing from its schedules in 1960. The other networks followed suit.

The reaction from boxing, which had become totally reliant on tv as its gates tumbled, was that television had "destroyed" and "taken the personality out of boxing," as the New York State Athletic Commissioner put it (quoted in Sammons, 1988: 174–5). Both the sport and the medium had merely followed the market. But the signs were clear: much of sport was getting deeply implicated in a comfortable and highly profitable relationship; it was also baring its throat. By exposing itself so completely to television, sport was risking possible ruin itself if tv decided to pull out, as it did from boxing, or becoming totally dependent for its existence on the networks. Apart from boxing, North American television's sporting energy came from wrestling and roller derby in the

1950s. They were relatively easy sports to produce: fixed orthicon cameras trained on small, finite areas of action insulated from natural weather conditions were perfect for the then technically naive television networks. The two principal powers were CBS and NBC and these identified sports events as being of interest predominantly to men. They were able to recruit beer and razor manufacturers as sponsors. The tv competitors had a relatively peaceful coexistence, carving up the big events between them. Then, came ABC.

Trailing way behind in the viewing ratings, ABC pursued a different strategy: instead of accepting the "natural" appeal of big sporting occasions and reflecting this in its programs, it set about creating interest. The premise was much the same as that of the advertisers on whose revenue ABC ultimately depended: if the demand is not there to begin with, build it. And the way they built it was by taking an obscure sport and adding something to it, something that only television could possibly provide.

ABC's cameras ventured to the top of cliffs, peered over the edge, then drew back to view a diver hurtling into the sea below, where another camera joined him or her in the water. Close-up action converted the dive into drama. Minority sports and activities that were barely competitive sports at all attracted ABC's cameras. Rodeos, demolition derbies and even the bizarre firemen's bucket-filling contests were all fair game for ABC. Inspired by the iconoclastic philosophies of Roone Arledge, ABC vandalized the established traditions and made an overt appeal to younger audiences which were not bound by the fidelities of their parents. ABC sought more women viewers and it wanted to move upscale to the more demographically appealing sectors of the market. The network was shamelessly populist, projecting personalities, highlighting unusual features, reducing almost any activity to its most basic competitive elements. Frog jumping contests were not out of place in ABC's sports panoply. Gillette, traditionally one of North America's biggest sports sponsors, linked up with ABC to present a regular Friday night boxing show; boxing's gates were already in steep decline, but its popularity with television viewers was steadfast. "How are you fixed for blades?" asked Gillette's hyperactive parrot during the boxing show. Gillette's money enabled ABC to bid successfully for the NCAA football in the 1960/61 season and this was the first of its many coups.

As ABC went from strength to strength, professional American football sprung to the fore as a major sport. The established National Football League (NFL) came under pressure from the fledgling American Football league (AFL) in 1960. The AFL was a second-rate outfit, full of players who could not make the grade with the rival league; but, it was competitive and was able to progress in the slipstream of the NFL, which had previously been less popular than either baseball or college football. NFL commissioner Bert Bell had made an important concession to television in 1958 when he permitted "television time-outs;" in other words, stoppages specifically to allow networks to screen commercials. CBS was delighted with the result: as more homes acquired tv sets, so the popularity of professional football grew all over the nation.

ABC had no reservations about featuring a strictly fabricated league created for the sole purpose of giving it more leverage with advertisers. In fact, the AFL had a contract with ABC even prior to a ball being kicked. It existed only for television. In its first five years, its credibility solidified, so that, in 1965, the AFL was able to loose ABC's apron strings and negotiate independently. A deal with NBC television brought the league $42 million for five years' coverage. The extra revenue enabled the AFL to sign better players and become a legitimate equal of the NFL. Too equal for comfort, in fact: fearing the upstart, the NFL, in 1966, agreed to a merger which resulted in the NFL as we now know it. If television was a vague factor in 1960, the end of its take-off period, it was not by 1966. And there was naught sports could do to hold tv at bay.

If any event symbolizes the thickening liaison, it came in 1962. The Telstar satellite made "live" transatlantic television possible and the first spectacle to be bounced from the USA to Europe was not the US President, as planned, but a baseball game from Chicago. "Perhaps it's only fitting that a sporting event, one of civilization's earliest ceremonials, be the first event to be televised across the seas," announced the tv presenter. It was an unscheduled screening, forced by the fact that Telstar's orbit made the link too early. But it was not inappropriate.

In 1966, the year of the NFL–AFL merger, BBC realized the potential of television to exploit a large-scale sporting tournament in the form of soccer's World Cup Finals. BBC television beamed the games "live" from various parts of England quite literally to the world. It was soccer, the most popular sport in the world, showcasing its most prestigious tournament on a genuinely global scale, not two weeks after it had occurred, but as it happened. The BBC, in its broadcast, also introduced viewers to arguably its most ingenious and, overall, most significant piece of technology: the instant replay. With this small addition to its repertoire, television showed that it was more than a match for actual attendance. What the naked eye missed, television caught, replayed, slowed down, froze, and showed again and again and again.

The English team's third goal in the final game against West Germany arrived gift-wrapped for television: a Geoff Hurst shot that thundered against the underside of the German goal's crossbar and appeared to bounce momentarily over the goal-line before flying back into play. If the whole ball crossed the plane of the line, it was a goal. But, it happened so quickly that no one quite knew; though a linesman thought he did and advised the referee who declared a goal, much to the anger of the German team. Television slowed down the shot, followed the ball's trajectory, froze frames as it bounced, changed angles; and it still could not prove conclusively whether or not the ball actually crossed the line. The debate spiralled and BBC television kept repeating one of its most valuable pieces of footage. Even today, the BBC can guarantee a lively argument by wheeling out the "was it a goal?" episode.

In the years since, the same technique has been employed countless times, especially in sports such as football and hockey where the camera can pick up a ball or puck breaking – or not – the plane of a goal-line. The eye sometimes misses, but not the camera, thus proving that watching tv was in many ways superior to being there. Positioning cameras in the quarterback's helmet, in front of the bobsleigh, in the cockpit of a racing car, in the swimming pool and other unusual places gave television viewers angles of vision inaccessible to spectators. Such gimmicks were ABC's trademark and the vehicle it used to carry them was *Monday Night Football*, a US sports program intended to widen the appeal of what had previously been an afternoon, male-centered activity. Arledge was again behind what became an immensely successful attempt to integrate components of variety shows, political events and drama into sports coverage. The search for minor sports continued, but the conversion of a sport into a mainstream primetime entertainment became ABC's priority. Close-ups, replays slo-mos, split-screens; they were all in there, as were personality close-ups, emphasizing the "human" side of players and coaches. The main commentator was Howard Cosell, an often disagreeable man who unfailingly provoked controversy. No device was left unexplored. The result: from the beginning of the Monday night games in the 1970s, ABC stormed to a one-third share of the audience. It had paid the NFL $8.5 million per year for 13 games and claimed this back by charging advertisers $65,000 per minute during the game. By the end of the decade, it was regularly the eighth most watched program in the country, enabling ABC to charge $110,000 for a 30-second commercial slot.

The program became something of a blueprint for other sports coverage, including major league baseball, basketball and, to a more limited extent, hockey. Others, like golf and tennis also drew audiences to television's attention. During the 1970s, the annual number of US network hours sports programming increased from 787 to 1,356; by 1984, the figure was 1,700. Advertisers looked on with relish: by the mid-1980s, the three networks were selling over $1 billion in commercials for sports slots. Guided by the logic of the market, television networks set about finding competitions to cover. Where they could not find them, they made them.

Tennis struck a Faustian bargain with CBS television in the 1970s, staging – fraudulently as it turned out – a series of special "winner-takes-all" matches. The bogus competition in which prize money, contrary to publicity claims, was guaranteed, was one of a number of stagey competitions involving made-for-television sport. Other competitions tailored for television included the American Basketball Association, the World Hockey League and the United States Football League (USFL), this last initiative having been squashed in 1986 after an antitrust suit in which the USFL claimed the NFL had a monopoly on network broadcast rights payments. The USFL received only a token dollar. The NFL's power was enhanced by the fact that it could negotiate as a total unit with the media, rather than allow teams to arrange their own deals (the Sports Broadcasting Act, 1961 permitted this). The apparently cozy relationship between the NFL and the major networks, while occasionally strained, hinted at the kind of protectionism so despised officially in the land of opportunity. One of the arguments that came out during the USFL case was that a perfect market situation was severely compromised by restraining the league's ability to obtain a proper price for its commodity. Television networks, too, ostensibly oppose any element of protectionism, though, theoretically, any one of them could strike up a deal for exclusive rights to potentially any event. In practice, Congress could and probably would try to intervene if, say, HBO, Showtime or any other cable channel closed an exclusive deal for the Super Bowl or the World Series.

Events of this stature were legally protected in Britain until the late 1980s. Major sports events, including the FA Cup Final and Wimbledon, were regarded like listed buildings: historic monuments which needed protection from Visigoth property developers who would bulldoze them to make way for office blocks. British legislators traditionally preserved the right of all television viewers, regardless of income or geography, to watch the big events free of charge. The inclusion of a clause guaranteeing the BBC "live" coverage of such events was prompted in 1955 by the beginning of commercial television and was justified then by the localized nature of the Independent Television (ITV) system. Exclusive ITV coverage would have left many areas of the country without access to big events, an omission the then Conservative government would not countenance. From 1955 – and long after ITV became a legitimate national network – the clause became part of the broadcasting landscape and was kept intact through the passages of the 1981 and 1984 Broadcasting Acts.

The BBC's British hegemony went virtually unchallenged until the mid-1960s. Its Wednesday evening magazine-style program *Sportsview* broadened its appeal to a general audience, rather than the traditionally male one. It accentuated personalities and the "human interest" elements of sport. Complementing this was a primetime Saturday program geared to the soccer fan and featuring, among other things, highlights of the games played earlier in the day. By 1959, the BBC had added a Saturday afternoon show, *Grandstand*, comprising a results service, "live" horse racing and other items of topical interest. The anchor held an important role, linking disparate events together for 4½ hours.

Faced with such forbidding competition the commercial web of ITV shrunk from a fight over sport. Unlike the major US tv networks, which have a number of regional, affiliated television stations which buy programs from the network-supplier then sell off advertising space, the British commercial system comprised a series of relatively autonomous franchises based in different regions. Granada, for instance, was located in Manchester and operated from Monday to Friday, serving the northwest but sharing the mix of programs from other franchises, like Associated Rediffusion in the southeast. There were originally four companies in total, each favoring different ideologies. Granada regarded itself as the commercial counterpart of BBC, a guardian of culture. Rediffusion was more tabloid in its approach. One hesitates to call it sport, but wrestling gave ITV its first major success in a head-to-head with the BBC's sports. It was the kind of trashy, populist spectacle despised by the BBC; but its Saturday afternoon ratings topped-out at a steady five million viewers, compared with four million for *Grandstand*.

But Saturday afternoon wrestling apart, Independent Television was a poor second to the BBC. It's splintered structure, with each franchise following its own philosophies; prevented the emergence of a united attack. Whannel speculates that an alternative arrangement with different franchises representing program types rather than geographical regions would have placed ITV in a stronger position to make an assault (1992: 49). It is interesting to imagine what might have happened had a single contractor been given the task of developing sports in the 1950s. In the USA, ESPN and, later, a clutch of other networks demonstrated the level of technical excellence to be achieved from concentrating only on sport.

Not until 1966 did ITV step towards consistent policy on sport by creating a special unit to acquire broadcasting rights and plan overall programming. Within a year, ITV had captured cricket's Gillette Cup, Brands Hatch motor racing and soccer's Football League Cup, a trophy which was to undergo several incarnations, each time bearing the name of its sponsors, viz. Coca-Cola Cup, Littlewoods Cup and so on. ITV's approach from that point bore similarities to ABC's in the States: new camera angles, close-ups, slo-mos run *ad nauseam* and recognizable presenters, some ex-BBC. Wrestling was a mainstay, but, otherwise ITV fought shy of overdoing the entertainment and opted for credible sports events.

The coincidence of ABC's and ITV's vigorous pursuit of sports on either side of the Atlantic in the mid-1960s suggests a realization that new markets were waiting to be harvested. Leisure patterns had changed as a direct results of tv's lichen-like spread into the homes of all classes. Traditional forms of entertainment, including sport, were changed by the magnetic quality of television. Some sports, as we have seen, were affected adversely by television viewers' preference for staying at home rather than witnessing events firsthand. Others, as we have also seen, were "made" by television's exposing them to a wide audience. Sport in the 1950s was not a proven commodity. Huge viewing audiences were a boon, but an infrequent one: big baseball games in the US, show-jumping in Britain and grand-slam tennis tournaments were very dependable, as they drew mixed-sex audiences from throughout the class structure. Most others attracted predominantly male, working-class audiences, which did not excite advertisers so much. Both ABC and ITV tried to move away from this syndrome.

Added to this market expansion was an awareness of the gigantic audience potential of global events, such as soccer's World Cup and the Olympic Games. In Britain, ITV fought bitterly for exclusive access to these, only to be beaten by the BBC which persistently used the by then dated legislation in its defense. ITV's eventual strategy was to forego events for which it would not secure exclusive coverage, while out-bidding BBC wherever possible for sole rights to specific events. The policy took time to reap rewards, but, in the 1980s, with BBC groggy from a decade in which political sentiment discouraged public spending, ITV snared major prey in the form of British track and field, along with regular championship boxing and, in 1991, rugby's World Cup. It also screened exclusively the Seoul Olympics of 1988.

In the late 1980s, two satellites flew out into the firmament readied to bounce signals back to dishes all over Europe. Sky and BSB offered three all-sports channels, plus a full complement of other specialist services, for the cost of a three-foot-diameter dish and a monthly subscription. BSB stayed airborne for only months before merging with Sky to form BSkyB. The alliance proved troublesome to the existing terrestrial networks, outbidding them for many prestige events, including world title fights, cricket's World Cup and, as stated before, English soccer's FA Cup and Premiership. The latter was secured in 1992, after an acrimonious bidding war, culminating in a legal protest from ITV at the manner in which BSkyB had negotiated its £304 million deal for exclusive "live" coverage of top soccer. It was a bitter pill for ITV to swallow and only a marginally sweeter one for BBC which had to settle for showing edited highlights on a Saturday night tape delay. ITV's counter was to screen "live" soccer from the Italian *serie A* on Channel 4, a service previously reserved for more unusual sports such as sumo, Australian Rules football and NFL, which seemed strange when they were introduced to Britain on a weekly basis in 1985, but which quickly attracted a following.

Sales of satellite dishes did not leap dramatically despite BSkyB's acquisition. During the first season, 1992/93, the games were relayed to about 4.4 million receivers, some in hotels and clubs, but mostly in domestic use. Such poor figures after the bumper pay-out may well have inspired panic, had it not been BSkyB's intention to convert the whole program to pay-per-view (ppv). Advertisers would find little temptation in the dish-owning market and the satellite network's awareness of this inclined it towards the strategies of HBO in the US and Canal Plus in France: raise subscription rates and disregard advertisers.

The ppv approach in the 1990s was to make more specific demands on consumers by isolating events and charging a fixed price, usually discounted if purchased well in advance. In 1980, for example, the first ppv sports event was the Ray Leonard v. Roberto Duran fight. 170,000 viewers each paid $15. Rock concerts and operas followed sporadically, until the advent of TVKO, an agency owned by Time Warner, which also owned HBO. With HBO, as with BSkyB, the viewer paid a monthly fee, come what may. TVKO struggled to established itself as an alternative, more selective method of viewing. In 1991, it made a killing with its exclusive coverage of Evander Holyfield's heavyweight title defense against George Foreman. An estimated 1.45 million homes bought the fight at $34.93. By comparison, only a tenth of this number of homes chose to buy a Guns 'n' Roses concert for $24.95 in 1992 and just 34,000 homes took a $34.95

Pavarotti concert in 1991. Perhaps the biggest debacle was NBC's 1992 Olympic Triplecast, a 15-day package of Olympic events, 24 hours a day for a total of $125, or $19.95 by the day. About 20 million US homes were then cabled and so had access to ppv; only 165,000 took the whole package and 35,000 took the single days.

Of all the disparate events, only boxing seemed suited to the ppv medium; and even then, only with very prestigious promotions. One suspects that events for which there is elastic demand could slide profitably into the ppv portfolio in the future. The mere mention of Super Bowl, the World Series or the National Basketball Association (NBA) finals going ppv elicits outcries from North American fans; but the day may yet come when they have to pay directly for premium events. Now that the rumpus over BSkyB's annexing of soccer has abated, British television audiences have accommodated the new ppv arrangements. US college football fans have taken ppv at regional levels, coughing up for local games that arouse parochial, but not national, interest. One hesitates before declaring that tv audiences accept virtually anything foisted on them, but, for some sports, demand is strong enough to justify new ways of extracting profit; ppv is one of them.

the goose that lays the golden eggs

Former president of NBC, Sylvester Weaver, is often credited with the aphorism: "We are first of all in the advertising business – for that is where our revenue comes from." By implication, sports are also in the advertising business. One needs only to watch three minutes of televised sport to realize that a cascade of advertisements is flowing over the action. Racing cars, not a square inch of their body work uncovered by ads, zip across the screen; even their drivers are plastered from head to foot in logos. Tennis players are ambulant commercials, today's equivalent of sandwich boardmen. Increasingly, the stadia in which sports take place are devoted to advertising hoardings and billboards. Even when invisible, commercial products and companies are unavoidable, mentioned when commentators utter the name of the competition, which may bear a name like the "Carling Premiership", the "Pepsi 500", the "Virginia Slims Tournament" or the "Nike Golf Tour." The playing field, or court, has become an extension of the marketplace.

Gillette was one of the first companies to recognize the potential of televised sport as a vehicle for advertising its products, the staple one being razor blades. In the days before razors were designed for women, Gillette's main ambition was to sell to men. And, as televised sport was watched mainly by men, it made sense to get involved in broadcasting. As far back as 1915, Gillette was featuring baseball scores in its newspaper advertisements. A sports review radio slot on NBC in the 1920s was sponsored by the makers of the famous blades. Its sponsorship of the radio transmission of the Max Baer v. Jim Braddock heavyweight title of 1935 spanned 26 weeks and incorporated a drama series in which Baer played a private eye. The bad news for Gillette was that Braddock won. Not that the result necessarily mattered; the exposure was more important, even limited exposure, as the World Series of 1939 showed. Gillette paid $100,000 for the radio rights and packaged its blades especially to tie in. In four straight games, out of a possible seven, Yankees beat the Cincinnati Reds. It seemed a disastrously short series for Gillette, who got minimum exposure. Yet sales rose 350 per cent in the immediate aftermath of the games and encouraged the company to pursue an association with other sports. As mentioned earlier, Gillette invested in the American Football League and virtually bankrolled ABC television's commitment to sport in the mid-1960s. Its venture into weekly boxing solidified Gillette's position as the premier commercial sports supporter of the period.

Makers of beer, cars, tires, after shave and other products aimed at a male market followed. We noticed in chapter six that there is no cause-and-effect way of assessing the precise influence of advertising or sales. But the willingness of corporations to part with large sums of money suggests that they and their advertising agents are satisfied that there is certainly a relationship between sport-related ads and sales. Some kind of evidence comes from Macintosh's experience in 1989, when it launched a new computer with a series of spots during the Super Bowl. The following day, $3.5 million-worth of said computer were sold. This sales figure increased to $155 million over the following 90 days. A typical American football game in the 1990s features fourteen car commercials amounting to seven minutes. Automobile makers want to reach men aged between 18 and 49 and football delivers them.

The use of a major sports event for advertising reached its apogee in 1984 at the Olympic Games held at Los Angeles and enshrined in history as the "hamburger Olympics" because of the overt use of one of its sponsor's logo, two arches forming a large letter "M." Commenting on the blatancy of the advertising in all aspects of the television coverage, Sut Jhally wrote: "Given the prevalence of brand names in the athletic events themselves and the use made of sporting themes in the advertisements that appeared between events, the blurring of the line between the two realms was so complete that, at times, it was difficult to tell what one was watching" (1989: 79).

In the US, commercials typically surround sports action and are studded into it in the form of discrete commercials. In Britain, the ads are actually on display in the process of the activity itself: on hoardings, on players' apparel, on panels of cars, on equipment. The structure of advertising in the States would make it impossible, for example, for the NFL to countenance football players' wearing of shirts emblazoned with, say, Valvoline when the tv network screening the game has sold advertising time to a competitor, such as Castrol. In Britain, such situations have been a sore point, but it is exceptional nowadays to find any sports performer appearing on television who is not adorned with at least one brand name or logo on his or her clothing. In a sense, this flies in the face of the BBC's historical strictures against commercialism, which must once have been a source of frustration for potential advertisers chasing disposable income in Britain.

Tobacco companies out of necessity contrived an effective way to advertise on the BBC when they began to sponsor major televised sports events and attach brand names to the tournaments, like the John Player Cup and the Benson and Hedges Trophy. This was brought about principally by the British government's banning of cigarette commercials on television in 1965. Sports sponsorship was worth less than £1 million in 1966; by 1976 it was £16 million and television, realizing its conventions were being flouted, refused to show any further tobacco-sponsored events. Other sponsors of major sports events continued to enjoy coverage by the BBC.

Television brokers sport in the sense that it sells events to advertising agencies, having already bought the right to televise. The difference between outlay and income keeps the relationship going. An additional beauty of the relationship is that, from the 1960s, television has been able to justify charging more for advertising spots simply by pointing to the spiraling ratings. But, is it a straightforward as that? W. M. Leonard quotes William MacPhail, who, on his appointment as director of CBS Sports, said: "Sports is a bad investment, generally speaking. The network needs it for prestige, for image . . . The rights have gotten so costly that we do sports as a public service rather than a profit-maker. We're doing great if we break even" (1988: 437). The statement may not have the ring of truth to it, but there is at least some proof that the halcyon days are over for television and that the patterns of the past thirty years or so may be breaking.

BSkyB's seemingly boundless generosity in securing exclusive "live" rights to British Premier League soccer reflects the satellite's confidence in the consumers' desire for sport. It made no bones about the fact that it intended to use sport as a lever for promoting subscriptions, which were ailing in 1992. BSkyB would surely concur with the view of an ESPN executive who, at the 1980 launch of the USA's first 24-hour, all-sports cable announced: "We believe the appetite for sports in this country is 'insatiable'" (quoted in McChesney, 1989: 65).

It is a view endorsed by academic writers such as Whannel, who argued that "if sport gains a lot of airtime . . . it will almost by definition get a large mixed audience" (1992: 196). Exposure is a "major determinant." Most of the evidence backs up this type of claim; but, there are examples of fools rushing in, assuming the audience is completely manipulable. Witness, for example, the major misjudgement made by ABC in conjunction with the USA cable network and the NFL, when they launched the obviously contrived World League of American Football which featured North American players temporarily drafted to such incongruous places as Barcelona and Frankfurt just to give the impression of a global league. In 1992, after two undistinguished seasons with little interest from US viewers, a moratorium was announced. (A revamped version started in 1994.)

In Britain, snooker's popularity sunk as abruptly as a pink ball into the corner pocket after its initial surge with the advent of color television in 1969. The game was rather meaningless in black-and-white, of course. As a postscript to this, an attempt in the early 1990s to revive snooker's televisual fortunes involved a "race against the clock" snooker game in which players tried to pot as many colors as possible in a limited timeframe.

There are signs elsewhere that the saturation point ESPN once thought unreachable may be nearer than ever. Consider first how much sport was on US television in 1992: end to end, about 75-days' worth (1,800 hours) on network, plus many more times that amount on cables and an unknown quantity on regional independent stations. To listen to the networks themselves, the same sports they have so vigorously featured from the 1960s are beginning to become an encumbrance.

After a couple of decades of profitably televising sports, the three US networks suffered a reverse in 1985, when advertising revenue failed to match outlay for NFL games and the three US networks lost $45 million collectively. This presaged further setbacks, particularly in the other national game, baseball: ABC's primetime ratings for regular season games ranged from 8.7 to 9.5 in the late 1980s; entertainment shows dipping below a 15 rating risk cancellation. The network cut back drastically on the number of games televised to avoid losses. Regular season games are a different creature to the climactic end-of-season World Series and the apparent slump in general interest did not deter

CBS from paying $1.1 billion for the exclusive rights to show the jewels of major league baseball for a four-year period starting 1990. The cost was about 25 per cent more than the previous contract for the games, shared by ABC and NBC. Such a high price, coming after NBC had bid a comparatively paltry $400 million for the 1992 Summer Olympics, indicated the lengths to which networks would go to wrench prestige programming from competitors.

But the scale of the deal doomed it from the start: television viewing figures for baseball had been falling since 1978, so advertising revenue was never likely to cover the cost. The only way the deal could have gone into the black for CBS was if all the best-of-seven-games series went to sixth and seventh games. Then, between 40–50 per cent of all US homes typically tune in and advertisers clamor to buy time.

In the event, the 1990 series was concluded in only four games but CBS was prepared to absorb losses in the expectation that it could use the World Series to include October promotions for its primetime shows in the crucial fall/autumn season, from which ratings are extrapolated. CBS effectively wanted to use sport as an instrument for generating interest in future entertainment programs. The deal meant that each baseball team started the 1990 season with about $10 million in its coffers before a single ticket had been sold. CBS measured its loss in nine figures, despite the 1991 and 1992 series' going to seven games. It did not attempt to renew its contract in 1993, when ABC and NBC stepped in with a joint venture. Even ESPN had to buy its way out of a $100 million yearly contract with major league baseball after a series of punishing losses estimated at $36 million per year in the 1990–92 period.

In the same period, American football's televisual fortunes were also slipping. NBC paid $752 million for four years of nonexclusive NFL games, the lowest outlay of the three main networks among whom the games are apportioned (ABC paid $900 million, CBS paid $1.06 billion). Having lost $100 million overall, $40 million in the 1992/93 season alone, NBC saved its financial face only by having been allocated the final Super Bowl game. It charged $850,000 per 30-second commercial spot, anticipating 56 units that would yield $45.9 million, a figure reduced to $40 million after ad agency commissions. The network's profit derived from the $6–10 million earned from spots in the 150 minutes of pregame build-up and postgame analysis, plus commercial fees from NBC-owned stations. No other television program in the world can consistently demand anything close to the Super Bowl commercial price, of course; it gathers almost 120 million US viewers to their sets. NBC in 1993 sold its commercial time with ease. Not so in the previous year when CBS sold its final 30 seconds only 24 hours before game time. The kinds of factors that affect this are competition from rival networks and which teams appear in the game.

Clearly, any event that can gross nearly $46 million in three hours is an exceptional commodity. There would be no rationality in tv networks releasing it to ppv. Yet it has become, as *New York Times* writer Richard Sandomir put it, "like a luscious crème brûlée after a long dyspeptic dinner" (January 26 1993). Take away the desert and all you have left is the kind of bellyache that may make certain sports – the expensive ones – less attractive in the future. There may be a whiff of gamesmanship about television's whining. In his *Baseball and Billions*, Andrew Zimbalist remarked cynically: "The [CBS] network's sudden diffidence might arouse some suspicion about whether it is engaging in a public relations game in a bid for smaller contracts the next time around" (1992: 160). Zimbalist scrutinized the figures and, while finding that the CBS baseball losses were probably not nearly as colossal ($170 million and $190 million from all sports) as it claimed, projected that a prudent sports executive should expect less tv money in the future.

If the networks scaled down their bids, the league would surely consider alternative outlets, ppv being the most compatible. The die may already be cast in Britain with the BBC relinquishing its once unrivaled supremacy in sport and ITV having to content itself with minority-interest events. Cost–benefit calculations may suggest in the future, sports programs will lose viability. Sport is no longer a cheap production number that draws good audience figures. Production has become more elaborate and expensive. The costs of rights have risen as more bidders have entered the fray. Sport may once have been the goose that lays the golden eggs, but now it is a grouchy cock that needs to be cosseted before dispensing its favors.

The question arises of whether sports could actually function without some kind of televisual outlet, whether it be regular or ppv transmission. A short answer is: Yes*. The * in this instance means that: the sport involved would diminish in popularity and adjust to existing on decreased revenue. Television has altered the structure and content of many sports to make them more tv-user-friendly, but it has also changed the very nature of the audience's relation with sport. First, it has made many sports widely accessible to national and international audiences. McChesney observed how: "In the early 1950s, pro football was a minor attraction, relative to baseball and the college game" (1989: 62). In the 1990s, it was not only the most popular sport in the States, but had audiences in every corner of the globe, thanks solely to television. It by far outstripped baseball and college football, which had also gained huge followings. Public fascination with certain sports has come about as a result of their availability.

While Whannel's point about sheer exposure guaranteeing viewing figures may not hold good for all situations, it is good for a great many. Television has elevated interest in sometimes obscure sports, like snooker or gymnastics. It seems unreasonable to suggest it could not reverse the process by pulling the plugs on some sports. Major sports will have learned lessons in how to package and present their product and could no doubt venture into ppv or some ancillary service independent of the mass media corporations (which they may well do, regardless). If they do not, a decline in general popularity will be certain. Sports are driven by much the same commercial imperatives as television and, if, as recent evidence indicates, there is a strain in the relationship, then those sports with resources enough to go it alone will do so.

made-to-measure

The first uncertain forays of television into sport may have yielded a fairly static recording of events. But, as television improved its technology and techniques, it was able to combine documentary accuracy with fast tension worthy of the most thrill-packed adventure series. The high-gloss presentations had analyses of slow-motion replays, and frozen moments, knowledgeable commentaries-cum-evaluations and detailed close-ups that captured facial – and sometimes verbal – expressions that attending fans could never pick up. Around the activity, tv came to edit events down to lean action and pad out with previews, postscripts and all sorts of information designed to make viewing from home a more enriching experience. In contrast to the swirl of tv coverage, attendance must have seemed quite pedestrian. The freshness and appeal of tv sports were undeniable and sport had no magic strong enough to resist it. It would be a mistake to think that television still just reports sport, if it ever did.

Television's presence in sport is invasive enough to convince some writers, like John Goldlust, that it actually determines the organization and administration of sports. In his book *Playing for Keeps*, he advances the view that tv's calculated intervention has been a "critical and possibly decisive factor" affecting the overall development of sport (1988: 164).

Goldlust cites the crisis of cricket in the 1970s as an illustration of his point. In 1976, one of Australia's major commercial networks chaired by Kerry Packer, offered the Australian Cricket Board (ACB) a deal for the exclusive rights to screen Australian cricket for five years. The offer was refused, so Packer decided to run his own tournament called World Series Cricket, for which he secured the services of 35 international star players. The "rebel" competition was networked by Packer's own Nine Channel, but in a way that offended traditionalists. It was not simply that players were asked to wear brightly colored uniforms (as opposed to "whites") and play under floodlights with a yellow ball; but the monitoring techniques intruded so as to make each match observable (eight cameras were employed per game) and audible (microphones were sensitive enough to pick up players' often blasphemous remarks). Its single-day format was, as Goldlust put it, "unabashedly spectator oriented, geared towards providing entertainment, tight finishes, big hitting and aggressive play . . . ideally suited for television" (1988: 163).

The cricket that Packer televised was barely recognizable as the nineteenth-century pursuit of gentlemen, but people watched it. After a nervous first season, viewing figures and, interestingly, attendances rose, enabling the Nine Channel to attract more advertisers. While the established cricket organizations, including England's MCC, opposed the wanton commercialism they capitulated after legal pressure from Packer whose marketing subsidiary PBL Sports, in 1979, signed a ten-year contract to organize the sponsorship of official cricket. Packer's attempt to capture exclusive broadcasting rights succeeded and, by the mid-1980s, he had virtually taken control of Australian cricket. Crowds continued to attend and, more importantly, more viewers watched on television. The players earned more money, the organizing bodies took a substantial fee for the rights and the network increased its advertising revenue by selling more commercial time in the normally quiet summer season. The arrangement suited everyone except those who wished to see cricket as having more than a faint resemblance to the game that was once played with a straight bat and a stiff upper lip. To this group, cricket *pace* Packer was short, violent and battered to distortion.

In contrast, there have been very occasional instances of sports that seem to have been plucked from their natural environs and boldly reconstructed without too much damage to their integrity. Darts, a game traditionally played over a few beers in smoky British pubs, was transferred intact to the small screen, as was gymnastics, which enjoyed a bonanza following the 1972 Olympics yet made no modifications to its context or format. Olga Korbut, of the Soviet Union, became the improbable epitome of ABC's "thrill and agony" slogan, leaping euphorically at every triumph, dissolving into tears when setbacks threatened.

The gymnastics event was more spontaneous, surprising and, therefore, enthralling than anything even Roone Arledge could have dreamt up. Television viewers were infatuated by Korbut's gentle play at the aesthetic borders between sport and art. It was a case of a virginal sport – and gymnastics was virginal in more ways than one, featuring many fresh-faced young cherubs – showcased almost by accident, yet producing a visual extravaganza that captured the imagination. Television's relationship with sport has thrown up very few cases of "natural" sports unaffected by the stare of the cameras. A miscellany of state-of-the-art devices have since framed gymnastics in new and interesting ways. But, it was the plain-as-a-pikestaff recordings of the Korbut Olympics that made gymnastics a discovery rather than an artifice. It remains an exception.

This may be saddening for those who mourn the days when sport was really "sport," but, as Jhally pointed out, "this seems to imply that before the influence of the media, there was something that was pure sports" (1989: 80). Roone Arledge has often defended his network's use of synthetic sports by reminding critics that sports were not delivered by god, rules inscribed on tablets of stone. They are completely artificial contests designed purely to challenge ourselves in what Arledge calls "preconceived settings." Teams of firefighters competing over how many buckets of water they can carry from point A to point Z is no more or less of a pure sport than eleven men trying to move an inflated leather ball in the opposite direction to another eleven men. We snicker at one, yet clamor to see the other. The comparison reminds us that one of the oldest preoccupations in the world is that of challenge: attempting to surmount obstacles, natural or artificial, has provided us with endless episodes of triumph or folly and, sometimes, disaster. Where the challenges do not exist, we make them to measure. And, in this sense, television has not so much transformed sports as extended and reshaped them. The change is not always as dramatic as many writers seem to think: over the past fifty years, there has been a drip-by-drip titration, some sports gradually moving from one state to another. Sports have always been evolving, anyway. Rules, duration, start times, methods of evaluation, etc., have been changing since the mid-nineteenth century, when loose-knit activities began to resemble what we now recognize as sports. Television has imposed change rather than wait for it to happen. And the audience has responded.

Sport in the raw is insufficient for the tv viewer: he or she wants it packaged and presented, rather like any other commodity. After all, when viewers are asked to pay for the product, as increasingly seems to be the case, they want more than roving-eye-style presentation; as, for example, the US cable C-Span covers court hearings, just flipping on the camera and letting the action speak for itself. In sports, the action does not speak for itself: it needs the direction and narration that produce drama.

There is now a warrantable second generation of people reared on televised sports, the kind of people who prefer waiting for videos to going to the movies and playing computer games at home rather than playing ball in the park. Attendance at sports events must seem terribly one dimensional to them. The tension in the atmosphere of a stadium or arena can never be even remotely approximated by watching at home, of course. Yet, one can almost hear the groans: "Where are the captions and statistics?" "I missed that piece of action; how about the replay?" "I'd like to see that from a different angle or slowed down, or even just explained to me by an erudite commentator."

Expectations and perceptions of sport have changed, as have patterns of viewing. Television has encouraged us to see the play differently. We may be watching the same piece of action as our grandparents, but we will see and read it differently. We are also likely to watch more of it, if only because of the volume on the air, or through the cables. The need for diligence has all but disappeared. Television's facilities for replays allows us to relax our concentration. Missing a goal, a touchdown, a hole-in-one, or an ace is not a disaster when the same piece of action can be reviewed several times over and from different vantage points. This, plus the comments, summaries and statistics that accompany the action, encourages an analytical posture. The viewer sits as an argus, assimilating all manner of information, visual and audial, on the action. One hesitates before suggesting it, but pre- and post-event analyses have all but supplanted the actual competition. Certainly, there is more time spent chewing the bread than the meat in the sandwich. Analyzing has become an integral part of televised sport and the better-informed viewers cast a more clinical eye today than ever before. The irony is that they can do so with less play-by-play concentration on the activity itself.

For television, sport might be nearing obsolescence: its price might assure it of new media in the future. But, in the golden years of the 1960s and 1970s, sport was as valuable a commodity as television executives could have imagined: relatively inexpensive (no salaries, or heavy production costs) and very watchable, as viewing figures attested. It was a dream match. Viewers seemed to warm to any activity that was vaguely competitive. In another book, *Making Sense of Sport*, I have argued that the basic impulse underlying the fascination with competition is primeval in origin. It dates back to the attempts to recreate artificially the hunting once practiced by our ancestors. We no longer need to hunt, of course, but we crave the tension and excitement that accompanied it. Sports express our efforts to introduce those emotions into otherwise bureaucratized predictable lives. In transferring these efforts to television, sport acquired all sorts of new dimensions, heightened the intensity and enhanced the drama of the contest. Critics would scoff and respond that we are simply gullible, with neither the wit nor wisdom to see through television's manipulations. Such a view gains plausibility when set against a background of competing log choppers and racing firefighters. Activities like these are only devices to keep our attention; some work, some do not. But maybe the reason we watch them is not so much because we are dopes, but because we can identify with the "ancient ceremonial" of competition. Sport's global popularity has been boosted inestimably by television exposure, but there was enthusiasm for smaller scale competition before tv and, even with it, people are prepared to spend small fortunes to witness big events firsthand.

To be sure, sport has been a splendidly serviceable instrument, bringing viewers to their tv sets and keeping their focus fixed, sometimes for hours at a stretch, while commercials prime their shopping sensibilities. But sport's ability to do this, though generously augmented by television, is based on something more than mere manipulation. The reason why sport has been and is used so fulsomely by television's advertisers is because viewers voluntarily submit themselves to becoming involved. Sports are products of an imagination ingenious enough to create artificial situations that human evolution has rendered irrelevant. Once created, they seem to exert a control and power of their own, eliciting in audiences and participants a pleasurable thrill that encapsulates the "rush" of a hunt, yet carries few, if any, of the attendant risks.

This is expressed in contemporary society's encouragement of individual and group attempts to measure themselves against others. Television has changed the shape of the framework in which the competition takes place; it has also sharpened spectators' perceptions of what elements go into the competition. But it has not created the underlying impulse that feeds enthusiasm for sports. Humans are not just like hockey pucks, banged around by factors outside their control. Certainly, there is a complementarity between the way in which sport is organized and the functions it fulfills for television on the one hand, and the requirements of consumerism on the other. Yet to accentuate this, at the same time devaluing sport and castigating television, means that we miss completely the human activity that makes this complementarity possible. The rise of television has been twinned with the growth of organized sports.

We are hard pressed to find a rival activity that unerringly fascinates viewers as much as sport has over the past decades; but crime comes close. Television has exploited and dramatized crime as thoroughly as it has sport. Next, we will discover how and, perhaps more relevantly, why.

chapter ten

arresting viewing

crimes that always pay

"Who says that crime doesn't pay?" asks actor John Glover, staring out from the television screen at the close of an episode of NBC's *Crime and Punishment*. He explains how he has escaped to Brazil with $17 million worth of jewels from a heist he has schemed. His accomplices were captured but, "they're pros; they know the rules." The gangleader adds that, in contrast to them, he has "hot and cold running servants." The testimony he gives to his offscreen interviewer (a sort of surrogate for viewers) works as a sharp counterpoint to the moral messages of many detective series. Glover's bright eyes and cool, alleycat smile suggest satisfaction with a good job well done. He signifies success. Time was when successful criminals were a rarity. Law enforcement on television typically laid out its stories as flat as a "Clue" game board. In shows like *Perry Mason* and *Columbo* – the latter still being produced – crimes were committed, perpetrators were caught and brought to book; and viewers went to bed in no doubt about who wins when good and evil clash.

In the 1990s, plots have crinkles in them. Ambiguity has rumpled contemporary crime shows. Colonel Mustard might be as guilty as sin, but he will sometimes get away with murder; or even let Miss Scarlet take the rap for him. Series like *Homicide: Life on the Street*, *Law and Order* and the BBC's *Between the Lines* did not show crime detection as a boardgame. Older simplifications were replaced by complexity: the good lie and deceive almost as often as the bad, deals are done instead of justice being served, culprits do not always get caught. Corporate or white-collar crimes may not arouse public anxieties as much as crimes against the person. But, in the newer shows, there is an attempt to show that crimes of the rich and powerful have human consequences too. A property developer illegally uses cheap construction products and, years later, an office block collapses killing dozens of people. A black youth is killed on the street as an indirect result of a drugs deal that originates in the luxurious villa of a Colombian government bureaucrat.

It took cop shows the best part of 40 years to mature. Flat parables of good and evil dominated North American and British crime drama until the 1990s. Even now, one could argue that in numerical terms, the morally clear shows remain the majority. Ambivalent drama though has effectively redefined the genre, often using stories that bear close resemblance to real events. If crime shows were once about the continual revalidation of the criminal justice system, it could be argued that many of today's shows ask questions of that same system. Why did this change come about? Answering this implicates us in a baser question: why were the flatter programs so incredibly popular in the first place? After all, they were never plausible: week after week, criminals would be caught and loose ends neatly tied up. Even a cursory glance at a daily newspaper tells the reader that this is a hopelessly inaccurate reflection of what really happens.

Yet, crime drama regularly occupies 20 per cent of program time and commands high ratings, not to mention viewer loyalty. The aforementioned *Perry Mason*, for example, first aired for CBS in 1957, and *Columbo* started life in 1968 as an NBC pilot *Prescription: Murder*. These two dinosaurs are exceptionally robust; turnover usually accounts for most cop shows within a few years. But, the genre of which they are part beats that of soaps in terms of longevity. While moods and tastes have shifted over the decades, crime drama has been television's *terra firma*. Explaining this presents us with a riddle as brain-teasing as any Miss Marple or Ellery Queen mystery. We will proceed like any good detective, first by examining the evidence.

opening the cases

Crime, particularly mysterious and violent crime, fascinates us. We have known this at least since the publication in 1871 of Wilkie Collins' *The Moonstone*, conventionally regarded as the first detective mystery novel. In the years since, crime fiction has established and maintained itself as a popular genre, perhaps unrivaled by any other. Crime titles today account for at least 10 per cent of all paperbacks and there are no signs that interest is abating. A miscellany of forms and styles is collected under the crime rubric: whodunits, procedurals, thrillers and pathologists' memoirs are among the subgenres. Some aspect of the appeal surely lies in the fact that it is about the nearest fiction gets to nonfiction.

Often, the plots are plucked from reality and fashioned into fiction with only minor changes. Even the more outrageous stories have at least some tenuous relationship with events consumers have heard of, read about or can believe in.

During the early days, it seemed almost natural that television would appropriate such a sturdy and commercially successful genre as crime. Radio and film had exploited this. One British film, *The Blue Lamp* released in 1950, was the inspiration for BBC's first major crime series *Dixon of Dock Green*. The London police constable George Dixon had been shot and killed twenty minutes into the movie, but this small fact was conveniently glossed over when the resurrection took place in 1956. Dixon was the archetypal British bobby: homely, principled and reassuringly ordinary. The cases he dealt with featured minor offenses, like post office robberies or burglary. Truncheons (batons) were occasionally needed to restore order, rarely guns. Actually, almost nothing happened in Dixon's world. The mundane adventures were hardly even leavened by slam-bang action. For the most part, the boys in blue wandered about London's environs hunting for lost dogs or stolen bicycles. The Britain Dixon policed was a country shrugging off the austerity of the postwar period, its population enjoying an economic boom that brought the tonic of full employment and soaring wages. Dixon and his colleagues were partners with the public; consensual policing was the order of the day.

As if to emphasize this, Dixon himself would open each show directly facing the camera and tipping his helmet in mock subservience. "Evening, all," he would greet tv audiences. To close, he would offer a tidy summary with some *bon mots* to encourage the belief that justice is always served, come what may. This sort of condescending address seemed horribly out of place in the 1960s and, by the 1970s, the whole series had become tiresome and irrelevant. Doubts over the consensus portrayed by the series turned to cynicism and, eventually, Dixon and co. had become caricatures of the bygone age. The show was taken off air in 1974 after a remarkable run of eighteen years.

Like *Dixon*, the US show *Dragnet* transferred from another medium, this time radio. The majority of early US crime shows were taken from successful radio series. Also like *Dixon*, *Dragnet* indulged in moralizing. "This is the city," sergeant Joe Friday monotoned over the opening titles. "Los Angeles, California. I work here. I carry a badge." Making sure the audience understood that the good guys always win in life as well as on the screen, the series announced that its plots were taken from police cases, only "the names have been changed to protect the innocent." Each show concluded like *Dixon*, with a report on how the culprits were sentenced. The NBC television series began in 1952, spun off *Badge 714* the following year, disappeared in 1959, only to return as *Dragnet '67*. The last television production was a feature-length episode broadcast in 1969. Its life, like that of *Dixon* was eighteen years. Apart from similarities in narration and posturing, the two shows were poles apart. Whereas Dixon depicted a relatively calm, almost tranquil London, disturbed but rarely menaced by miscreants, *Dragnet* showed LA as nasty, and alive with criminal intent. The show did not neglect the mundane aspects of detection, but kept the action rolling. British viewers, who had access to both shows, were no doubt thrilled by the dangers of LA, but glad to be secure at home, where threats could always be handled inside the community.

Dragnet clones were too numerous to mention. Even today, some detective series show the hallmarks of the early show. *The Untouchables*, a period series about FBI attempts to crack down on Chicago's Mafia, started in 1959, and stuck to a very similar pattern. Offense is committed; chase takes place; arrests are made. This type of formula proved resistant to change. Among the deviant strains was the mystery thriller, often featuring private investigators who sometimes straddled a shadowline between the police and criminals. The classic model for this was, of course, Sherlock Holmes. Conan Doyle's sleuth has inspired television portrayals from 1954, with a US series featuring Ronald Howard, to the 1990s and Granada's show with Jeremy Brett.

The private investigator (pi) series typically de-emphasized thrills and spills in favor of intrigue, hoping to absorb the viewers, tantalize them with clues and tempt them into guessing culprits incorrectly. Ellery Queen, like Holmes, came from the pages of literature. He too was an intellectual magnifying glass carrier with a penchant for detail. The first television adaptation came in 1950. Seven series and seven different lead actors later, the character seemed exhausted and ready to hand over the glass to the likes of Hercule Poirot and Jessica of *Murder, She Wrote*, who continued to reveal who done it, how it was done, with what and why.

Attempts to bridge the two subgenres and combine active detection with thoughtful mystery have been hit-and-miss affairs. Britain bought a steady series of successful North American shows in the later 1950s and 1960s, including *77 Sunset Strip* and *Hawaiian Eye*, both centering on detective agencies in parts of the world never visited by rain and cold weather. The former, which stopped production in 1964, had a direct line to teenagers in the form of "Kooky," a valet parking attendant intended to be on the fringes of the show, who cultivated a devoted following with his "hip" language ("buzzed by germsville" = being ill) and tendency to comb his well-greased hair at every occasion. The show's ratings dropped when he left and never recovered, even when he returned as a licensed pi.

These two, along with many other, not so successful variants, were less cerebral than the mysteries and less visceral than the cops and robbers programs. But, they were more visual than either: landscapes of sunbaked Hollywood and Honolulu were the backgrounds for average plots and ritualized action. Perhaps the forces of wish-fulfillment were at work in promoting the shows in places like Detroit or Glasgow. If so, they were also instrumental in the success of *The Rockford Files*, *Magnum pi* and *Hawaii Five-O*, all strangers to bad weather. *Strip*, *Eye* and their sibling *Surfside Six* were moldbreaking in their own way. Their cinematography was bright, their characters radiated good health, and their plots were lightened with humor. This contrasted with the darker, heavier, sometimes even dolorous shows that preceded them. An obvious appeal to youth in a period when young people were opening what was then called the generation gap was timely. Music and fashion were two major items that young people used to define themselves, and the detective shows had plenty of both. The *Strip* theme became a successful record, as did that of another cop show, *Peter Gunn*, an earnest series about an LA detective with a liking for jazz.

Climactic courtroom drama has long been a virtual guarantee of box office success for films. No matter if we have to endure telegraphed dialogue and acting for three-quarters of a movie; a few unexpected revelations in front of the jury at the end and we go home satisfied. The formula was taken by television, adjusted minimally to accommodate some perfunctory detective work and turned into *Perry Mason*. Principal actor Raymond Burr periodically left the show, but always returned to his most bankable role. Others like *The Grand Jury* and *Behind Closed Doors*, tried to repeat the formula, but without even coming close to Perry Mason's success. The show remains something of a phenomenon among detective series. The spell of the courtroom remains unbroken, as *LA Law* and *Civil Wars* attest.

The 1960s emphasis on detection, as opposed to policing, became evident in a number of British shows also. Detectives, plainclothes or uniformed, institutional or private, came to the fore in several shows. A half-hour show syndicated in the States as *Scotland Yard*, was a sort of harbinger. It allowed the viewer to trace the course of detection, aided by narrator Edgar Lustgarten, a self-appointed criminologist. *No Hiding*

Place was another of the many series revolving around Scotland Yard. An exception was *Z Cars*, which underwent several mutations during its sixteen-year run from 1962, without ever losing the earthy feel of the northwest of England. The title referred to the patrol cars which were then replacing the beat. The popularity of detection drama from the US inclined *Z Cars* towards featuring more and longer investigations. It grew to an hour format, then spun off series which concentrated solely on detection, as the title of one, *Softly Softly*, suggests. A central and, in many ways, symbolic character in these shows was Charlie, later Charles Barlowe. Changes in his rank and accent were tracked, his upward social mobility a metaphor for a nation climbing towards affluence and the status it typically brings.

Britain's series relied on the documentary traditions of British cinema in the 1930s. They were grainy and unglamorous; part of their effort was to remain plausible, in contrast to their US counterparts whose exotic locations and fanciful plots made them fantasies rather than believable accounts.

In 1974, Euston Films produced a show for Independent Television that was to change the direction of British detective shows. *The Sweeney* was based on the exploits of two members of the London Metropolitan Police's Flying Squad, neither of whom had much respect for authority, or regard for procedural rules. Jack Regan and George Carter operated on the assumption that ends always justified means. Regan, in particular, came straight from an American school that was well-established by the mid-1970s: the maverick cop, who did things his way. Many of these cops were abstracted from movies. *McCloud*, for instance, could have ridden his horse straight out of *Coogan's Bluff*, which also featured a cowboy-style detective adrift in the big city. Detectives Columbo, Kojak, and Madigan also fell into the category. But, while the US characters were always exaggerations, Regan strove for authenticity. He was an unswerving and, possibly, dangerous cop who pulled out all the stops to secure a conviction. *The Sweeney* gave him plots often drawn from newspaper stories and fictional criminals who closely resembled real ones.

Regan habitually got drunk; he womanized; and, at one point, ended up behind bars under suspicion of corruption. The relentlessness with which he pursued his prey often bordered on obsession. There was more than a hint of malice in his character.

Also in 1974, a new character in the maverick mold arrived on US screens. Jim Rockford was a pi living in a mobile home on Malibu Beach. Like Regan, he despised bureaucracy and police hierarchy.

Frequently, he found himself at odds with the LAPD as well as lawbreakers. Not that the two were entirely separable: Rockford often ran into corruption, bribery and graft in the force. *The Rockford Files* was the creation of producers Roy Huggins and Stephen Cannell and as Richard Meyers explained in his book *TV Detectives*: "The initial idea was that Rockford would take on cases the police had closed . . . when the cops closed their files Rockford reopened them" (1981: 213). Jim Rockford, unlike Regan, was not a loose cannon. An ex-cop who had served time in prison, he avoided violence whenever possible, choosing the most expedient method of closing his case. All he wanted was his $200 a day fee and a quiet life, which, of course, he never got. The series ran until 1980, but the timelessness of its themes ensured that it still runs today – as does *The Sweeney*.

critical realism

In *The Sweeney* and *The Rockford Files*, we find a distinct movement away from what we might call the classical crime show, in which the salient features included: restraint; reason; simplicity; attention to due process; respect for tradition; commitment to justice and fairness; and a clear and severe division between good and evil. The term referring to realistic fiction which criticized aspects of society between 1875 and 1920 was critical realism, one American school of which was known as "the muckrakers." Regan and Rockford were like muckrakers: their work involved them in solving crimes, but also in exposing dishonest methods and unscrupulous motives in big business, the police force and, sometimes, in politics. Yet, beyond all this, both shows presented a vision of a criminal justice system that might have a few rotten apples, but which was basically fine. Another less successful series bravely suggested that a least one police department was entirely rotten.

Emboldened by the success of Rockford, Huggins and Cannell, in 1976, ventured further along the critical path with *City of Angels*, which was effectively an extension of Roman Polanski's 1974 movie *Chinatown*, in which the Philip Marlowe replica Jake Geddes burrows into Southern California's political system in the 1930s. Huggins and Cannell modeled their pi on Geddes, even using his first name. Jake Axminster was a straightish pi in a world of cops so bent they could collar people around corners. Each episode started with a voiceover explaining that the LAPD might now be considered one of the least corrupt police forces, "but it wasn't always that way." There was never a suggestion that the corruption found by Axminster was isolated or aberrant: it was integrally part of the system. Nor did this show conclude with homilies from the hero. Perpetrators of crime were often politicians, business executives or police officials eager to put private gain before public good.

The plausible recreation of place and period, plus the critical cutting edge augured well for the series. Yet it flopped after a single season. Setting the show in the 1930s seemed a clever device; but the messages were too clear for comfort. The city dissected was analogous to any big city, any time. *Law and Order*, a four-part BBC drama set in London, showed policing to be even more corrupt than *City of Angels*. The fact that it was contemporary and written by an ex-police officer, G. F. Newman, gave it added authenticity. Protests from the police and controversy followed its screening and it was buried.

In terms of muckraking, *Lou Grant* rivaled *City of Angels*. It lasted longer, ending in 1982 after seven years. The series was not about crime *per se*, though the crimes of the rich and powerful frequently featured in the scripts, all of which involved a journalist, played by Ed Asner, whose own liberal politics made it possible for viewers to conflate the role and the man. This worked to the show's advantage in early years, but, in the 1980s, the suspicion grew that Grant's/Asner's crusades were becoming an embarrassment to CBS, especially after he publicly presented a check for $25,000 for medical aid to El Salvador. Todd Gitlin revealed how a slip in ratings for *Lou Grant* was the given reason for its cancellation; but, compared to other shows, its ratings were still quite respectable (1985). As *Lou Grant* closed, the series conventionally regarded as its logical successor began to build its considerable following. While *Hill Street Blues* had a similar humanism and attention to detail, its subversive qualities were in its presentation rather than content, which was rarely political in an overt way.

Hill Street Blues explored the anima and personae of policing, allowing a fast-moving camera to document public lives, but never neglecting to show the faltering individuals behind the badge. It abandoned linear plots and discrete episodes, opting instead for multiple themes, and an open, almost soap operatic framing device. It offered sober accounts of policing enlivened by the occasional dramatic incident. But, for all its agitated semi-documentary style, it sets its sights too low to be considered critical, certainly in the 1980s. It involved the viewer in the particulars of crime and justice, never the generalities.

Whereas Hill Street's cops traveled in patrol cars, the *Miami Vice* detectives sped around in a gleaming black Ferrari. It was part of their cover: Crockett and Tubbs spent most of their time pursuing major drug dealers, usually ignoring all danger signs and dividing lines between cops and criminals. Often, they would find themselves in the art-deco lairs of drug barons, dressed in Hugo Boss outfits and bearing beatific grins as they sampled the "merch." Subtler themes on police corruption and conflicting loyalties were introduced, but usually drowned out by the incessant rock music that gave the show the atmosphere of an elongated music video.

There was much more to it than that; certainly in the first couple of series between 1985 and 1986 when investigations typically started on the streets but moved upscale to the stratospheres of white-collar crime, corporate dealings and political graft. Crimes had no initiation or resolution: they were part of a continuing process, whose cycle could be disturbed, but not broken. The separation of heroes and villains was as provisional as a line drawn in Miami Beach sand.

And, while there was an implicit morality in *Miami Vice*, it stayed that way: the crooks were often powerful and clever enough to avoid prosecution, or important enough to be beyond suspicion.

The cogency of early series gave way to hokum when flying saucers began featuring and the plots became glib and predictable. It was almost as if the series tried to live down to its critics' expectations that it was a designer show in which style overwhelmed content. Eventually, it did. The show's producer, Michael Mann, had less success with another series *Crime Story*, which, in its own way, was as ambitious in its intentions as *Miami Vice*. Set in the 1960s, the show swung like a pendulum between a white youth's progression through the echelons of a crime syndicate and a fixated cop's attempts to bring him down. No other television crime drama had allowed the criminals to share centerstage with the cops. Hollywood has for years invested some of its most serious artistic aspirations in loathsome offenders; movies such as *Reservoir Dogs*, *Bugsy*, and *GoodFellas* demonstrated audiences' interest in the picaresque. Television has not tried to exploit the apparent attraction. *Crime Story* came nearest, but folded after two seasons in the mid-1980s.

Spurning the ravage-revenge-redemption action served up by *Crime Story* and its own *The Sweeney*, British television sought inspiration in the work of crime novelists. Stalwarts Conan Doyle and Agatha Christie were brought back into service in the 1980s and 1990s; and contemporary writers like P. D. James and Ruth Rendell were the sources of new mystery series. One of the efforts in this period was to provincialize crime. *Inspector Morse*, for instance, was based incongruously in Oxford. *Spender* operated out of Newcastle-upon-Tyne in the northeast of England. *Taggart* was a member of Glasgow's police force. The success of all three seemed to originate not from the plots or frameworks, which were classical, but from the eccentricities of the chief characters.

Morse, played by John Thaw, who was also Jack Regan in *The Sweeney*, was an unsmiling bachelor devoted to opera and classical music. He drove a red Jaguar XJ6, appreciated natural beer and could not bear the sight of blood. In one 1993 episode, "Fat Chance," he gets to vent his spleen grumpily on, among other things, denominational religion in the form of men who are determined to keep women out of the priesthood. After discovering a scandal, Morse is told by a priest: "May God forgive you." He replies: "I doubt if your God would have much truck with me; at least I hope he wouldn't." Another successful series was more regressive: *The Bill* was little more than *Z Cars* with different accents. Only in its occasional series, like *Between the Lines*, did British crime drama push against the boundaries of tradition.

In the early 1990s, three NBC series took the lustrous, cynical intentions of *Miami Vice* and gave them a matt finish. *Law and Order*, set in New York City, and *Crime and Punishment* in LA, were both creations of Dick Wolf. The critical realism of both was enhanced by their plots, which were often fictionalized versions of real cases. Justice was invariably served by a deal done by district attorneys and defendants' lawyers. Crime was seen as the product of diffuse causes. Usually, securing a conviction meant a triage: ordering a hierarchy of blame in which several perpetrators were granted impunity in order to capture one. The criminal justice system was seen as an altogether shakier piece of apparatus than that portrayed in earlier series. Viewers were always paid the compliment of having to figure out the rights and wrongs, so vague and ambiguous were the signifiers.

In a 1993 *Law and Order* episode, for instance, a crack addict is killed by her own mother. It was based on a real New York case; but the show's writers turned the actual working-class family into black bourgeoisie. The investigators learn how the addict pulled a gun on her grandmother while stealing her life's savings and that she eventually begged her mother to kill her. An African American assistant district attorney (DA) reacts to the suggestion of his peers that charges might be dropped. "Do blacks have a special right to kill their children?" he asks, adding that the coded message sent out by such a decision would be that a black girl's life does not matter.

In *Crime and Punishment*, embezzlement becomes a "business opportunity" and revenge killings become rough-hewn justice. Often, the whodunit element remains deliberately indistinct. A teenager shoots dead another in a school playground and the investigation forges causal links that lead back to a family man who legally buys a pistol for his son. Gun is sold, stolen, then traded twice, before it gets exchanged for homework. Who is to blame? The teenager squeezing the trigger, the purchaser of the gun, any one of the intervening possessors of the weapon, or all of the above? Or, the second amendment of the constitution that allows US citizens the right to bear arms?

Homicide: Life on the Street, which first aired in 1993, was another crime drama in which signifiers blew like a hailstorm. One notable episode was devoted entirely to a night-long interrogation of a black male, suspected of murdering a ten-year-old black girl in Baltimore. Two detectives, one black, one white, circle the old man, who sells fruit and vegetables for a living; they threaten, entice, cajole, at one point even appealing to his sense of decency. The long confrontation smolders with racial resentments, until the suspect explodes with a tirade against the status-seeking black detective. In the end, the old man walks free; yet nothing is resolved. The audience is denied its classical privilege of omniscience. One more unsolved case.

Homicide and the others owed police documentaries such as *Cops* and *Top Cops* at least a small debt. The latter featured handheld cameras pursuing police officers, themselves pursuing suspects. Much of the fly-on-the-wall material resembled scenes from the dramas. The lack of certainty that pervaded much of *Cops* was, of course, central to the aesthetic success of the NBC trio.

justice for nearly all

Television crime dramas are not equal opportunity employers: women, ethnic minorities and disabled persons have been underrepresented in central roles over the years. Series featuring such groups have, historically, been distinguished by the unusual casting rather than the strength of plots. In 1974, for example, NBC screened an episode of its series *Police Story*, with Angie Dickinson as a vice officer. Encouraged by a positive audience reaction, the networks spun off *Police Woman* with Dickinson reprising a similar part. The temptation to revert to type was too much for the network which capitulated to macho tendencies by thrusting Dickinson into compromising positions and showing her flesh virtually every week. Meyers noted how protests from then the growing feminist lobby forced producers to change their approach over the remainder of the show's three-year life (1981: 203).

In the same period, another show, *Get Christie Love!*, was purpose-built to capitalize on both interest in women as active, rather than passive, characters and in blacks as subjects rather than objects. *Roots*, as we have seen, had already raised the profile of blacks on television and a spate of blaxploitation movies (including *Shaft* and *Superfly*) had been good box office. *Get Christie Love!* was imitative and artificial. The tv version of John Shaft was only marginally more successful, artistically and commercially. The *Shaft* movie series became sterile when transferred to the smaller screen. The language lost its profanity, the characters their intensity and the plots their substance.

Charlie's Angels made no pretense to assist or appease the women's movement: it cast three white women in implausible roles, dropped them into fantastic situations and charged them with the responsibility of looking good for the cameras. Despite personnel changes, the series had commercial success in the USA and Britain and lasted until 1980. *Cagney and Lacey* was, in many senses, the antidote to *Charlie's Angels*, but it had a torrid time in its first two years and had to be rescued from oblivion by its committed producers, abetted by the National Organization for Women. Once established, it generated its own momentum and is still regarded as a symbolic series for women. Stereotypes were blasted and plots seemed to reflect much of what the women's movement had been insisting for years: the personal is political. In older narratives, women were the prey, the hunted; but, as the conventions of crime genre changed, so women, in the persons of the female investigators, became hunters. This became more than a simple role reversal in which victim turns aggressor. Later, it was to be a transformation in which potential victims, by becoming active and vigilant, avoid and help others avoid victimization.

Cagney and Lacey had a black colleague, who also struck at stereotypes: a mild-mannered family man, he was as straight as a die and too serious in his approach to work for some of his colleagues. Generally though, blacks were cast in the role of villains, accomplices, or sidekicks. An exception was *Paris*, which told of a black detective who moonlighted as a criminology professor. James Earl Jones played the title role. In Britain, an ambitious project called *The Chinese Detective* featured David Yip roving around London, proving he was better educated and better spoken than most of the native population. There seems to have been a niche reserved for East Asian detectives from the earliest days of television, when both British and US networks produced versions of *Charlie Chan*, a character that had been popular in books, radio and film since the 1920s.

Women and ethnic minorities heave into view in most contemporary crime series. In the age of political correctness, there is woe for any series neglecting them. In previous chapters, we have noticed how roles have become more multidimensional and, thankfully, less tokenistic. Some crime shows have invited viewers to understand the particular problems faced by such groups, yet without making the message too macroscopic. British series *The Gentle Touch* and *Juliet Bravo* both attempted this, casting women in traditionally male senior roles and observing the consequences.

A more successful illustration came with Granada's *Prime Suspect*, which first aired in Britain in 1992. In the sequel, Detective Chief Inspector Jane Tennison still feels the sting of sexism so evident among her colleagues in the original production. Now, she heads the investigation into a decomposed body of a young black woman found in a predominantly Afro-Caribbean area of London, where residents are not especially fond of the police. Nobody is reduced to type. And sexuality defies expectation and categorization. In the opening scene, Tennison questions a black male about a reported rape. He talks insinuatingly about how "some whites like it rough" and she responds that the thought of a woman's being humiliated does not turn her on. The confrontation intrigues, only to dupe the viewer: for the whole scene is revealed to be part of a police seminar on rape. A second surprise quickly follows as Tennison and the interviewee, who is really a police detective, are seen together again, this time *in flagrante*. "I hope I can rely on you to be discrete," Tennison tells her lover. He coldly warns her: "I don't like being treated as a black stud." The tensions of their staged encounter resurface and take on new aspects when he is assigned to her case simply because he is black; she begins to boss him around, neglecting the fact that the tokenistic nature of his appointment closely parallels her own as a woman.

Tennison is a "unique figment of popular culture:" a figure who, as Patricia Craig and Mary Cadogan put it in their book *The Lady Investigates*: "stands out as the most economical, the most striking and the most agreeable embodiment of two qualities often disallowed for women in the past: the power of action and practical intelligence" (1986: 245). It is interesting that those very qualities have been accorded to a number of fictional detectives who have been in some way disabled.

The most celebrated of these was *Ironside*, the paraplegic investigator played by Raymond Burr, in his *inter regnum* between Perry Mason series. The show was first shown in 1967. Four years later, a blind martial artist detective named *Longstreet* appeared. As early as 1955, a sight-impaired *Colonel March of the Yard*, played by Boris Karloff, was produced in Britain and syndicated in the States. Another Yard detective, this time with only one arm, *Saber of London* formed the basis of a series which ran between 1957 and 1959.

In the 1990s, *Reasonable Doubts* ushered in Marlee Matlin, herself deaf, as a district attorney with a male investigator who is adept at sign language. The series was challenging without ever becoming pedagogical.

Lest I be accused of an "-ism" myself, let me note the virtual absence of elderly detectives from the genre. Joan Hickson played Miss Marple into her eighties. The Agatha Christie character showed she could still run rings around police officers half (or a third of) her age. In the early 1970s, when British and US networks were flushed with the success of "odd cops" such as *Cannon*, who was overweight, *Sarge*, who was a priest, and *Randall and Hopkirk (Deceased)*, the latter of whom was a ghost, an aged cop seemed an almost natural complement.

Barnaby Jones premiered in 1973: it featured Buddy Ebsen as a retired police officer who is drawn back into the fray. It shot to the top of the US ratings in its first season.

Television crime drama is something like the precinct in *Hill Street Blues*, a human menagerie where ladies of the night jostle with bums, double-breasted attorneys trade verbal blows with uniformed officers and an assortment of different social types clatter together. Crime drama, as my brief and far from comprehensive history tells us, is as varied a genre as one can imagine. Some shows are electrifying, others absorbing, still others plain silly. For the most part, they are gratifying. Otherwise, why so many for so long with no sign of a demise?

Many see the crime drama taking over from the western. But the western's big country landscapes were ill-suited to the small screen and, in any case, the civil rights movement put a stop to the depiction of Native Americans as villains. Crime drama had no comparable problem. Its villains could come from any social group and the tight action images and suspense it purveyed were right for a twenty-odd-inch screen. The appeal of the western to movie audiences, especially Americans, is understandable: its origins lie in Anglo-Saxons' abundant appetite for empirical proof of their superiority over the natural inhabitants of the land they occupied. Television cop shows may have similarly reassuring effects, but the source of the desire for them is quite different, as we will now see.

the anxious viewer

Do we grow anxious as a result of watching crime on television, or are we already anxious before we even switch on the set? This is the kind of question addressed by Richard Sparks in his book *Television and the Drama of Crime* (1992). Sparks investigated the relationship between tv crime shows and public fear, alarm and anxiety over crime. The relationship holds the key to understanding our continual attraction to crime series. Sparks' thesis is that it is not plausible to suggest tv shows actually cause fear "in any important degree." But: "it is both interesting and plausible to think that they can address fears, play upon them, exploit or reassure them" (1992: 155). The relationship that concerned Sparks had been analyzed previously but not satisfactorily. One approach had been to see tv shows as the cause of anxieties about crime, particularly violent crime. Another had been to treat crime as depicted on television as a reflection of crime in the outside world and public apprehension about it.

George Gerbner's research exemplifies the former. In chapter five, we examined his "cultivation effects," specifically in relation to violence on television and how this violence can impact on an audience. Basically, Gerbner argued that there is a very strong relationship between watching television "heavily" and anxiety. The violence on the screen is seen as bearing a close resemblance to what is going on in society and viewers grow fearful of the mean streets outside. Television then has independent and decisive influence on our perceptions of crime and cultivates an image of a "scary world" in which we feel insecure, perhaps excessively so. Our reactions to this feeling may actually help create or at least commission more crime.

Sparks found such a view untenable, principally because it never specifies either viewers' "motivations to engage in television viewing, nor affiliations towards what is viewed" (1992: 89–90). His objections were broadly those aired earlier in this book: insufficient emphasis is placed on the role of viewing as an activity, rather than a passive timewaster. Television is mistakenly given "causal force" in determining viewers' thoughts and emotions. Although published after Spark's book, Michael Medved's assailing *Hollywood vs America* would presumably be subject to similar objections. Medved's book concentrated on the film industry, though he also noted television's violent tendencies. He agreed with Gerbner that the anxious view of the world conveyed contributes powerfully to "insecurity and paranoia" and that these in turn facilitate increased levels of criminal activity. How? "A fearful attitude makes it far more likely that average Americans [*sic*] will huddle protectively together in their homes, taking no responsibility for the state of their neighborhoods and their communities" (1993: 198). As people become more privatized and isolated, they leave the streets unattended, so that they become fertile grounds for violent criminals, who can operate with relatively little restraint. Television mirrors a reality it has helped cultivate.

Alan Clarke's article about British tv crime drama, "Holding the blue lamp", took a different approach. "Contained within the format of the entertainment of the crime series are some of the values which inform the interpretation of policing in modern societies," wrote Clarke (1982: 45). As concern about crime is aggravated by politicians' rhetoric about law and order, so cop shows "confront the crime problem, the problem of increasing levels in of violence in crime, and each week return undefeated by bending the rules to facilitate their investigations" (1982: 49). Clarke cited *The Sweeney* as evidence of this and reckoned each arrest made in the show "helped prepare the ground for the official recognition of more authoritarian methods [of policing]" (1982: 49). He was emphatic that: "production teams pick up on trends, ideas, and debates that they witness on the political terrain and fit the most welcome ones into the presentation of their work" (1982: 49).

Sparks agreed that: "What is clear for present purposes is that shifts in the manifest public debates about law and order find echoes in the representation of crime and policing in television and other media, in fiction as well as reportage" (1992: 21). The transition from the moral clarity of early series to the more ambiguous series, like *The Sweeney*, or *Starsky and Hutch*, in which rules were there to be broken, did two things. First it represented changes in the nature and patterns of crime and policing. Second it legitimated the harder forms of policing that were introduced in the 1970s and 1980s. So the movement from the likes of *Dixon*, *Dragnet*, and *77 Sunset Strip*, where even private investigators follow "procedure," to *Kojak*, *Rockford et al.* suggests both a change in actual policing and a change in society's awareness. Sparks accepted the logic of this argument, but reckons Clarke's approach, which blurs the distinction between fictional and actual crime, runs the risk of seeing tv cop shows as straightforward historical documents. It might give television shows undue weight in "bringing about the events they seem to describe" (1992: 29).

Neither of these perspectives allows us to understand the undoubted appeal of crime drama. But, in constructing his alternative, Sparks opened up an interesting possibility. One dimension of the appeal, argued Sparks, relates to viewers' beliefs and anxieties over crime. The origin of such anxieties may or may not lie in actual criminal events. They could lie in gossip, speculation, fantasy or, of course, television.

Philip Jenkins' book *Intimate Enemies*, supports the view that anxiety has become pervasive (1993). For Britain's population at least, the 1980s were a decade of panic. Public awareness of serial killings, sexual abuse, Satanism and other menaces was constructed by a variety of interest groups, according to Jenkins. Specifically on crime: "There was a widespread perception that growing violence and unrest were related to a decline of public order, and an increase of violent demonstrations and riots" (1993: 33). Women became scared to wander out alone at night, and families began installing alarms in their homes as traditional civility was thought to decay.

It is a terrible world out there, people concluded. The crime figure has grown to hideous proportions; we are right to feel worried about our personal safety and that of our families. This would be a typical reaction to the recurrent wave of panic. So far, so tenable. We know television can whip up some scares that play on public anxiety, but can it alleviate anxiety? Perhaps, by providing dramas with outcomes in which justice usually prevails, it can. We are conscious of crime and probably fearful of it; the way television depicts crime may seem credible to us; and it confirms our anxiety. Television might exploit our anxieties, but it does not directly cause them. At the same time, the formulaic *denouements* of most of them gives them the status of fables, in that they convey moral messages. As Sparks wrote: "Television crime drama involves the routine introduction of fictive critical situations, precisely in order that they may be resolved" (1992: 50). We should add: most of the time. All crime fiction, in literature as well as television, has this ideological slant. Stephen Knight specifically addressed thriller novels, but may well have included tv cop shows, when he wrote that the literary form always contained a sense of peril or threat. "But if most powerful and successful thrillers include such a threat," wrote Knight, "they also resolve the threat by extirpating its human activators, and so they return the narrative and its audience to a newly established conservative statis" (1990: 175). We are now approaching an explanation: (1) we are anxious about crime; (2) crime drama appeals to us because it addresses that anxiety; (3) most cop shows conclude with a restoration of order; (4) we find this an acceptable resolution that reinforces our sense of propriety.

This argument still leaves an important question unanswered: why should viewers find the outcome of cop shows, complete with coded morality, reassuring? Surely, we cannot seriously expect them to be docile or gullible enough to accept the often strained, implausible conclusions as reflections of reality. Suggesting that tv cop drama effects a satisfying solution to widely felt problems and so alleviates fear is appealing in theory, but, in practice, it will not wash. Let us try a different angle.

There is much that is drab in today's society and the security it apparently offers. Security is something we seek, yet do not necessarily want. Because predictability and calculability are such powerful organizing principles, spontaneity and randomness are refreshing diversions; but, in large doses, they can prove disruptive and even threatening. Still, there is residual attraction in something that has unknown, perhaps even dangerous consequences. Were this to invade our working or public lives, it would be disorienting. But, once out of the office, we can retreat to our homes and act out our resistance.

Unlike characters in cop shows, most of us are not habitually exposed to danger. The most hazardous part of our day, statistically speaking, is driving to work. Fictional detectives face personal injury, loss or death virtually every week. There is a nice tension in watching a crime show: in identifying with figures who are perpetually at risk. Perhaps it is the kind of risk we crave as a contrast to our own security. Sparks may be right in stressing the role of anxiety in our relationship with tv cop shows; but total security is just as terrifying. I am not suggesting we would like to live in mortal fear. But, I find nothing exceptional in proposing that we value *frisson.* Most tv crime shows do not make viewers shriek; not in the same way as some movies, at any rate. But, they deliberately try to involve the viewers, drawing them into labyrinthine mysteries. Other methods work like a gun to the head: they demand viewers' attention, like a robber at a bank teller's window.

We, as viewers, are able vicariously to share the risk in the safety of our own homes and with a reasonable certainty that the morally right characters will come to no harm. We may not find the outcomes plausible at all. But, we are prepared to await the often predictable conclusions because we have been involved by the attractive vicarious danger on offer. Formulas have changed, especially since the early 1990s brand of critical realism in which outcomes did not inevitably code a clear moral structure. But, even a series like *Law and Order* did not lastingly expose the frailties of the criminal justice system. Perpetrators of crimes would often walk free and morally right persons would be wronged by technical circumstances. These were not shown as anomalies, either. Graham Murdock, in a paper on television's presentation of crime, once speculated that such shows, far from allaying anxiety, may reinforce "popular skepticism about police performance" (1982: 118). Yet which is better: a faulty system, or no system at all? The show would invite the viewer to answer.

Cop shows in the future will no doubt mix up signifiers with the same ambiguity while coding similar preferred meanings. The "conservative statis" ensures that we can expect only rarely to glimpse a television equivalent of radical thriller novels in which the convention of engaging the fears of the audience is followed, but a consoling resolution is elided.

Dashiel Hammett's novels of the 1920s and 1930s were considered suitable for film, but only an anemic version of his *The Thin Man* ever made it to television. Contemporary writers like June Cook, Peter Dunant and Gillian Slovo work in a left-leaning radical vein. The statis will no doubt also discourage the adaptation of novels featuring homosexual investigators. The work of Joseph Hansen, whose hero is a gay male, or Mary Wings, whose books feature a street-tough lesbian who often enjoys the spoils of the corruption she finds everywhere she looks, may not have networks clamoring. But nor will the blander shows which are already showing their age and will seem ridiculous to a generation that knows of drug-dealing billionaires, expatriate embezzlers, fraudulent politicians and corporate tax evaders. This generation is likely to ask the same question that opened this chapter.

chapter eleven

political hype and hyperreality

politics is good for television. . .

As if it were not enough that consumers are expected to watch and listen to politicians, they may soon be asked to read their words as well. Political broadcasts have a canny knack of following the same formats as commercial advertisements. And why shouldn't they? If the likes of Pepsi-Cola, Jaguar cars and Citibank can discover a potent strategy to stimulate viewers into buying their products, politicians might use it to sell theirs. One of the trends favored by advertisers in the 1990s has been to capture the attention of restless viewers, who are wont to graze channels with their remote controls, with kinetic typography. Words come rolling, floating, scrolling, dissolving, shrinking expanding, leaping and hopping their way up, down, across and even through the screen to underscore points being made by a voiceover announcer.

The strategy is not without irony: readers will recall Neil Postman's bemoaning the demise of the written word as we vegetables become accustomed to *Amusing Ourselves to Death*. Postman himself would be amused by the triumph of typography in a medium that has, in many senses, superseded print. Here is the printed word reasserting its power. If advertisers are convinced of its efficacy, politicians will follow. After all, politics has virtually copied advertising catchphrases, logos, ciphers and images; all are basic advertising tools that have been adopted and adapted by politics in the attempt to attract voters. The mechanisms involved in persuading people to vote in particular ways are not so different from those entailed in making them part with their money. In each case, something has to be sold.

Thirty years ago, this would have sounded cynical and alarmist. Now, it is a truism. We have not become more gullible; politics has become more mischievously enthralling. We have been ensnared by the maxim "seeing is believing." Not only do we hear our masters' voices, but we see the masters themselves recorded by the camera. Politicians have either followed or been unable to avoid being carried along by the imperatives of consumerism. There is no finer medium than one that can reach several million voters in far-flung places simultaneously and allow them the indulgence of choosing whether to watch or not. Political broadcasts are not the great turn-off one might suppose: people actually do want to see and listen to their would-be rulers.

So, is the advent of onscreen typography in television commercials portentous? We might once have dismissed the idea of politicians consenting to being made up and appearing on tv in what could have been regarded as an unseemly and debasing effort to catch votes. Today, the concept of Bill Clinton or John Major uttering platitudes with a moving strap of type reinforcing the spiel seems ordinary, if somewhat patronizing ("like, they think we can't hear them, without having it spelt out.") But politicians have made it clear they will use any facility the medium can offer to influence consumer behavior in the way they desire. We can trace the beginnings of this back to a period when the Western world was finally shrugging off the austerity and restraint of the postwar era.

From 1948, television cameras began peering at political conventions, conferences and speeches. Television acted principally as an instrument of record, monitoring events and messages without intentionally intruding in the political process. Dwight D. Eisenhower, in 1952, took advice from the advertising agency Batten, Barton, Durstine and Osborn, about how to enhance his presence on television. The agency handled the accounts of, among others, General Electric and American Tobacco. Eisenhower purchased advertising time on tv in much the same way as manufacturers of consumer products, a fact noted sarcastically by his presidential rival Adlai Stevenson, who proclaimed to the US public that he did not wish politics to be merchandised "like a breakfast food." Stevenson lost.

More than 55 million people, that was over 61 per cent of the US population, watched some part of television's coverage of politics in 1952. At peak periods, in excess of 60 per cent of homes with televisions tuned in. It was the first time the medium had comprehensively covered national politics across the USA. In the process, the networks discovered that there was an audience for political news and events. Added to the commercials, television's coverage set something of a standard for the future.

It looked to have played a significant part in Eisenhower's election, though the networks downplayed their influence, insisting they merely recorded. By the end of the decade, it was plain for all to see that this was not the case. Television played an undeniably active role in the outcome of a presidential race. It was able to do so precisely because it did not just record: it also created.

1960 is conventionally thought of as a watershed year in US politics. It was the year in which a close presidential election was swung by a television appearance. From that point, all political races involved an additional player. The "great debates," as they became known, took place between John F. Kennedy and Richard M. Nixon before CBS television cameras. This was made possible by an amendment to Section 315 of the Communications Act. As if to highlight the power of image added to informational content, Kennedy emerged victorious, his tanned, healthy appearance a total contrast to the pale, craggy-faced Nixon, shaving shadow cosmetically covered by a pink cream that melted under the heat of the studio lights. Image, it seemed, carried as much, if not more weight than substance. "Among those who heard the first debate on radio, Nixon apparently held his own," wrote Eric Barnouw. "Only on television had he seemed to lose" (1990: 274). Radio listeners actually thought Nixon had won the war of words. While Nixon fared better visually in subsequent tv debates, the impact of his almost ghostly appearance in the opener was disastrous to his campaign, giving momentum to the ultimately successful opponent.

The debates magnified features that had no relevance to the ability to govern. George Washington would have lost debates in front of cameras, the historian Henry S. Commager once speculated. Being telegenic was a vital attribute in presidential elections: appearance, coolness and adroitness supplanted wisdom. The campaign uncovered the significance of television for politics. Parties and candidates were made forcibly aware that tv could make or break them. There was no question about whether or not to use television. As more and more homes acquired sets, television became a pivotal tool of persuasion. In a sense, the distinction between overtly commercial political advertisements and other forms of less-rehearsed exposure was meaningless. Whether the slot was paid for, or not, an appearance on television was a commercial.

The Kennedy–Nixon debates thumped home the clear message that was to structure televised politics for decades. Ostensibly, politics falls into the "hard" category of program content. It is news documentary, informational in expression and educational in intent; not entertainment, purely to occupy viewers pleasantly or divert their attentions from earthly matters. Yet, in television, the demarcation line is so ill-defined as to be meaningless. Television may inform, document and educate. But, to do so effectively – effectively, here, meaning to sustain attention – it must frame its content entertainingly. Kennedy's and Nixon's messages may have been comparable in quality, scope and insight for most intents and purposes, but not all. Kennedy, it seemed, presented a more congenial visual image; one that entertained people, in other words.

Political parties grew increasingly sensitive to this. One-on-one interviews, forums, speeches and even debates had the capacity to bore as well as thrill. The impact of television was emphasized in *The Unseeing Eye*, a study of the 1972 election campaign by Thomas Patterson and Robert McClure (1976). One of the study's conclusions was that commercials were oriented to communicating substantive positions on issues: ads provided voters with information about issues four times as often as news. As such, they were the primary source of information about election issues for voters. News, by comparison, lacked substance. Patterson and McClure argued that commercials influenced the voting patterns of 3 per cent of the total electorate.

Patterson and McClure further concluded that what they called "mindless" and "emotional" short commercials played only an insignificant role. This particular finding was later challenged by Montague Kern in his book *30-Second Politics*, the title of which sums up his argument (1989). Politics in the 1980s were played out in short bursts of entertaining messages, media blitzes. The groundbreaking effort of Ronald Reagan in 1984, duplicated by George Bush in 1988, made the already unclear line between news and commercials even fuzzier: the commercials themselves made the news. Reagan carefully coordinated advertising strategy with news according to single-message advertising principles: establising specific themes – say, abortion or taxes – and focusing on them exclusively, one at a time. The idea was to give each theme so much attention that the media were virtually compelled to cover the same issue; hence the integration of advertising and news. Reagan effectively controlled the television agenda. Kern argues that the manipulation involved in this coordination was "unthinkable" in the early 1970s.

Another area that Kern believed was profitably exploited from the 1980s was that of negative advertising. He argued that burgeoning cynicism and mistrust of politicians created a climate conclusive to campaigns based on accentuating opponents' flaws. But, Kern seems to have overlooked that this type of approach had precedents in the 1960s. John F. Kennedy's successor, Lyndon B. Johnson, appointed the ad agency Doyle Dane Bernbach (DDB) to develop his media campaign against Republican candidate Barry Goldwater in the 1964 presidential election. The agency produced an ingeniously conceived series of tv spots, highlighting a contrast between a sensitive, caring LBJ and a reckless and extreme Goldwater, alien even to elements in his own party.

Earlier, Kennedy had muddied the political waters with what was later to be called "dirty" campaigning: commercials designed to show his opponent, Nixon, in the worst possible light with no attempt to foreground Kennedy's positive features. Johnson's attempts went further; too far, as things turned out. A commercial melding the sights and sounds of a young girl pulling petals from a daisy, while the countdown to the launch of a nuclear warhead progressed, was intended to point up the consequences of insensitive leadership in the nuclear age. "These are the stakes," said Johnson as the count reached zero and the screen went blank, "To make a world in which all God's children can live, or go into the dark." As Goldwater had earlier opposed a test ban treaty, the inference was clear enough.

Entertaining and creative as the film was, it pushed matters beyond the pale and was pulled off the air amid Goldwater's shock-horror protests. Enraged Goldwater ripped into Johnson for what he called "weird television," probably unaware that he was playing up to the role the Democrats had set out for him: belligerent and trigger-happy. Although it aired only once, the girl-with-daisy commercial remains the most controversial piece of televisual politics of all time. It foreshadowed the development of contemporary political media in that DDB targeted precisely its market: moderate Republicans and independents (floating voters). Its dynamic was to establish Johnson as the only rational choice for these crucial groups of voters and it did this by dismantling the credibility of Goldwater. In 1960, Kennedy had won the presidential election for the Democrats by a hairline 100,000 votes. Johnson, in 1964, won by a landslide. The value of focusing on an opponents' deficiencies had been brilliantly realized.

While Kern saw the negative device working more effectively in the 1980s, the 1964 campaign certainly created a benchmark. Later ads were to dovetail visual and linguistic messages in much the same way as the Johnson commercial had, simultaneously allowing the viewer scope to interpret and decode the message. A visual of a rotund Tip O'Neil to accompany a verbal message that Democrats waste money was one example. In another, the right-wing Republican from North Carolina, Jesse Helms, used a picture of Jesse Jackson assisting in voter registration activities captioned with: "Is this a proper use of your tax dollars?" Ostensibly, it carried no racial significance, but it aimed to stir white voters with its evocative imagery. Another commercial in 1991 coded a similar theme, this time featuring a white hand holding an employer's letter of rejection; the simple message carried no explicit reference to the affirmative action programs it addressed.

Perhaps the most dismayingly effective endeavor in this vein was George Bush's deployment of the image of convicted murderer Willie Horton during the 1988 presidential election. Horton, an African American, murdered while on furlough from prison in Massachusetts, where Bush's opponent Michael Dukakis was Governor. With Horton's visage, Bush was able to draw on all manner of sentiment and mobilize it against Dukakis. The full chronicle of sleazy ads that have proved so effective is in the book *Unsilent Revolution* by Robert Donovan and Ray Scherer, who argued that television has changed the political process from "top to bottom" (1992). While Kern saw a new spirit of negativism in political commercials from 1985, there is at least some evidence that the form has been employed continuously since the early years of television itself. Kern believes such commercials became more persuasive as dispositions towards politicians turned sour.

Political parties typically claim their commercials improve public awareness – usually of their opponents' apparent weaknesses. But, occasionally, the commercial is so contrived that it distorts. The British Labour Party's attempt to expose the gaps in the Conservative Party's health policy in the 1992 General Election backfired when it was found how Labour had put the commercial together. Jennifer Bennett, a five-year-old who suffered from an ear ailment, was used to focus attention on the problems of children being made to wait long periods for operations, unless their parents could afford private care. The child was featured anonymously but was soon identified, precipitating a rush of media attention. The parents (one a Conservative, the other undecided), angered by the frequent intrusions, bickered in public. Soon a stressful environment swirled around the child and the Labour Party was culpable.

The staging of the minidrama was close to scandalous and may have cost the party votes. On the other hand it may have fulfilled its three functions. According to Kern there are three components in televised political advertising. Obviously, like all television, it has to entertain, arousing and holding the viewer's attention albeit for a short span. It must have some sort of message, frequently about character and issues. And, it must "attempt to provoke a reaction, surprise, excitement, recognition, affect, or an action message" (1989: 1). The Labour Party commercial certainly contained all three, provoking a reaction that kept the story behind the ad on the front pages of national newspapers for days.

It barely needs emphasizing that political advertising in both the USA and Britain has grown closer to the advertising formats popularly used by manufacturers. It has become affect-heavy; as Kern put it, "freighted with entertainment values and what are described as emotional appeals" (1989: 207). This alignment has developed since the early 1970s, when political spots used a more documentary model with a leaning towards news styles of delivery. "The purpose of political advertising has also changed," wrote Kern. Consumers read less and rely more on television as their source of information about the world. Political parties have opted increasingly for short, but repetitious single-issue messages that dovetail the visual and the oral. Like commercial advertisers, political parties try to draw viewers into the ad, to make them "experience" it. The kind of referential advertising cited earlier epitomizes this approach: showing a signifier loaded with meaning that can be transferred by the viewer to a different context. Signifiers might include people (Horton, Jackson) or body parts (hands) or anything that refers to something else, the signified (sick girl = decline of National Health Service).

Kern suggests that political advertising has now "overwhelmed" news, probably because it has fine-tuned itself to the requirements of popular entertainment better. Since the publication of Kern's analysis in 1989, there has been a leaning towards the mood and structure of music videos; clichéd plots and moral certitudes being carried along by sleek visuals. The style that made MTV such compelling viewing, for the young at least, has been appropriated with minor modifications for political purposes. The Democratic Party in the 1992 election campaign elevated Fleetwood Mac's "Don't Stop Thinking About Tomorrow" into a virtual anthem, and soloists like Don Henley served the same functions as Billy Bragg for the British Labour Party. Some groaned at the overt appeal to youth, but the move was only logical for parties with an eye on the baby-boom generation.

By contrast, political news seems staid. Kern's conclusions that news "still focuses on horserace coverage, and on a category of noncandidate coverage relating to the election process in general, to such questions as turnout and voting patterns" may not be completely valid; but, even with the advent of tabloid-style tv news, the form still lacks the entertaining punch of dazzling plot-laden commercials, where fact meets fiction and the difference between the two is not always apparent.

Perhaps the most overt switch away from this and towards a more straightforward informational approach was made by 1992 independent presidential candidate Ross Perot, badly beaten at the polls but odd enough to insist on serious attention. His economically directed commercials consisted of monologue and text. In this sense, they approximated more than any other political commercial the dynamic typography described at the start of this section. The almost naive integrity that Perot brought to the election was reflected in the scrolling words that visually reinforced the voiceover message. In his longer "infomercials," as they became known, he assumed a schoolmasterly role, lecturing the audience, aided by charts and an assortment of visual devices.

Short of a test pattern, the most off-putting sight on television must be a diminutive old man with big ears, lecturing about the country's economic ills. Honest and sublunary virtues are all very nice; but they do not make entertaining television. And, basically, that is all televised politics has ever done: entertain.

A Harvard University study in 1991 cited three "problems" with television's coverage of politics, though it is by no means certain that either political parties or tv networks would regard them as such. First, was that not enough airtime was devoted to political affairs. Second, coverage was superficial, always striving for the "lowest common denominator." Third, that politicians, aware of the constraints of time, limit their addresses to "nine-second soundbites" (Gersh 1991: 18). There have been many other similar studies in the USA and Europe, and beyond their differences they all reach broadly similar conclusions: that the actual information carried by tv is, at best, superficial, at worst misleading; and that the primary function of televised politics is, like all other television programs, to entertain.

While the Harvard study's findings were intended as a critique of politics on television, they might well have been used as directives for parties wishing to promote themselves on tv. Collapsing complex policies into messages as simple as "this is Dick, this is Jane" and subordinating content to image became something of a *sine qua non* for parties, especially when self-consciously styling their own messages through paid commercials.

This may seem judgemental. But it really is not. Television viewers who dote on the tube might be accused of being too lazy or apathetic to read about politics in newspapers, where coverage is frequently more dense and analytical. What of readers of *USA Today*, or Britain's the *Sun*? Politics are hardly treated with depth or complexity in these and many other newspapers. Television's treatment looks highbrow by comparison. The fact that it has been able to entertain at the same time is something of an accomplishment.

The volume of advertising bought by parties means valuable revenue to television companies. Politicians, realizing the possible benefits of television exposure, are willing and inexpensive interviewees or discussants on news and current affairs programs. The excitement and interest generated by elections keeps viewer ratings up. Even the normally boring party conventions or conferences attract solid viewing audiences. Undoubtedly, politics has been good for television. But, is the opposite true? The answer is: yes, television has been good for politics. Not only in the obvious sense of promoting parties. Beneath the surface, television has performed a variety of functions, the effects of which are of great benefit to the political system; we examine these effects in the next section.

. . . but is television good for politics?

News is not neutral. We have any number of studies to show that the media's depiction of national and international events is partial, biased and often political in perspective (for example, Franks 1973; Gans, 1980; Glasgow Media Group 1977, 1980). The very process of selecting, editing, structuring and then presenting stories makes any claim to journalistic objectivity nonsensical. The instant potential news becomes "news," it becomes subject to processes that will eventually render it into a form that can be easily assimilated by viewers, readers and listeners. During this extrusion, news is defined, interpreted and communicated by a variety of people, each of whom give it an inflexion, or a "spin."

In *Media, Power, Politics*, David Paletz and Robert Entman gave an apposite illustration. Consider a television news story on massage parlors in which the theme is "illicit behavior." Related subthemes might typically include sexual exchanges, drug use, organized crime and venereal disease and the story would be fashioned in such a way as to reflect this. "But," Paletz and Entman argued, "the massage parlor story could have been discussed from such other perspectives as good health, sexual satisfaction, onerous government regulations, free enterprise, and career opportunities" (1981: 22).

Viable as the second set of themes might be, they would strike the consumer as strange, falling as they do outside the range of the accepted news discourse. We might find one of the more adventurous cable channels on the US public access systems essaying such a presentation. But, it would be at some variance with the mainstream treatment, the "preferred," meaning.

Television, more so than other media, stays within a very narrow scope of preferred themes. Its tendency to squeeze mixed and contrasting events into a highly formalized and structured format means that a certain mode of presentation, with recurring themes, keeps repeating itself. There is a predictable, perhaps ritualistic quality to television news. No matter how unexpected, untoward or exotic events are, they can be channeled into existing themes and made to seem reassuringly familiar. The presence of a recognizable anchorperson bolsters the reassurance; that person is typically an urbane figure and must be trustworthy, as the plausibility of the news depends on how credible he or she is.

News sources may be uncertain, knowledge conditional and facts disputed; yet an anchor's dress, demeanor and vocal tone should absorb enough interest to deter the viewer's skepticism. If the anchor is seen as legitimate, then the news selection, framing and contextualizing will appear natural, an accurate reflection of reality.

Trifling matters such as politicians' peccadillos are unearthed periodically and cause embarrassment rather than catastrophe. The mass media regard them as rare and unusual, if not exotic. But events on the scale of Watergate possess the potential to destroy the credibility of governments if not the entire political system. Watergate was made intelligible by the media as a highly untypical occurrence and one likely never to be repeated. By covering such an event in this way, the integrity, responsiveness and representativeness of the polity was not threatened. Quite the reverse: by encouraging the belief that Watergate was an oddity, the media fortified the political system's legitimacy.

Paletz and Entman discerned five effects of the mass media on public opinion, all of them political in nature: "They stabilize prevailing opinions, set priorities, elevate events and issues, sometimes change opinions, and ultimately limit options" (1981: 189). While their analysis underestimates the curiosity, interpretative guile and sheer skepticism of consumers, it offers at least a frame of reference for understanding the political potential, if not exact effects of television. In encountering the new, novel and puzzling, we tend to see what the familiar has taught us to expect. Journalists, scriptwriters, presenters and all others involved in television programs are not different: they describe, explain or convey in terms of their own pre-existing attitudes and expectations. They need to pique viewers without interrupting them. This is referred to as "stabilizing:" screening new developments in a way that fits them "in a frame of existing beliefs and by failing to present a complete picture that might challenge audiences existing thoughts" (1981: 189).

When Paletz and Entman wrote of "priority setting," they referred to the way the media give primacy to some topics and not to others. A scandal in the British royal family, research findings on the causes of breast cancer and civil war in Central America may all rate higher on news agenda than, say, rising interest rates, school closures and changes in health care. The coverage afforded some issues ensures they are widely regarded as serious and important, even though they may not reflect viewers' specific priority interests. Since the publication of Paletz and Entman's work, the Reagan media blitz strategy has shown how possible it is to influence the media's priority setting.

Closely linked to this is "elevation," the process through which sometimes obscure events are elevated into "big" new stories. Nuclear power prior to 1979 was not a huge topic; but the accident at the Three Mile Island plant instantly catalyzed media interest and transformed the issue.

These effects are largely a function of news coverage rather than drama, but the fourth effect analyzed by Paletz and Entman can equally be brought about by either. Three Mile Island was covered not as an isolated disaster, but as a symptom of a more general threat. The nature of the treatment had the effect of "changing opinions" about nuclear power. The British docudrama *Who Bombed Birmingham?* was a reconstruction of an investigation into the IRA bombings of 1974, which revealed evidence that the "culprits," who were imprisoned, were innocent. Public sentiment changed as did official opinion and, later, the convicted men were released. Cases of straight fiction altering public opinion are legion. Sometimes, the changes have been overnight. Britain's *Cathy Come Home* is the most widely documented program of this kind. Several episodes of *Lou Grant* caused opinions to shift. The authenticity of such shows helped dispel commonsense notions. Cartoon villains and simplistic resolutions to problems were ditched in these and other credible and, sometimes, mordant dramas that purported to deal with real issues. Shown as a television film, *The Burning Bed* forced viewers to rethink their opinions on women who are brutalized by their menfolk. Farrah Fawcett's tremulous depiction of a woman at her wits' end who kills her husband, achieved the distinction of being covered as a news item as well as a drama and prompted extensive public discussion.

"Limiting options" smacks a bit of conspiracy theory, but Paletz and Entman argued that it involves only keeping issues "within the boundaries laid out by consensus values." Returning briefly to *Prime Suspect 2* (from chapter ten), even a slightly different inflection might damage the legitimacy of the criminal justice system. A suspect kills himself while in custody. The incident is treated deftly and ambiguously enough to suggest the police were not completely to blame for the death: the interrogation that preceded the suicide was harsh, but perhaps not unjustified given the severity of the offense, a murder. The US series *Law and Order* shadow-boxed with the notion that the criminal justice system sometimes serves anything but justice, but without punching holes in the legitimacy of the system itself. It acknowledged the system has imperfections, while asserting its basic soundness.

News is more overt in its practice of closing options for questioning: it screens out views that might threaten mainstream social institutions, seeing neither "problems or solutions in system-threatening ways," as Paletz and Entman observed (1981: 193). While the "political effects" analysis of Paletz and Entman would not satisfy the demands of cultural studies, there is a symmetry between their conclusions about the propensities of the media to fashion its output in such a way as to conserve or restore, not change or challenge.

There is a further political effect neglected by Paletz and Entman, but picked up by Shanto Iyengar in *Is Anyone Responsible? How television frames political issues* (1992). Television generally and news especially shape out attributions of responsibility. Social psychologists have long argued that people are highly sensitive to context when they are asked to make decisions or offer an opinion. The way the choice is framed can be an important contextual factor. For instance, surgery is regarded as a more attractive choice by both doctors and patients when survival rates are used to describe its effects rather than mortality rates. Iyengar simply extended this logic to television's coverage of politics: the way issues, events and politicians are covered dramatically affects the way viewers evaluate them; specifically who and what they blame or credit.

Television news is dominated by two types of stories: episodic (events, concrete issues) and thematic (abstract, background pieces), which produce contradictory attributions of responsibility. Episodic stories incline viewers towards focusing on the individuals in the stories, rather than less tangible social trends or impersonal economic factors. Iyengar found an emphasis on episodic coverage of crime and terrorism raised viewer support for the death penalty and military intervention. Similarly, episodic coverage of poverty reduced support for government programs and increased public approval of political leaders wanting to abolish such programs. Anxiety over law and order have come about not only because of political opinion-leaders advocating a clampdown on crime, but because of television's treatment.

A related and arguably more important conclusion of the study was that television's accent on individual issues as if they were unique, or even idiosyncratic, distracts viewers' attention from fundamental causes. One consequence of this is that they do not hold politicians or parties responsible, even though their policies may have contributed to the causes of a chronic problem, such as poverty, homelessness or violent crime. The title of Iyengar's book invited a question, the answer to which, according to tv viewers, must be "no." Television prods us into thinking about issues, at the same time delivering into our homes the kind of bland interpretation that effectively protects politicians and government. Television in Iyengar's study is a political shield behind which governments may hide.

distraction + distortion + deception = reality

Television news up till the 1960s had been seen as a necessary evil: costly to produce, especially at local level where audience size was limited, unattractive to advertisers, it was produced principally to satisfy legal requirements for public service and informational broadcasting. An ancillary benefit for US-affiliated stations was in being able to project a more homely, caring image for local viewers. This changed in the late 1960s, when television for the first time became privy to a "live" war. By this time, television had the technique and resources to cover Vietnam as the conflict raged. Harrowing barbarism and cruelty were exposed graphically by television crews. Vietnam was transformed from what seemed to Americans to be an insignificant sliver of land in Indochina into a daily living-room spectacle. Unlike other wars, Vietnam was lived through by all North Americans: the distance between the USA and Vietnam was shrunk by television. This was not a war from which consumers could detach themselves.

In early phases, the war was as black-and-white morally as it was visually. Viewers were left in no doubt about whom to hiss. But, as the bodycount grew, so did the moral gray areas. Support changed to ambivalence and, among many, opposition, as the gruesome saga trudged on.

Television captured the atmosphere of war in a way that escaped newsreel and Hollywood. Its immediacy and vividness was astounding in the 1960s; it engaged audiences and challenged them too. Vietnam changed the nature and impact of news. With its coverage of the war, television realized its potential, both as a spectacle and as an audience magnet. Recognizing this, networks, in the 1970s, began to concentrate their attentions on producing attractive news. As competition from cable intensified, the established stations were forced to find new elements in their schedules. News gathering and presentation took on new importance.

What took place might be described as a "tabloidization' of television news. As many popular newspapers became successful through their selection and compression of stories and their subjective method of presentation, so television news reflected these features. Bulletin-like presentation of condensed summaries, sometimes augmented with "expert" comment and analysis were refined. Crime, corruption, scandal, tragedy and other symptoms of what Graham Knight called "moral disorder" were and still are daily ingredients. Knight's analysis of "tabloid television news" throws out some interesting arguments, one of which is that: "Television is a medium that mixes fiction and non-fiction yet it takes their distinction very seriously and goes to great pains to ensure the boundaries are clearly marked" (1989: 122).

And yet, "conventions associated primarily with one spill over into the other." The pace, movement, narrative and editing of news has edged near to drama action. But, according to Knight, there has been a cost. News is intended to be the most truthful depiction of reality available on television; but in shadowing the styles of drama it loses its "transparency." In becoming more interesting and attractive to viewers, it has grown less "realistic." To counter this, television news has developed what Knight calls a "hyper-active effect," bludgeoning viewers with fast, staccato action, sharp comments and plenty of visual cutaway shots to give the impression of speed and change. In this, television news has even more closely approximated the tabloid style of such newspapers as the *Sun* and *USA Today*, which offer an undemanding, cursory view of the world and one that keeps the reader's eye moving across the pages. Television news aims to keep the eye fixed while it moves the pages. The "loss of the real" is compensated for with a "heightened realism and circumstantial detail;" through the substitution of reality with "reality effects." In broaching this subject, Knight finds himself in agreement with the postmodernist philosopher Jean Baudrillard. Western culture, according to Baudrillard, has passed through three historical phases when images and appearance changed their relationship to reality. The latest phase, or "order," is one in which the electronic media has come to dominate and is known as hyperreal (1983).

In the hyperreal age, we have become preoccupied with authenticity: we value the original, the genuine article, the real thing. There is a premium placed on anything authentic; which is why "based on a true story" enhances the value of a miniseries, or fly-on-the-wall documentaries have added appeal, or *vox populi* formats have a realistic quality that evades conventional interviews. Television news more than any other medium places great store on its access to reality, raw and unprocessed – or "unplugged," to use MTV's conceit. Perhaps the consummate moment in any news program is when it is able to go 'live' to any given place or person to reveal reality as it is happening.

The actual phrase "we are able to go 'live' to . . . " was never used so copiously nor to such effect as in the coverage of the Gulf War of 1991. "I am looking directly west from the hotel and through the entire sky," reported ABC News' Gary Shepard at precisely 6.35 p.m. (EST) on January 16. "It appears to be some sort of anti aircraft fire. Couple of flashes on the horizon, something is definitely underway here" (quoted in *Broadcasting*, January 21, 1991: 23). Shepard was talking to millions of US viewers from Baghdad during the first moments of the US air attack. The remarks opened the marathon broadcast coverage of Desert Storm, the war against Iraq. The US networks' constantly updated treatment of the conflict and, especially, the cable CNN's comprehensive, twenty-four hour coverage harnessed all the elements of what Baudrillard calls simulacra, which are representations or copies of events and objects. Simulacra are in theater, fashion, in anything in which a representation of reality is effected. In the postmodern society such as exists today, simulacra dominate life: models or copies no longer just represent reality; they are reality. This is what is meant by hyperreal society, "where the distinction between real and unreal is no longer apparent or valid and where simulacra constitute and count as 'the real'," as Douglas Kellner put it (1988: 243). Workout videos, childcare manuals, homeshopping catalogs; these are examples of simulation models that represent other things, yet have become things in themselves. DisneyWorld is a grandly effected simulacrum, in which the representation is not reality; the fantasy it is thought to represent is actually subordinate to the reality of DisneyWorld itself.

CNN's Desert War was another example, a media representation of events that became the event itself. *Los Angeles Times* tv critic Howard Rosenberg understated the position when he wrote at the time that: "Television . . . has almost become part of the war." A case could be made for television's having supplanted the war.

The case would comprise the unyielding attention afforded the war by CNN and the three major networks. As might be expected, given the virtually universal interest in the Gulf, the four US channels dominated the ratings. Apart from ratings, the prestige at stake was enormous. So enormous that the three networks were prepared to lose between $5–$9 million each for every day they went without advertisements. As it turned out, none of the networks went more than sixteen hours without a commercial.

Another factor can be summed up by quoting Chair of the Joint Chiefs of Staff, Colin Powell: "We have done considerable damage – at least according to what [CNN correspondent] Bernie Shaw tells me" (quoted in *Broadcasting*, January 21, 1991, p. 24). This may or may not have been uttered in jest; it was a senior-ranking member of the military involved in the war acknowledging that the source of this intelligence was television. The US Defense Secretary Richard Cheney made a similar admission. So saturated was CNN's coverage that, within days, it took on an oracular role, informing not only consumers, but strategically based players in the conflict. In early phases of the war at least, CNN was the primary source of information for all. But, as the days wore on and focus on the region shifted from Baghdad to Tel Aviv, the reports took on the status of the emperor's new clothes. One cynical voice alerted everyone that tv's version of events might not be the only one. Reports of stupendously successful scud missile attacks on Iraqi weapon bases in Tel Aviv were not well substantiated. Telephone testimonies from Tel Aviv and sporadic pictures after the missiles had landed were the only pieces of evidence before some poor quality footage was smuggled out of Iraq into Amman.

But the euphoria greeting the apparent success evaporated within days. The networks, it seems, had acted with too much haste and too little attention to detail in their efforts to capture audiences. Cries of "misinformation" tempered the praises. It was clear that both the public and government leaders, as well as the military, were relying on television to the point where they were believing a fabricated definition of reality. Cheney later conceded that the media had predicted success too early.

A further point on the "different reality" theme. CNN, more so than the other channels, played up the conflict for all it was worth. As a 24-hours cable specializing exclusively in news, it had time and resources to mount the most lavish television coverage of a war in history. In fact, it reproduced more than just covered: it transformed the conflict into something akin to epic drama, slapping a specially designed slogan and graphic across the screen to enhance the impression that this was something being contested on our screens, not in the desert. It was an exercise conducive to flag-waving, teeshirts bearing "Screw Saddam" messages and "Desert Storm" car bumper stickers. CNN did nothing to remind its viewers of the violence, pain, mutilation and innocent lives lost, not to mention the reason why the battles were fought in the first place. The pace and the spectacle effectively dehumanized the war. Even the reports of United Nations forces mistakenly killing their own allies were dismissed with the neat oxymoron "friendly fire." The grandiloquent television coverage was a construction that pandered to simple-minded partisanship. It was as if Gary

Shepard's early remark as he witnessed the opening salvos was taken to heart: "It's like fireworks on the fourth of July multiplied by 100."

Great upheavals like the American War of Independence are distorted in the memory by fireworks and celebration. In the Gulf War's case, the distortion began from the word "go." And there was a further twist: research (cited in the introduction) indicated that television viewers actually did not mind being fed erroneous information, as long as the "national interest" was served. I am reminded here of an illustration of the function of ideology provided by Peter Berger, in his *Invitation to Sociology* (1971). Berger tells of an imaginary preindustrial society where food could be procured only by traveling through treacherous shark-infested waters.

Twice a year, the men of the tribe set out in the flimsy canoes, believing as an article of faith in the society's religion that stated that any man failing to go on the voyage would lose his virility – except the priests whose virility was not affected and who could stay safely at home. We suspect, of course, that it was the priests themselves who originally devised the theory to protect their own skins. "A priestly ideology," Berger called it, adding, "this does not mean that the latter is not functional for the society as a whole – after all, somebody must go or there will be starvation' (1971: 130). The canoeists who risk life and limb are like viewers of the CNN Gulf War coverage in the sense that they might suspect or know they are being duped, but are prepared to go along with the deception as long as it is for the greater good of the society. In this view, political hype may not be such a bad thing.

Critics did not see it this way: they wondered whose interests were served by misinformation – or was it disinformation (i.e. designed, not achieved by accident)? In his *New York Times* column, Walter Goodwin asked: "Is [CNN correspondent] Arnett sending out enemy propaganda? Is he only doing the journalist's job?" (quoted in Diamond and Kasindorf, 1991: 32). Others noticed how perspective buckled under the sheer weight of factual data constantly fed through the cables.

Of course, wars do not self-direct and events rarely live up to television's demands for pace and visuals. Intolerable *longueurs* were bridged with testimonies from tame experts and endless recaps, inviting the comment that CNN's "coverage is a mile wide and an inch deep" (quoted in Diamond and Kasindorf, 1991: 32). Lack of profundity is rarely a problem for US networks and it was not for CNN: it gained the highest viewer ratings in its history, reaching between 4.7 million to 10.9 million homes in primetime hours, compared to less than 930,000 before the crisis.

In his appraisal of CNN's increasingly influential role in creating news, Jay Rosen concluded that: "CNN represents a new dimension of an emerging global culture that is already heavily Americanized" (1991: 622). As CNN has grown into a television world news service, it has become "another vehicle for the spread of American values.'

Rosen argued that television, being the visual medium it is, seeks stories and information accompanied by images with maximum "oomph value." This means that important items are subordinated or even wiped out by "arresting irrelevance"; like American crews extinguishing fires in Kuwait, or babies being rescued from wells – stories with pictures that captivate the world. This has political consequences, according to Rosen. "In the Gulf War, for example, it worked to the advantage of the US military in favoring repeated showings of laser-guided missiles hitting their targets squarely and spectacularly" (1991: 623). But, it also dictated that "CNN would show scenes of what Iraq said was a civilian shelter destroyed by allied bombs." The very fact that the network will opt for, or perhaps even create, stories with visual appeal is political in his view. CNN, in particular, will develop the "power to create global distractions." He meant that significant events without a visual dimension will escape world notice because image-hungry procedures need to grab people and keep them watching.

CNN's "fetishizing of the live," as Rosen called it, has the advantage of allowing viewers to watch news conferences, announcements and hearings in their entirety, "avoiding the tyranny of the sound bite and the tv reporter's breezy, overly facile wrap-up" (1991: 623). But the selection of newsworthy subjects will, Rosen ventures, be dictated by dramatic impact which means that events that are "fundamentally non visual" are destined to be of only negligible interest to the network. This will have even greater significance "as CNN begins to constitute – rather than merely inform – the global public sphere" (1991: 623). In other words, a television news service with the worldwide penetration of CNN, rivaled only by the BBC, will assume power not only to report news, but to govern what counts as news and to construct the reality of that news for a global audience.

Rosen's attempt to temper this forbidding scenario by adding that more "live" coverage enables viewers to watch, listen and decide for themselves' seems a small gain. Other writers are troubled by television's transformation from an electronic magic lantern to a virtual-reality helmet. Too much televisual politics makes us impotent, they argue. Then again, that is what the priests told the stay-at-homes.

the impotent generation

The CNN–Gulf War phenomenon figures to be a masterwork of what Michael Parenti calls *Inventing Reality*. Published in 1986 before the war, Parenti's book is an analysis of "the politics of the news media" and examines how armies of federal government employees have assumed positions as sources of news. Their function is to frame information in such a way as to complement order and protect the status quo and, by implication, all groups that have an interest in the status quo. The Gulf War shows that such an arrangement may not be so one-sided, nor as manipulative as previously supposed. The media themselves, in particular television, may operate perfectly independently of governments and interest groups and reverse the flow by becoming their source of information.

There may be a covert understanding that potentially destabilizing news is suppressed or reworked so as to assist some interests while damaging others. But this is not the product of some conspiracy. For the less governing groups wish to have recourse to violence, the more they need to rely on various consensual norms to legitimize their power. As we have seen previously, television has become a vital apparatus through which those consensual norms are disseminated.

In this sense, television's conservative influence is undeniable; but is it undemocratic? It is, if we accept a different interpretation of the viewer: not as actively engaged, but as inertly vacant. William Greider, in his scaremongering book, *Who Will Tell the People*, did exactly that. Subtitled *The Betrayal of American Democracy*, Greider's argument encompasses television's role in today's political system. "If the mass-media culture has permanently robbed people of their democratic capacities, then the deeper governing problems – or their remedies – will have no meaning to ordinary citizens," wrote Greider, somewhat fatalistically (1992: 313).

Disconcerted by what he felt were the politically damaging effects of tv, Greider wrote: "People whom tv taught to be hip and wary and impatient naturally lose interest in what seems opaque and distant. The remoteness makes them feel passive, impotent' (1992: 317). And, later: "Most younger people are more inward-looking in their lives, concentrating on the well-being of family and friends and themselves, convinced that nothing they can do can have much effect on the larger problems, especially in politics." This, according to Greider, is "a practical response to the political reality of impotent citizens" (1992: 319).

It is an understandable analysis of the politically neutering consequences of watching television, but based too much on a one-way-traffic image. The reason for such an interpretation is that writers like Greider have their noses pressed so tightly against the tv screen that they cannot notice what is going on behind them. Perhaps viewers are not so passive or do not feel so "impotent" as Greider supposes. When he writes of a "brain-dead citizenry" produced by television, Greider almost parodies Adorno and repeats the same error. In one telling phrase, Greider countenances that "younger viewers are able to see things through television that are really not visible to their elders" (1992: 316). Maybe televisual politics is not so opaque to those accustomed to it. The MTV generation of which Greider expects so little might just have rumbled that a lot of what passes for news, analysis and comment is familiar, superficial, and bland. Viewers today are too sardonic to mistake the alleged revelations of television for anything more than old plots rehashed with new characters.

MTV's 25 million viewers (mostly 18–25-year-olds) in the US are not nearly as vacant as critics like Greider suppose. Witness the music cable's coverage of the Gulf War and, more relevantly, the entire 1992 Presidential Election campaign, which it reported daily with the theme "Choose or lose," aimed at encouraging involvement in the political process. MTV's director of news, Dave Slrulnick made the point: "Our audience has grown up in a real media-savvy world." He defended the fast pace and video style of presentation: "It's how our audience is used to getting information" (quoted in *Atlanta Journal*, March 30, 1992: A2).

Maybe the post-boomer generation has learned to assimilate a store of information in the three minutes it takes to show a music video. Maybe they focus more attentively when George Michael or the Red Hot Chili Peppers are playing in the background. Maybe they find more meaning in an interview conducted by a young, uninhibited rock correspondent rather than a mannered journalist. True, the coverage looks facile. Yet, this makes MTV's politics no more radical or conservative, better or worse than other channels. Just attuned to the hyperreal order and the young people who populate it.

This might tend to flatter the viewer, especially after my earlier propositions about the political effects of television and the advent of "30-second politics." But it has the virtue of recognizing that we have consciousness. We are not crushed into compliance by governing powers and their propaganda machines, though this can happen, as history tells us. Typically our affiliation to a political system is established more by collusion.

Much of this chapter has concentrated on the political nature of television, its functions and effects. Viewers are as much products of a political system as is television. They learn to object, oppose, protest and resist in the same culture where they learn to defend, guard, sustain and, mostly, just endure. Accepting ourselves as products does not mean we need to see ourselves, as many writers do, as anesthetized patsies. In becoming socialized into society, we might acquire patterns and limits for our emotions and imaginations. Society penetrates our minds as well as surrounds us. Why should this result in a loss of our critical faculties? We acquire the ability to question and challenge, just as we do the ability to accept and conform.

Television has become the premier medium bar none for the transmission of political messages, appeals and promises. It sells political ideas much as it does tires and toothpaste. Politics has been commodified and television's *raison d'être* is to sell commodities. Its putative functions may include educating, informing and expanding cultural awareness. But what it does best is: sell. It owes its existence to a political system that encourages this role. So, there would be little rationality in fearlessly condemning and criticizing a system of which it has become an integral part. One does not have to be a Marxist to realize that television will inevitably reflect vested interests; it too has an interest in seeing the system stable and secure.

But challenge is as important as support to the validity of a political system. It affirms the system's ability to absorb and respond to criticism. And, while many writers point out the obviously conservative functions and effects of television, we should also take note of its role in investigating, probing and questioning; plus the ability of its viewers to extract meaning, judge the credibility of stories, assess their merits. Television encourages them to recognize a certain security, reassurance and authority in its statements; it does so with the language it uses, the symbols it expresses and the signifiers it gives off. But it cannot pummel viewers into submission. Maybe we are held in some sort of bondage by our political system. If we are, we are betrayed into captivity with our own cooperation.

chapter twelve

tomorrow, the world

cultural lingua franca

"American popular culture is the closest approximation there is today to a global lingua franca," declared Todd Gitlin in a 1992 *New York Times* article, "World leaders: Mickey, *et al.*" – an allusion to the ascendant cultural hegemony of all things Disney (May 3, section A).

Without mentioning the word "globalization," Gitlin produced one of the most significant statements on this phenomenon in recent years. The USA now exports its culture to, well, everywhere. It does so through its entertainment. While others might have busied themselves with cultural elevation or didactic enrichment, the commercial nature of US television ensured a narrower cultural ambition. Nothing wrong with this: no other culture comes close to the USA's in consistently creating compelling and consummately amusing product that can be rapidly transported and appreciated anywhere via television, film or music. Gitlin believed that the three media were helping plug "most nations into a single cultural zone." Homer Simpson, Arnold Schwarzenegger and co. were not actually replacing local cultures, went the argument; yet they were finding sufficient space, whether in Norway or Namibia, to co-exist.

US culture "doesn't necessarily supplant local traditions," wrote Gitlin, "but it does activate a certain cultural bilingualism." This may underestimate the power of television. Think of what tv has done to American and British culture alone. Riffle through the previous chapters of this book to remind yourself of all the ways, some of them hardly perceptible, in which television has influenced you and the culture of which you are part. Then imagine how other unsuspecting parts of the world may be prey to the same forces, most emanating from the US.

It is happening and will continue to happen in the future, probably at an accelerated pace. One reason we can be confident of this is economies of scale. Gitlin pointed out that a Copenhagen programmer can lease an hour-long episode of *Dallas* for under $5,000; that is less than the cost of producing a single original minute of Danish drama.

But there are other, aesthetic reasons. Americans have defined the form television should take and this has become virtually irresistible. Formulas for narratives, characters and plots are pretested like any other marketable product. Approval ratings with focus groups are taken very seriously by networks, keen to seize new initiatives but circumspect enough not to turn away advertisers. The result is frequently a back-of-an-envelope idea approach, programs being reduced to their blandest, most user-friendly essentials. Commercially risky shows, such as *Twin Peaks* look like anomalies, but are made more secure by having high profile directors, in this case David Lynch, at the helm. This in itself sounds perfectly innocuous; until the American formulas become converted into universal conventions to be copied by all. It does not matter too much where you watch television, the output is barely distinguishable nowadays.

When the British, in particular, are not importing American shows, they are mimicking them. In many cases, Brits do not even bother thinking about new names: the USA's *It's Gary Shandling's Show* turned *Sean's Show*; *American Gladiators* became just *Gladiators*. Formats have been plundered. Jonathan Ross' British talk show was a contrived David Letterman rip-off. Robert Kilroy-Silk even looked a little like Phil Donahue. And black female Chrystal Rose was an ersatz Oprah. British ITV's projected removal of its "News at Ten" so as not to interrupt primetime entertainment with audience-losing news, follows the US network's policy.

The world-shrinking effects of television include not only the exporting of US-produced programs to the rest of the world, but the importing of audiences to America. Not literally, of course; but multinational corporations are ever eager to widen their markets. And television is the primary instrument for achieving this. As markets grow wider, there looms the danger of death-by-blandness.

Freshness and originality may be being slaughtered as American conventions establish their supremacy. And yet, it has to be said that no one would adopt, or copy, such conventions unless they worked. But, what does "work" mean, exactly? Advertisers, the *primum mobile* of television, are not concerned with the intrinsic value of programs; only their extrinsic worth. If sitcoms, sports and soaps deliver audiences, they "work." Craft and imagination are all very nice; but common or garden stock typically draws audiences to the screen.

Writing of film, Gitlin invoked a version of Gresham's Law – in economic terms: if two coins of equal nominal value but of different bullion content are in circulation, the "dearer" money will be extracted and saved, leaving the money of lower intrinsic value to circulate. Because free market principles rule in entertainment, local or particularistic programs that are not readily exportable are driven out of circulation by more generic products. The global growth of television has meant a "massification" of populations of a type and on a scale never envisioned by Adorno and his colleagues. Television has been the catalyst for a new kind of cultural assimilation: symbols, phrases and images have become ubiquitous and recognizable. Imagine a world in which a black LA Raiders cap with silver insignia had no meaning. Or no one had heard anyone say, "Party on, Garth," or could identify the single zigzagging strip of the type that forms the logo of CNN. Or knew of the aforementioned *Twin Peaks*, or Michael Jordan.

Are television audiences everywhere being melted into monoculture? Homogenization was once a fear, but perhaps the entertainment industry does not envision its market as uniform, as it did between the 1950s and 1980s. "The audience is no longer regarded as a homogeneous mass but rather as an amalgamation of microcultural groups." wrote Jim Collins: "Appealing to a 'mass audience' now involves putting together a series of interlocking appeals to a number of discrete but potentially interconnected audiences" (1992: 342). Television enhances the interconnectedness of groups around the world.

There's many a slip twixt signifier and signified, of course; and cultural studies alerts us to the pratfalls of assuming that globalization leads to identical discourses. "Audiences in Italy may read *Miami Vice* differently than audiences in the United States," cautioned James Hay (1992: 360). Looking through this end of the telescope, we see variegated audiences producing meanings according to their own logics and codings. Through the other end, we see them behaving with remarkable similarity: replacing old with new Hyundais, buying U2 albums, drinking Budweiser, wearing Nikes; we could go on. Television viewers are not just viewers: they are consumers in an unrelieved international market.

Global television sounds alive with possibilities for cultural osmosis and international artistic exchange. But, more likely, we will witness a Pan-American automatism in which programs all but reproduce themselves, according to market requirements. This is precisely the kind of prospect Christopher Lasch despaired of: it is a culture gnawed to the bone by a voracious consumer capitalism eager to create and exploit markets everywhere. Lasch, whose work has supplied a principal theme in this book's argument, wrote of a "producers' view of the world" predicated on an idea of universal access to a proliferating supply of goods (1991). Television projects this kind of beguiling view: it issues notices to consumers to become aspirational and embrace the visions of the good life portrayed. All the time it is enticing them into the cultural zone written of by Gitlin.

Auntie v. market forces

Market forces, I argue, ultimately drive all television, even those ostensibly committed to other ambitions. Britain's Channel 4, for example, began with an official remit to cater for audiences not served by existing British networks. Its innovations in sports, original films and "alternative" comedy have influenced mainstream programs. Despite its aesthetic triumphs, Channel 4 found itself under pressure in the early 1990s, as the satellite channels and fifth terrestrial network forced it to produce work that was at once both innovative and attractive to advertisers. Market forces traditionally lead to imitation, not originality. Channel 4's dilemma was compounded by the fact that it was and still is ostensibly non-profit-making. Yet it has to swim in the same waters as overtly commercial stations when it bids for advertisers' money.

Much the same could be said for a clutch of the USA's cable stations, which cater for specific tastes (like comedy fans), or linguistic groups (Spanish-speakers), or ethnic minorities. The preference of financiers is for global product. Unless the channel can survive by buying old series and films, as did the SciFi cable, then it will be torn by conflicting priorities when it comes to production. Self-censorship in the name of anticipating market demands is likely. Specialist channels will be under pressure to convince advertisers that they can reach a demographically exact segment of the population, the segment particular advertisers want to target.

One way of thinking of the BBC's position in all this is by imagining an enfeebled old lady battling stubbornly with her umbrella against a ferocious storm. Try as she may to defy the elements, the storm's blast pushes her against her intended direction. The image of the BBC as an old lady has been a popular one: "Auntie Beeb," as the Corporation is known in Britain, has long been regarded as the secure and reliable preserver of culture and good taste in a cheap and cheery world. Since its inception, the BBC has maintained its position as a purveyor of public – i.e. not commercial – broadcasting financed by a license fee, rather than advertising. Given my comments about globalization, we might ques- tion whether the Beeb's position is still tenable.

Actually, BBC television's position in the mid-1990s seems more tenable than it was in the mid-1980s when Margaret Thatcher was in power. Few then would have thought it possible that a BBC funded by a license fee was even the remotest possibility for the future. The 1986 report of a committee headed by Professor, now Sir Alan Peacock concluded that the main issue confronting the BBC in the remaining fourteen years of the millennium was whether a publicly financed network should, or even could exist in an increasingly competitive broadcasting market. Economists buoyed by Thatcher's free enterprise ethic, wanted to abolish public funding completely and push the BBC into an unsubsidized perfect market in which satellite and cable channels would proliferate.

The Corporation experienced a torrid period in the Thatcher years. It was made to apologize and pay damages with costs to two Conservative ministers whom it libeled. After the BBC's reporting of a Libyan bombing raid, Norman Tebbit, then Chairman of the Conservative Party, produced a dossier alleging bias in the coverage and urging a reappraisal of BBC standards. The final *faux pas* was the forced withdrawal of *Project Zircon*, a BBC program on Britain's secret spy satellite.

By 1992, the expected satellites and cables had arrived and the BBC faced a contracting share of the television audience. By the BBC's own forecasts satellite and cable subscriptions were likely to be 40 per cent more than the monies collected by the license fees. But, the unbridled *laissez-faire* Thatcher approach had given way to John Major's cautious conservatism and the BBC's place as an "establishment" institution, impervious to market forces, was guaranteed with a government green paper. The "high ground" traditionally sought and frequently occupied by BBC television was confirmed. It should remain in British broadcasting, said the document, and the BBC should be protected in its quest for it. The paper affirmed the BBC's right to exist in a publicly funded fashion: it should build on its "best traditions," reflecting all aspects of "British culture" and resisting the populist forms of program favored by its commercial counterparts.

The trouble with this kind of affirmation was that it seemed to assume that the BBC was still, in 1992, the sentinel of taste and culture it was when Lord Reith first made his proclamations. A glance at the program profile of the BBC over the past several years reveals prestigious peaks of drama, comedy and quality news and documentary. There were also uninspired dramas, comedies with derivative formats and unchallenging game shows taken from American "originals," themselves minimally adjusted versions of programs pioneered in the 1950s. Worse still: in the early 1990s, the BBC regularly screened old troopers recruited from commercial television; for example Bruce Forsyth (*The Generation Game*, *Bruce's Guest Night*), Paul Daniels (*Every Second Counts*, *The Paul Daniels Magic Show*), Les Dennis and Anneka Rice.

As late as 1992, an inspiration-starved BBC copied the LWT/Granada make-fools-of-the-public *Game For a Laugh*, which was effectively *Candid Camera*, the old CBS stalwart. BBC1 unashamedly duplicated *Blind Date* with its *Old Flames*. Its *Caught in the Act* was a compilation of private mishaps caught on amateur video tape *à la America's Funniest Home Videos*; cheap productions like this have been copied all over the world. The Beeb took Bobby Davro and gave him a show in which he performed the same role as Jeremy Beadle had in LWT's *Beadle's About*.

There are other examples, but these serve to illustrate that, despite its mission to serve the public interest, BBC has consistently given in to the urge to beat commercial television at its own game. And, in terms of viewing figures, it has lost: all of the above averaged less than 10 million viewers, while most of ITV's lighter material ranged between 10 and 18 million. Cloning competitors' programs, themselves cloned from US originals, was not a successful strategy for BBC; its stated intention to return to its natural habitat of the "high ground" was more expedient than quixotic.

No one doubts the BBC's track record in quality productions, especially in drama and documentary. *The Ascent of Man* and *Civilization*, in particular, are televisual landmarks. But, in addition to poaching rivals' formats, the Beeb has not been averse to filling primetime with US imports like *Dynasty*, or Australian cast-offs like *Neighbours*, or foisting on its viewers extravagant flops like *Eldorado*, or even abstracting its documentary topics from the pages of tabloids (as it did with its "Teenage Virgins Sold into Sex Slavery' opener to the *Inside Story* 1992/3 season). There has been an underside to BBC's international image.

If, as the 1992 consultative document suggested, the BBC abandons its search for ratings and resumes its public service task, then it will be resisting what seems to be a global trend. For all its grand traditions, the BBC will have to settle for a much smaller portion of viewing audiences. That much is certain. What is not so certain is whether it will still be able to produce high-quality programs, especially with a £100 million deficit. Expensive programs can be made in a commercial market if they attract large audiences. The more fragmented the market becomes, the harder, it is to assemble a critical mass of viewers. As a result, broadcasting markets naturally tend to become concentrated in the hands of a small group of big competitors. These can deliver the large audiences to advertisers, who will continue to play the dominant role in financing broadcasting. But, the experience of the past few decades indicates that advertising's pre-eminence and its search for global markets will also limit the choices available to viewers.

Attempts to attract viewers to specialist events through pay-per-view means have enjoyed mixed successes, as we saw in chapter nine. Yet the spread of ppv seems ineluctable as we head towards the next century. In crude terms, the options to viewers will be: (a) watch the proven commodities, the hugely popular audience-catchers that advertisers will invest in, for nothing; or (b) watch less popular programs and pay for them.

Back in 1986, the Peacock Committee recommended that all new television sets sold should be fitted with pay-tv technology. It was ignored amid the furore over the future of the BBC. Ironically, some time into the next century, the BBC may have to reckon with ppv either as competition, or even as an ancillary method of building revenue. Should it continue its public service obligation as a "theater of the air" it is at least conceivable that it will ask viewers to pay directly for its products, either in addition to or as an alternative to the license fees. The BBC can hardly expect to attract advertisers with the same magnetism of populist networks, even if it were to welcome them with open arms. A facility called BBC Select began as a subscription service, selling unused late-night airways to specialist producers. This will be another route for the BBC to explore.

As for advertising itself, Auntie's resolution has already started to crumble, as any sharp-eyed viewer can see. Since the early 1990s, there has been a rash of logos and brand names appearing on the bodies of shows. Some BBC programs, such as *The Clothes Show* and *Challenge Anneka*, were derided for their generosity in giving "free" publicity to companies. But, less obviously, the BBC has tolerated product placements. To take one small example: the network allowed, or invited, Thorn-EMI to construct a video rental store front for an *Eldorado* set. The cost to Thorn-EMI was £25,000. One ten-second exposure at 7.00–7.30 p.m. alone could be worth up to £200,000 in raising consumers' awareness.

A Balkanized market will mean less money to go round, giving rise perhaps to the temptation for a little discreet negotiation in raising extra cash. Advertisers, seeking airtime at cut-price rates, will enthuse. We can expect the identifiable corporate images of cars, airlines and brewers to skip stealthily across BBC screens in future. (As an aside, we might note that Brazilian soaps, or *novelas*, brazenly use brand-name merchandise and charge roughly the same as they would for commercial spots; the products are sometimes written into the plots, as when a police officer in *Perigosas Pervas* was almost stripped of his commission after modeling Jockey Y-fronts on billboards.)

time on our hands

It took about 28,000 years after the invention of the wheel before humans hit on the idea of attaching a set of them to an internal combustion engine and making a motor vehicle. Both artefacts brought momentous cultural changes. But it was only three decades after television first appeared that bright sparks augmented it with a piece of equipment that transformed television as dramatically as the engine had wheels. I refer to the video cassette recorder (VCR), a piece of equipment that sped off store shelves and into homes in the 1980s at a pace that rivaled the domestic growth of tv itself.

When Sony first introduced its Betamax machine for home use in 1975, it offered an extraordinary facility. Viewers could release themselves from television schedules and organize their viewing according to their own priorities. They, rather than the networks, would determine viewing patterns. In 1977, an alternative and incompatible system, VHS, was launched which subsequently went on to dominate the entire market. By 1985, about 30 per cent of tv-owning US households possessed a video hook-up, 40 per cent in Britain. The surge continued so that, by 1993, 75 per cent had VCRs. The growth was just as pronounced in continental Europe and even more pronounced in less-developed countries.

In passing, we might notice that, compared with the take-up of video, color tv's progression was sluggish; the message being that improvements in the actual quality of images mattered less than the widening of consumer control over leisure habits. Recovering the ability to organize one's time after decades of being dictated to, was met with enthusiastic approval.

At first a useful adjunct to television, video gradually developed into something of an alternative, as video rental stores tapped into a new market. Those for whom the effort of driving to a movie theater was too much, took advantage of the expanding video libraries opened up by such chains as Blockbuster – now the largest with over 2,000 outlets in the USA alone. While they were watching videos of months-old movies at home, they were not watching network television; nor were they watching first-release films at cinemas, of course. Research published in 1990 showed that 72 per cent of VCR use involved viewing movies

(Kubey and Csikszentmihalyi, 1990: 97). The study also indicated that "only slight experiential differences between VCR viewing of movies and regular viewing (non VCR) of movies on TV could be discerned." And that "the VCR has not substantially altered the subjective experience of relatively similar content" (1990: 97).

What the machine did substantially alter was the consumers' ability to determine what they watched and, more significantly, when they watched it. Timeshifting meant tv programs were under viewers' command. Program clash? No problem: watch one at transmission time, record the other and play back the tape at a later time, fast-forwarding at the commercials. Then watch it again, possibly repeating the good bits and editing out the boring parts. Alternatively – if the set has this facility – switch modes to accommodate two images on the same screen with one of the desired programs featuring in a "window." All this without leaving the armchair, if the remote control is at hand.

A few years into the next century, VCR machines will look like contraptions from another world. The technology that will render taping and replaying redundant is in preparation. It remains to be seen how long the "law of the suppression of radical potential" we encountered in chapter two will work to contain the diffusion of the technology, which would basically give viewers access to libraries of movies and regular television programs whenever they wished and without the inconvenience of leaving their homes. When this comes about, we will be able to decide when we want to watch particular programs and not have to bother with tapes.

The important legacy of video is choice. Already it is unthinkable for many that we once had to watch whatever programs were scheduled at times designated by the networks. This type of imposition will diminish even further with the arrival of high-definition digital television (which entails converting images into a stream of ones and zeroes that can be read by a computer and gives movie-quality pictures; analog transmission uses waves analogous to original images.) At first, this will necessitate digital video recorders, probably employing an alternative to the awkward and fragile videotape.

One of the main difficulties faced in moving from analog to digital television is to compress a vast amount of information into digital signals. As this is overcome, consumers will receive a treasure chest of channels, many of them encrypted, or scrambled, and available only by subscription or ppv. And, consumers will have to become accustomed to paying much more directly for what they watch. We speculated in chapter nine how sports are becoming more focused on narrow bands of interested consumers, who are prepared to pay for specialist events. The suggestion here is that this trend will spread, affecting all but the globally popular mainstream shows that enjoy the support and sponsorship of advertisers. Many items that currently attract a restricted or specialist audience will have to be paid for (as noted earlier, the BBC is currently renting out airtime for business programs that are scrambled and available only to subscribers). The added costs of television will build incrementally, so that, before we know it, we will be paying directly for virtually all our television.

Years hence parents will recount to their children the days when films were films, tv programs were tv programs, video games were . . . and so on. One of the consequences of digital compression is that we will be able to take a household's supply of entertainment and information from a single feed. All of the above will arrive at the home through a single cable about the diameter of a human hair, one that will also bring the mail plus daily newspaper for printing on a type of fax machine (or showing on a screen), access to a computer network and, of course, the telephone service, among other as yet unrealized services, all voice-activated.

In a curious way, this integration of media has artistic parallels. In 1993, for instance, *Super Mario Bros* leapt from computer games circuitry to the movie screen and left at least a few tv execs pondering the possibility of a children's series. Television has quite a tradition of snatching commercially successful products from the big screen and converting them into (usually less) commercially successful products (*In the Heat of the Night*, *Alien Nation et al.*). It has effected some ingenious conversions, as in the *Young Indiana Jones Chronicles*. But only in recent years has the process been reversed, with Hollywood searching for inspiration in sturdy television favorites; and veteran favorites at that (*Maverick*, *Sgt Bilko*, and so on). The cartoon cat and mouse Tom and Jerry boomeranged from the movies to tv, then back again in a full-length feature. Is this evidence of a film industry bereft of invention? Possibly. But it also says something about the symbiotic nature of all media. If you can sell a product in one medium, try it in another, then another. It is a safety-first policy that has ominous consequences for globalization.

I promised at the outset that this book would not be laden with prescriptions, of the "television is bad for your health" kind typical of many other works on the subject. Much of the panic over the role of television has been nursed by grim academic writers and cultural critics with a flair for the outrageous. Exaggerated claims often share space with indignation to produce dire forecasts. Neil Postman, whose own writing contains something of a health warning ("The problem is in *what* we watch. The solution must be found in *how* we watch"), believed that the medium, indeed any medium, has its dangers minimized in one swoop the instant viewers become aware of them. Our exact appraisal of the nature and magnitude of the problems is far less important for Postman than the fact that we think about them. Common sense not consensus is what counts. "To ask is to break the spell," wrote Postman (1985: 161). We can argue endlessly about the effects of television or the modes of consciousness employed when viewing or any other topic. That in itself is sufficient for Postman. Just inquiring about television will release us from its influence.

Wherever people write in terms of spells, there is an implied malevolence. My belief is that indulging in the pleasures of television does not commit us to such a fate and, to this extent, I disagree with Postman's conclusions. But I have no doubts at all about his injunction "to ask." Nor about the sufficiency of this: as long as we remain mindful of how television is changing the cultures in which we live, then we will reflect. Postman argues that there is presently not enough air between us and television to be able to reflect. I suggest that we already do reflect; we just need to do more of it. Given the projections I have sketched earlier in this chapter, we are going to have to anyway.

Viewers in Britain have not had the *embarras de choix* enjoyed by their American counterparts, at least since the advent of cable. But with the increasingly commercial competition (very different from the old-style non-commercial rivalry between the BBC and ITV) means consumers will play a more deliberating role in their viewing habits. Freedom of choice will be enlarged universally by the technologies that will soon supersede video and analog transmission. Major networks will adapt in the way I have indicated, offering safe, bankable commodities. Viewers will divide into smaller audiences, according to preferences and priorities. Choice encourages evaluation and this has the benefit of involving the viewer in the process. Younger viewers, already used to the franchise conferred on them by video, will become ever more selective. Objectors might insist that being selective does not mean being reflective. True; but the conceptual distance between the two is short enough to allay most of the gloomier fears. Exercising choice in the selection of what we watch may not involve much creativity; but it does at least set us thinking about the programs we watch. My feeling is that we will extend this to thinking about the medium itself.

The commercial imperatives of television may be herding us into markets; and we assuredly will continue to part with our hard-earned.

Television stimulates, provokes induces; we cannot help being affected, though our response is by no means as predictable or uncritical as some assume. Do we rush out and buy new products? Do we sneer critically at latent and blatant advertising? Do we rage at the banality and revel in enigma? Do we . . .? We do *all* these things. And for no other reason than that we are human beings, not mere respondents.

Recognizing this absurdly obvious but often overlooked dimension will certainly not budge some from their critical verdicts. Still others will scream "cop out" at the tameness of such a conclusion. But, my intention has not been to shock or console. The corrugated character of television resists such simplification. Nothing and no one compels us to watch television; yet we do so in numbers and with frequencies that alarm even ourselves. Like being startled at our own shadow: once we understand that it is only a reflection of ourselves, we can smile at our nervous ignorance. The contrived title of this book alerts us to the fact that television is not a force sent by divine ordination: it is our creation and, as such, can threaten only when we ignore that fact.

references

Adorno, T. W. (1991) *The Culture Industry*, London: Routledge.

Adorno, T. W., Frenkel-Brunswick, E., Levinson, D. and Santoro, R. (1950) *The Authoritarian Personality*, New York: Harper & Row.

Ang, I. (1991) *Watching Dallas*, London: Routledge.

Bandura, A. (1973) *Aggression: A Social Learning Analysis*, Englewood Cliffs, NJ: Prentice Hall.

Barnouw, E. (1990) *Tube of Plenty*, 2nd ed., New York: Oxford University Press.

Barwise, P. and Ehrenberg, A. (1988) *Television and its Audience*, London: Sage.

Baudrillard, J. (1983) *Simulation*, New York: Semiotext.

Benjamin, P. (1992) "Seeing is not believing," *Guardian* (May 5), p. 34.

Benn, L. (1990) "Whitenoise," *Village Voice*, vol. 35, no. 50 (December), pp. S14–16.

Berger, P. (1971) *Invitation to Sociology*, Harmondsworth, Middlesex: Penguin.

Berger, P. and Luckmann, T. (1966) *The Social Construction of Reality*, Garden City, NY: Doubleday.

Berkowitz, L. (1962) *Aggression: A Social Psychological Analysis*, New York: McGraw-Hill.

—— (1984) "Some effects of thoughts on anti and prosocial influences of media events," *Psychological Bulletin*, vol. 95, pp. 410–27.

Bernstein, J. M. (1991) "Introduction," pp. 1–25 in Adorno, T. W. *The Culture Industry*, London: Routledge.

Cashmore, E. (1990) *Making Sense of Sport*, London: Routledge.

Clarke, A. (1983) "Holding the blue lamp," *Crime and Social Justice*, vol. 19, no. 2 (summer), pp. 44–51.

Clark, E. (1989) *The Want Makers: How They Make You Buy*, New York: Viking.

Cole, B. (ed.) (1970) *Television*, New York: Free Press.

Collins, J. (1992) "Television and postmodernism," in Allen, R. C. (ed.) *Channels of Discourse, Reassembled*, London: Routledge.

Comstock, G. (1991) *Television in America*, 2nd ed., Newbury Park, CA: Sage.

Condry, J. (1989) *The Psychology of Television*, Hillsdale, NJ: Lawrence Erlbaum.

Craig, P. and Cadogan, M. (1986) *The Lady Investigates*, London: Oxford University Press.
Cumberbatch, G. and Howitt, D. (1989) *A Measure of Uncertainty*, London: John Libbey.
Davidson, H. (1987) *Offensive Marketing*, Harmondsworth, Middlesex: Penguin.
Davidson, J. H. (1985) *Offensive Marketing*, London: Penguin.
Davidson, M. (1992) *The Consumerist Manifesto*, London: Routledge.
Denzin, N. (1990) "Reading 'Wall Street'," pp. 31–44 in Turner, B. S. (ed.) *Theories of Modernity and Postmodernity*, Newbury Park, CA: Sage.
Diamond, E. and Kasindorft, J. (1991) "How CNN does it," *New York*, vol. 24, no. 6 (February 11), pp. 30–4.
Donohue, W. A. and Donohue, T. R. (1977) "Black, white, white gifted and emotionally disturbed children's perceptions of reality in television programming," *Human Relations*, vol. 30, no. 7, pp. 609–21.
Donovan, R. J. and Scherer, R. (1992) *Unsilent Revolution: Television and American Public Life*, New York: Cambridge University Press.
Drabman, R. and Thomas, M. (1974) "Does media violence increase children's toleration of real-life aggression?," *Developmental Psychology*, vol. 10, no. 3, pp. 418–21.
Dyer, G. (1982) *Advertising as Communication*, London: Methuen.
Eskin, L. (1989) "The Tonto syndrome," *Scholastic Update*, (May 26) pp. 21–3.
Ewen, S. (1976) *Captains of Consciousness*, New York: McGraw Hill.
Fiske, J. (1987) *Television Culture*, London: Routledge.
—— (1987) "British cultural studies and television," in Allen R. (ed.) *Channels of Discourse*, London: Methuen.
Fiske, J. and Hartley, J. (1990) *Reading Television*, London: Methuen.
Fowles, J. (1992) *Why Viewers Watch*, Newbury Park, CA: Sage.
Franks, R. S. (1973) *Message Dimensions of Television News*, Lexington, MA: Lexington Books.
Galbraith, J. K. (1992) *Culture of Contentment*, London: Sinclair Stevenson.
Gans, H. J. (1980) *Deciding What's News*, New York: Vintage Books.
Geraghty, C. (1992) *Women and Soap Opera*, Oxford: Polity Press.
Gerbner, G. (1970) "Cultural indicators: The case of violence in television drama," *Annals of the American Association of Political and Social Science*, vol. 338, pp. 69–81.
Gerbner, G. Gross, L., Jackson-Beeck, M., Jeffries-Fox, S. and Signorielli, N. (1978) "Cultural indicators," *Journal of Communication*, vol. 3, pp. 10–29.
Gerbner, G., Gross, L., Morgan, M. and Signorielli, N. (1980) "The 'mainstreaming' of America," *Journal of Communication*, vol. 30, pp. 10–29.
—— (1982) "Charting the mainstream," *Journal of Communication*, vol. 32, pp. 100–27.
Gersh, D. (1991) "Superficial tv," *Editor & Publisher*, vol. 123 (September 14).
Gitlin, T. (1980) *The Whole World is Watching*, Berkley, CA: University of California Press.
—— (1985) *Inside Prime Time*, New York: Pantheon.
—— (ed.) (1986) *Watching Television*, New York: Pantheon.
Glasgow Media Group (1977) *Bad News*, London: Routledge & Kegan Paul.
—— (1980) *More Bad News*, London: Routledge & Kegan Paul.

Goldlust, J. (1988) *Playing for Keeps*, Melbourne, Australia: Longman Cheshire.
Goodhardt, G. J., Ehrenberg, A. and Collins, M. A. (1987) *The Television Audience*, 2nd ed., Aldershot, Hants: Gower.
Graff, G. (1993) *Beyond the Culture Wars*, New York: Norton.
Greenberg, B. S. and Reeves, B. (1976) "Children and the perceived reality of television," *Journal of Sociological Issues*, vol. 32, pp. 86–97.
Greider, W. (1992) *Who Will Tell the People: The Betrayal of America*, New York: Simon & Schuster.
Gunter, B. and Wober, M. (1988) *Violence on Television: What the Viewers Think*, London: John Libbey.
Hall, S. (1980) "Encoding/decoding," pp. 128–39 in S. Hall *et al. Culture, Media, Language*, London: Hutchinson.
Hartley, J. (1987) "Invisible fictions," *Textual Practice*, vol. 1, no. 2 (summer), pp. 121–38.
Hartmann, P. and Husband, C. (1974) *Racism and the Mass Media*, London: Davis Poynter.
Hawkins, R. and Pingree, S. (1981) "Uniform content and habitual viewing," *Human Communications Research*, vol. 7, pp. 219–301.
Hay, J. (1992) "Afterword," pp. 354–85 in Allen, R. C. (ed.) *Channels of Discourse, Reassembled*, London: Routledge.
Hirsch, P. (1980) "The 'scary world' of the nonviewer and other anomalies," *Communication Research*, vol. 7, pp. 403–56.
—— (1981) "On not learning from one's own mistakes," *Communication Research*, vol. 8, pp. 3–37.
Hodge, R. and Tripp, D. (1986) *Children and Television*, Stanford, CA: Stanford University Press.
hooks, b. and West, C. (1991) *Breaking Bread*, Boston, MA: South End Press.
Huesmann, L. R. (1986) "Psychological processes promoting the relationship between exposure to media violence and aggressive behaviour in the viewer," *Journal of Social Issues*, vol. 42, no. 3, pp. 125–39.
Huesmann, L. R. and Eron, L. D. (1986) *Television and the Aggressive Child*, Hillsdale, NJ: Lawrence Erlbaum.
Huesmann, L. R. and Malamuth, N. M. (1986) "Media violence and antisocial behaviour," *Journal of Social Issues*, vol. 20, no. 4, pp. 707–16.
Hughes, R. (1993) *Culture of Complaint*, New York: Oxford University Press.
Huxley, A. (1932) *Brave New World*, New York: Harper & Bros.
Inglis, F. (1991) *Media Theory: An Introduction*, Oxford: Blackwell.
Iyengar, S. (1992) *Is Anyone Responsible? How Television Frames Political Issues*, Chicago: University of Chicago Press.
Jenkins, P. (1993) *Intimate Enemies*, New York: Aldine.
Jensen, K. B. (1990) "The politics of polysemy," *Media, Culture and Society*, vol. 12, pp. 57–77.
Jhally, S. (1989) "Cultural studies and the sports/media complex," in Webber, L. A. (ed.) *Media, Sports and Society*, Newbury Park, CA: Sage.
Johnson, W. (1970) "Television and Sport," parts 2–4 *Sports Illustrated*, vol. 32, nos. 1–3.
Kaplan, E. A. (ed.) (1983) *Regarding Television*, Los Angeles, CA: American Film Institute.

Katz, E. and Lazarsfeld, P. (1985) *Personal Influences*, Glencoe, NY: Free Press.

Katz, E. and Liebes, T. (1990) *The Export of Meaning*, London: Oxford University Press.

—— (1986) "Mutual aid in the decoding of *Dallas*," in Drummond, P. and Paterson, R. (eds) *Television in Transition*, London: British Film Institute.

Kellner, D. (1988) "Postmodernism as social theory," *Theory, Culture and Society*, vol. 5, nos 2–3 (June), pp. 239–69.

Kern, M. (1989) *30-Second Politics: Political advertising in the eighties*, New York: Prager.

Knight, G. (1989) "The reality effects of tabloid television news," in Raboy, M. and Bruck, P. (eds) *Communication For and Against Democracy*, Montreal: Black Rose Books.

Knight, S. (1990) "Radical thrillers," in Bell, I. and Daldry, G. (eds) *Watching the Detectives*, New York: St. Martin's Press.

Kottak, C. P. (1990) *Prime-Time Society*, Belmont, CA: Wadsworth.

Kubey, R. and Czikszentmihalyi, M. (1990) *Television and the Quality of Life*, Hillsdale, NJ: Lawrence Erlbaum.

Kuhn, T. (1970) *The Structure of Scientific Revolutions*, Chicago: University of Chicago Press.

Landry, B. (1988) *The New Black Middle Class*, Berkeley, CA: University of California Press.

Lasch, C. (1991) *The True and Only Heaven*, New York: Norton.

Lazarsfeld, P. and Merton, R. (1948) "Mass communication, popular taste, and organized social action," in Bryson, L. (ed.) *The Communication of Ideas*, New York: Free Press.

Lee, C.-C. (1979) *Media Imperialism Reconsidered*, Beverley Hills, CA: Sage.

Leonard, W. M. (1988) *A Sociological Perspective of Sport*, 3rd ed., New York: Macmillan.

Liebert, R. M. and Sprafkin, J. (1988) *The Early Window*, 3rd ed., New York: Pergamon.

Liebes, T. and Katz, E. (1990) *The Export of Meaning*, New York: Oxford University Press.

Livingstone, S. (1987) "Implicit representation of characters in *Dallas*" *Human Communication Research*, vol. 13, no. 3, pp. 339–420.

—— (1990) "Interpreting a television narrative," *Journal of Communication*, vol. 40, no. 1 (winter), pp. 72–85.

Lynd, R. and Lynd, H. (1929) *Middletown: A Study of Contemporary American Culture*, New York: Harcourt, Brace.

McChesney, R. (1989) "Media made sport," pp. 49–69 in Wenner, L. A. (ed.) *Media, Sports and Society*, Newbury Park, CA: Sage.

MacDonald, J. F. (1992) *Blacks and White TV*, 2nd ed., Chicago: Nelson-Hall.

McLuhan, M. (1964) *Understanding Media*, London: Routledge & Kegan Paul.

MacNeil, R. (1983) "Is television shortening our attention span?," *Educational Quarterly*, vol. 14, no. 2 (winter), pp. 2–5.

Mander, J. (1980) *Four Arguments for the Elimination of Television*, Brighton, England: Harvester.

Marc, D. (1989) "*Belles Lettres* about TV", *Journal of Communication*, vol. 39, no. 4, pp. 76–89.

Marcuse, H. (1964) *One Dimensional Man*, London: Routledge & Kegan Paul.
Marshall, J. and Tulley, M. (1992) "Untitled report," London: The Media Centre (DMB&B).
Medved, M. (1993) *Hollywood vs America*, New York: Harper Collins.
Merton, R. (1968) *Social Theory and Social Structure*, New York: Free Press.
Meyers, R. (1981) *TV Detectives*, San Diego, CA: A.S. Barnes.
Miller, M. C. (1986) "Divide and conquer," pp. 183–228 in Gitlin, T. (ed.) *Watching Television*, New York: Pantheon.
Miller, M. C. (1988) *Boxed In: The Culture of TV*, Evanston, IL: Northwestern University Press.
Montgomery, K. (1989) *Target: Prime Time*, New York: Oxford University Press.
Morley, D. and Silverstone, R. (1990) "Domestic communication – technologies and meanings," *Media, Culture and Society*, vol. 12, pp. 131–55.
Morrison, D. (1991) *Television and the Gulf War*, Leeds, England: Institute of Communication Studies, University of Leeds.
Murdock, G. (1982) "Disorderly images," in Summer, C. (ed.), *Crime, Justice and the Mass Media*, Cambridge: Cropwood Conference Series, no. 14.
National Federation for Educational Research (1992) *The Teaching of Initial Literacy*, Slough, Berks: NFER.
Packard, V. (1981) *The Hidden Persuaders*, Harmondsworth, Middlesex: Penguin.
Paletz, D. L. and Entman, R. M. (1981) *Media, Power, Politics*, New York: Free Press.
Parenti, M. (1986) *Inventing Reality*, New York: St. Martin's Press.
Patterson, S. (1963) *Dark Strangers*, London: Tavistock.
Patterson, T. E. and McClure, R. E. (1976) *The Unseeing Eye*, New York: Putnams.
Postman, N. (1985) *Amusing Ourselves to Death*, New York: Viking Penguin.
Ritzer, G. (1992) *The McDonaldization of Society*, Newbury Park, CA: Pine Forge Press.
Root, J. (1986) *Open the Box*, London: Comedia.
Rosen, J. (1991) "The whole world is watching CNN," *The Nation*, vol. 252, no. 18 (May 13), pp. 622–23.
Sammons, J. (1988) *Beyond the Ring*, Camden, NJ: University of Illinois Press.
Schramm, W., Lyle, V. and Parker, E. (1961) *Television in the Lives of Our Children*, Stanford, CA: Stanford University Press.
Scott, R. K. (1990) "Effect of sex on excitation transfer and recall of television news," *Psychological Reports*, no. 66, pp. 435–41.
Silverstone, R. (1991) "A new golden age?", *Journal of Communication*, vol. 41, no. 2 (spring), pp. 233–4.
Singer, J. L. and Singer, D. G. (1981) *Television, Imagination and Aggression*, Hillsdale, NJ: Lawrence Erlbaum.
—— (1986) "Family experiences and television viewing as predictors of children's imagination, restlessness and aggression," *Journal of Social Issues*, vol. 42, no. 3, pp. 107–24.
Skornia, H. (1965) *Television and Society*, New York: McGraw Hill.
Sparks, R. (1992) *Television and the Drama of Crime*, Buckingham, Middlesex: Open University Press.

Stewart, D. (1989) "Doing the dishes," *Smithsonian*, vol. 20, no. 7 (Oct), pp. 156–67.

Taylor, E. (1989) *Prime Time Families*, Berkley, CA: University of California Press.

Volti, R. (1992) *Society and Technological Change*, 2nd ed., New York: St. Martin's Press.

Whannel, G. (1992) *Fields in Vision*, London: Routledge.

Williams, R. (1974) *Television: Technology and Cultural Form*, London: Fontana.

Williamson, J. (1992) *Decoding Advertisements*: Marion Boyars.

Wilson, C. C. and Gutierrez, F. (1985) *Minorities and Media*, Newbury Park, CA: Sage.

Winick, M. and Winick, C. (1979) *The Television Experience: What Children See*, Beverly Hills, CA: Sage.

Winston, B. (1986) *Misunderstanding Media*, Cambridge, MA: Harvard University Press.

Wober, M. and Gunter, B. (1988) *Television and Social Control*, Aldershot, England: Avebury.

Wolfe, A. S. (1989) "Review of John Fiske's Television Culture," *Journal of Broadcasting and Electronic Media*, vol. 33, no. 3, pp. 342–44.

Zimbalist, A. (1992) *Baseball and Billions*, New York: Basic Books.

index